Maurice Goguel

J ESUS THE NAZARENE

Myth or History?

TRANSLATED BY
FREDERICK STEPHENS

WITH A NEW INTRODUCTION BY
R. JOSEPH HOFFMANN

PB Prometheus b
59 John Glenn Drive
Amherst, New York 14228–2197

Published 2006 by Prometheus Books

Inquiries should be addressed to
Prometheus Books
59 John Glenn Drive
Amherst, New York 14228–2197
VOICE: 716–691–0133, ext. 207
FAX: 716–564–2711
WWW.PROMETHEUSBOOKS.COM

10 09 08 07 06   5 4 3 2 1

Library of Congress Cataloging-in-Publication Data

Goguel, Maurice, 1880–1955.
    Jesus the Nazarene : myth or history? / by Maurice Goguel.
        p. cm.
    Originally published: New York : D. Appleton and Co., 1926.
    Includes bibliographical references and index.
    ISBN 1–59102–370–X (alk. paper)
    1. Jesus Christ—Historicity. I. Title.

BT303.2.G64 2006
232.9'08—dc22

                                                                              2005056608

Printed in the United States of America on acid-free paper

CONTENTS

INTRODUCTION

MAURICE GOGUEL AND THE "MYTH THEORY" OF CHRISTIAN ORIGINS

R. JOSEPH HOFFMANN

The theory that Jesus of Nazareth did not exist has a long and undistinguished history in the annals of theological speculation.[1] In part this is so because Christianity has never relinquished the belief that its difference from other faiths is uniquely based on the supernatural status of its founder—a distinction very different from those put forward by Judaism and Islam, where neither Moses nor Muhammad, for all their virtues, was thought to be a god-man. Moses the lawgiver and Muhammad the prophet belong to the ranks of religious heroes whose message did not include a doctrine about their personal divinity. Christianity, by contrast, especially that represented by Paul and the Fourth Gospel, is incomprehensible without the founder's proclamation of himself as revealer, savior, and resurrected Lord of life. Judaism survived in spite of the destruction of its holiest shrine, the Temple, by Roman armies in 70 CE. It survived largely as a system of legal and moral thought following the end of the sacrificial cult, the death of its last prophets, and the waning of its messianic hopes. A religion of political disappointment, succumbing first to a succession of occupying powers ranging from Babylon and Persia to Rome, and then the victim of Christian expansion and Muslim aggression, it was sustained by an ethico-ritual code and a romanticized literary history of its Davidic past which united it in dispersion. Islam survived because of its adherents' willingness to defend, violently if necessary, their belief that the Prophet was the last and authoritative expounder of God's will. As the youngest of the Book religions, it was also the most polemical and defensive of its right to a place at the scriptural table, a posture that sharpened its survival instinct to a fine edge.

Christianity survived, and succeeded as a world faith, for a different reason: It survived because it staked its message of forgiveness and salvation on an emotionally appealing belief in the resurrection of the dead and eternal life with God in heaven. It defended this belief by pointing directly to the "history" of its founder, Jesus of Nazareth, who was born of a virgin during the reign of the emperor Augustus, crucified during the governorship of Pontius Pilate in the province of Palestine, and subsequently raised from the dead.[2]

The early Christians regarded these events as "facts," not as myth, but (oddly) not facts that came to them out of their immediate environment. The events which formed the basis of their faith, and which they knew by hearsay and story, had happened in the distant province of Palestine. They knew the story—by oral transmission—in Greek, the *patois* of merchants, tradesmen, and shipmasters who plied the Middle Eastern trading routes. The legend that Jesus' followers were like them—boat owners, fishermen—would have been appealing; even the most significant of the early Christian book collectors, Marcion (second century, and later branded a heretic), is known to antiquity as a shipmaster himself, from the province of Pontus.[3] The origin of the Jesus story along the trading routes (where later Muhammad would learn the lore of Judaism and Christianity) is well established.[4] The tale the *proselytoi* accepted was preached to them in Syria, Rome, and Anatolia and then later written down in those places with increasing degrees of detail and editorial changes reflecting local preferences in storytelling. As with all legends, what began as a story about a man, perhaps a healer or magician, named Joshua ("he who saves") accumulated these details with a notable indifference to consistency, with the most popular elements (the stories of his birth and resurrection) showing the greatest fluidity of all. If the ordinary details of the life of the protagonist mattered to the tellers of the Jesus story, the missionaries (*apostoloi*), this interest is not reflected in the literary remnants of the tradition.

By the end of the first century, this heroic figure was not just another memorable prophet-teacher, nor even another garden variety failed messiah,[5] but the son of God who had been sent to take away the sins of the world, raised by God from the dead, and taken up to heaven to be with God until the "day of judgement"— the *eschatos*.[6] Also before the close of the century, belief was widespread that Jesus would come again and that, like him, those faithful to his message would be raised from the dead. The original meaning of "salvation" was thus an appealing blend of being saved from final death and being protected from the penalties of judgment.[7] Both ideas were present, if not emphatic, in first-century Judaism, but it was the cult of Christ that gave them a purchase on the popular imagination through its aggressive missionary outreach to the non-Jewish world.

*   *   *

If belief in resurrection was already present in sectarian (Pharisaic) Judaism, and would later be adopted dogmatically by Islam as well, it was only in Christianity that such belief was tied to the acceptance of the historical founder as the means of forgiveness and the way to salvation.[8] For him *not* to have existed removed not one doctrine among many, but the linchpin of Christianity as a theological system. In orthodox thought anyway, as the teaching of the church gradually settled on a set of well-defined propositions about Jesus, he was the way, the truth, and the way to eternal life (John 14.6) because he had lived a life on earth. To put the historicity question in boldest relief, as it often is not, the *day-to-day* facts of

Jesus' life (and the Gospels provide few or none)[9] were insignificant compared to the belief in his supernatural status, a fact which has dogged all critical attempts to humanize Jesus, to make him a superior ethical teacher, a moral exemplar, a liberal (or conservative) rabbi, or a failed political radical. In other words, his historical importance was determined completely by his suprahistorical significance for believers—those who sought "life in his name."[10] Was this the *same* as saying he had no objective historical significance at all? Had he *really* existed? Beginning actively in the nineteenth century, the historical foundations of the gospels began to crumble beneath the weight of questions which could no longer be shoved to the margins of biblical criticism: the two-source theory[11] deflated the notion that the church possessed four independent, corroborative sources for the life of Jesus. Critical-historical studies located parallels and origins for virtually every element of teaching thought once to be original to Jesus—especially his apocalyptic worldview. The study of late Mediterranean antiquity threw up dozens of parallels for miracle stories, healing gods, dying and rising saviors; and the study of Christianity within the context of pagan culture gave new life to a question the church fathers had once managed to bury with the bones of their last pagan opponents: Did the early Christian community simply *borrow* its ideas from Jewish scripture, pagan myth, and popular philosophy, and put its words into the mouth of a fabricated savior figure named Jesus? The theological establishment itself had been responsible for focusing almost all attention on the primitive *Gemeinde*, the community of believers, as the primary historical datum of the first century—so much so that it was not at all unusual to see the gospels described as *their*, that is, the church's biography.[12] Yet persuasive and as seemingly unavoidable as the question of the nonexistence of the historical Jesus was, the resounding verdict of Christian theology was, "Impossible."[13]

*   *   *

Beginning in the nineteenth century, the theory was broached that Jesus of Nazareth had never lived.[14] The details of the progress of that theory in Europe and America have yet to be charted in a historically satisfying way, but here it will do to cite three reasons for scholars to hold it at all:[15]

(a) First, the earliest Christian literature, the letters written by Paul, is completely silent about Jesus as a historical figure. The six or seven "genuine" letters of Paul,[16] written mainly in the fifties of the first century, know Jesus as the *kyrios Christos* (Christ the Lord) who died for the sins of the world, gaining forgiveness of humanity and a form of "immortality" for those who believed in him. There is little—one almost has to say *no*—reference in these letters to a Nazarene who taught by the sea of Galilee, healed the sick, and spoke in parables about the end and judgment of the world. There is next to nothing, and certainly nothing on the order of a historical narrative, about a public crucifixion and resurrection, merely a reference to "deliverance," death and resurrection as events of his life (see Galatians 6.14) which were understood to have bearing on the life of believers within the cult or "church." Problematically, indeed, the most explicit of these references (Philippians 2.5–11) is a hymn which seems to locate these events in a cosmic dimension that bears closer resemblance to Gnostic belief than to what emerges, in the end, as orthodox Christianity.[17] There is nothing to suggest that anything found in the Jesus tradition as Paul knew it in the fifties of the first century is significant or pertinent to being a Christian, beyond the bare datum that the overcoming of death by Jesus (or God raising him from the dead) provides a reason for the Christian to be confident of salvation and everlasting life.[18] While the whole meaning of Christian "faith" was predicated on the acceptance of a single event located in time (Paul does not specify the time, and seems to have an eschatological view of the days nearing completion: Romans 8.17–20), the earliest form of Christianity we know anything about yields not a *historical* Jesus, but a resurrection cult in search of a mythic hero.[19] It found this in the divine-man (*theios aner*) cult of Hellenistic Judaism.[20]

(b) In significantly similar ways, the gospels provide such a hero—but it would be better to say, provide the story of such a hero, a Galilean prophet named Jesus who teaches familiar lessons, performs routine miracles, and is crucified mistakenly by a caste of unbelievers in his divinity and their accomplices.[21] He proves them wrong, and himself divine (a "son of God"), by rising from the dead. Just as Paul knows nothing about this story, suggesting it was composed in the closing decades of the first century, the gospels—though written later than Paul's letters—do not know anything about Paul, or rather, do not expressly reflect Paul's belief that the resurrection of Jesus is a paradigm for the immortality of every Christian believer. It is by splicing the two traditions together, the Pauline and the Evangelical, as the New Testament canon does, that the theology of cross/death and resurrection becomes available. What this artificiality suggests to some scholars is that the myth arises out of the "mystical supper"[22] that forms the only significant nexus between the Pauline and evangelical traditions: a meal designed to ensure the benefits of salvation to the expectant messianic community of believers who had come to believe that their savior was also the expected deliverer of the last days. The myth was a synthesis of Passover liturgy (Galatians 4.4), apocalyptic thought (1 Thessalonians 4.13ff.), and biblical typology (Mark 9.1–8)—especially drawing on the familiar tale of the binding of Isaac and Jewish wisdom traditions (see Sirach 1.1ff.). Its most important deviation from Judaism was its emphasis on the divinity of the savior-redeemer, a hybridization of messianic and apocalyptic thought further complicated by being agglomerated with hero tales, miracle sagas (thaumaturgies), and features of the mystery religions and emperor cult, especially the signification of Jesus as a "son of the God." Complexity was nothing new to Hellenistic Judaism, an agglomerative phenomenon in its own right, but nothing as layered as the Christological complexity of the Jesus cult. This cult's dazzling array of beliefs about Jesus at once ensured its eventual prohibition in the conservative Palestinian synagogues where it was perhaps first preached, and its popularity as a message of liberation to dissident Jews and religion-hungry gentiles outside Judaea and Galilee (we know, for example, of its popularity in religiously mixed enclaves in Samaria and in Antioch, and the centrality of the meal as a sacramental ritual of rebirth at Corinth).[23] If stories about the virgin birth, death, and resurrection of the messiah were "heretical" from the standpoint of a later, settled rabbinical orthodoxy, they were not altogether unusual in the religiously charged atmosphere of Hellenized Palestine. The Jesus legend embodied in the gospel is significant proof of a syncretizing Judaism which invented and exported such stories to the Jewish diaspora in Rome and Syria.[24]

(c) A further reason for holding the accounts of Jesus in the Gospels to be legendary lay outside the boundaries of the New Testament canon and its immediate social environment. In general, the Gospels seem to be combinations of *traditions about* Jesus rather than the life story of a single individual. The myth theorists were quick to point out that there is virtually no part of the Gospel that has not been affected by existing tales then circulating throughout Rome and the provinces. The tales themselves are familiar from ancient stories of dying and rising (or recomposed) gods, ranging from Osiris and solar deities such as Mithras to Heracles and Prometheus. Jews, especially Palestinian Jews, did not accept such myths wholesale, as did the religiously generous Romans, but tended to domesticate them within the constructs of their own religious history. In the apocalyptic context belief in certain semidivine personages was at fever pitch prior to the outbreak of the first Jewish revolt in 66 CE. The most important of these mythical figures were the "Son of Man," linked in the popular mind to the *ben 'enosh* of Daniel 7–12; Sophia, or Wisdom (cf. Sirach [Wisdom] 1.6ff.; Matthew 12:42/ Luke 11:31); and even crudescences of the pre-Hebrew goddess Asherah (Ishtar) who was never successfully extirpated from the Jewish pantheon. Jesus in the synoptic Gospels is an uneven commixture of these idealized figures, while in John he is repainted as the Gnostic savior revealer, the *logos* of God, who is "identical" to God himself (John 10.29)—so that he can be said to have existed "from the beginning" (John 1.3–4; cf. Ecclesiasticus 24.1–5). The mythic features of Hellenistic Judaism as much as priesthood, calendar, and ritual held sway over the popular religious imagination. Of these, the eschatological figure of the Son of man, the Greek idea of the divine man, quasi-Gnostic constructions of the androgynous revealer goddess Sophia, and (especially for Paul) a theophanic view of messiahship as the appearance and return to heaven of a heavenly man (the *kyrios christos*) blended to form an inchoate tale that developed into a controlled structure only after written versions of the story began to supplant its weedlike variegations. Even so, the variegation is clear from differences between earlier gospels, such as Mark, and later gospels, such as Matthew and Luke, with their expanded accounts of the birth of the savior god and assorted accounts of his rising from the dead; and between the synoptic accounts and the "spiritual" gospel of John, an attempt to replace the messianic-apocalyptic figure with a heavily Gnosticized one. Looked at in this way, moreover, the wide variety of Gnostic gospels and apocryphal gospels contribute to a total picture in which the Jesus tradition was much less tidy than its defenders and propagators—the church fathers—would have wished for it to be in the third and fourth centuries, when it is at once subsumed and replaced by the "orthodox" dogma of the divine trinity, a belief for which the tangled myth itself provided no warrant.

*   *   *

Orthodoxy itself is best defined as the victory of the belief that Jesus had *actually* lived a full human existence over the belief that he was a mystical being or a man from heaven, greater than the angels (see Hebrews 2.1–18). Elemental to this victory was the canonization of the books which seemed to vouch for his historical existence: the Gospels. Paul's letters, without these later sources, would have provided but little ammunition against the docetic and Gnostic views (if indeed he did not share them) that Jesus had not been truly human.[25]

For Paul, most explicitly in his letter to the Galatians, the process of salvation is described in the language of myth: "When we were children we were slaves to the elemental spirits of the universe [*archontes tou kosmou*]. But when the time came, God sent forth his son [to be] born of a woman, born under the law, to redeem those who were under the law, so that we [too] might receive adoption as sons. . . . [So, then,] how can you turn again back to the weak and beggarly elemental spirits whose slaves you want to be once more?" (Galatians 4.3–6, 9). As Paul views history, a damned human race had been liberated from sin through the advent, death, and resurrection of a Jewish redeemer, who in significant respects resembled the savior gods of Hellenistic religion—especially Mithras. This "lord" had no personal biography, or rather the merest one ("born of a woman [Gk: *gyne*] under the law [i.e., into Judaism]," but the most important events of his sketchless life were his death and restoration—or rather revelation as a god. The so-called Christ hymn in the letter to the Philippians, perhaps a snippet of early Christian liturgy, makes the same point in versified form: Jesus Christ, a god by "birth," temporarily disavowed divinity and was born in the likeness of a man, was killed (crucified), and was then restored to full divinity by his Father-god (Philippians 2.5–11). A number of generic stories, including the pro-Gnostic "Hymn of the Pearl," tell the same story.[26] Paul's claim is not primarily that Jesus was the long-awaited Messiah of the Jews—though that message is incorporated into his more ambitious one—but that Jesus was a dying and rising savior God, a "redeemer" given to the Jews in the same way that Mithras had

been given to the gentiles. Like the Jesus believers, the worshipers
of Mithras held strong beliefs in a celestial heaven and a world of
evil. They believed that the benevolent powers of good would sym-
pathize with their suffering and grant them the final justice of
immortality and eternal salvation in the world to come. They
looked forward to a final day of judgment in which the dead would
be raised, and to a final (eschatological) conflict that would destroy
the existing order of all things to bring about the triumph of light
over darkness. Purification through a ritualistic baptism was
required of the faithful, who also took part in a ceremony in which
they drank wine and ate bread to symbolize the body and blood of
the god. The "day of the Sun" was held sacred, and the birth of the
god was celebrated annually in late December.[27] Could Christianity
be a Judaic or Jewish-Gnostic recollection of one of these earlier
myths? Theorists in the nineteenth century making use of a variety
of analogues ranging from pertinent to absurd began to be convinced it could.

Though the case was argued in many ways, and often badly, the
basic premises were sound: stated here with dangerous brevity,

1. The gospels are written later than the letters of Paul, and the
   letters of Paul are founded on the myth and liturgy of the
   dying and rising god, Jesus Christ.
2. The gospels can be seen as the simple expansion of this
   foundation, over time, to provide a *mise en scene* for the life
   of the god.
3. This *pattern* of "expansion" is familiar from the development of myth and hero legends of the Roman *oikoumene*,
   especially the myths of Horus, Mithras, and Dionysus,
   though it can be asserted of religious myth in general. It is
   not a pattern one sees in chronicle and historical narrative,
   even making allowance for legendary embellishment in
   ancient historical writing.
4. Characteristic *differences* between Græco-Roman and

Jewish-Gnostic mythology (reflected in the gospels) can be explained by Judaism's religious conservatism, its reluctance to separate the religious from the historical, and its belief that the supernatural and temporal interact in specific rather than arbitrary ways: that is to say, Greek and Roman myth, because of its understanding of god and fate, tends to be amoral, whereas Jewish myth tends to be ethical: concepts of law and justice are integral to its theology, and hence are not absent from the teaching ascribed to Jesus. The depiction of Jesus as a wisdom teacher and espouser of virtue comes from the Jewish tranche of speculation. His (differently accented) theophanous status in Paul's letters and John emerges from the wider Hellenistic context. The myth theorists, however, did not see the second as an *elaboration* of the first: both are mythical or ideal representations conditioned by geographical occurrence.

5. In order to establish the historicity of the gospels, one would need multiple "firsthand" accounts for purposes of corroboration (as one sometimes has, though not often, in the case of other ancient historical events). Source-theory of the gospels, however, had destroyed the whole notion of corroboration, in the doctrine that Matthew and Luke are actually derived forms of an "original" written story narrated by Mark; further, that in those portions where Mark is *not* a source (e.g., the birth narratives) we are quite clearly dealing with unvarnished or lightly coated Greek myth. In the independently composed gospel named John, we are in the neighborhood of a pure Gnostic mythology which has been only superficially historicized.

6. A positive verdict on the historicity of the gospels would also have to depend on an assessment of the kind of literature a gospel is: the early myth theorists were often more forthright than their theological opponents in this regard, saying that the gospels were examples of first-century religious propa-

ganda, created for the purpose of winning allies for the new movement. One gospel explicitly (John 20.30; 21.25) and one by implication (Luke 1.3–4) serves this purpose. This should raise an alert with regard to any secondary, historical purposes a gospel writer *might* have had in telling the story of Jesus. But again, that question is ruled out by motive: the *only* reason for telling the story is to exhort and to persuade ("kerygmatize" is a polite term used by biblical scholars), not to provide evidence. Thus we are thrown back on the principle that the reason for the gospel's existence is to propagate the myth of the redeemer as someone situated in history (thus human) but whose true home was heaven above (divine). Whereas the traditional biblical exegete begins with a Jesus who "becomes" a divinity through flukes of history, biblical interpretation, and (finally) conciliar edict, the myth theorists had wondered since before Schweitzer's *Von Reimarus zu Wrede* (English translation: *The Quest of the Historical Jesus*, 1911)[28] why the myth is so pervasive that it yields *no* purely historical data—no information which is not, in the language of biblical studies, "Christological." Regarded strictly from the standpoint of the literary hypotheses of the nineteenth century, the movement is from *Christ to Jesus* and not *Jesus to Christ*,[29] and the famous Bultmannian dichotomy reckoned to save theology from its detractors—the distinction between the "Christ of Faith" and the "Jesus of History" disappears.[30] The number of scholars holding what became branded the "radical" view of the New Testament, a term that failed to convey sharp differences of opinion among adherents of the myth theory, swelled greatly in the late nineteenth and earlier twentieth century[31] before it was swept aside by a tide of historical scholarship that seemed to supplant its basic tenets with a succession of "quests" for more detailed information about the Jesus of history as he might be reconstructed from the gospels.[32]

The urgency of this project had two causes: the erosion of Christian metaphysics (i.e., the failure of the miraculous to provide a sufficient warrant for Christian belief) and the more radical position that Jesus himself was a fabrication of the early church, a position first vigorously argued by Bruno Bauer in 1839 and never decisively put to rest. These two positions could not be reconciled in liberal theology, for even if the church could do without the miraculous worldview of the first century, it could not do without the profound ethical teacher whose significance, perhaps mistakenly, was expressed in terms of the supernatural. In defending the historicity of Jesus against the radicals, liberal theology was waging a battle against a thesis it had created.

*   *   *

Maurice Goguel was the rare exception to the outraged academic theologians who repudiated the opinions of the myth theorists with a scorn unjustified by the nature of their weaponry, a task made easier, however, by "absurd" and reductionist claims like those of the British Egyptologist Gerald Massey (who saw Christianity as a reworking of Egyptian antetypes) and van den Bergh van Eysinga's brilliant but highly speculative efforts to find precise and minute parallels for all parts of the gospel tradition and Paul's theology.[33] Goguel's examination, and defense, of historicity in *Jesus the Nazarene: Myth or History?* can be roughly divided into the following parts:

(a) *The notices of opponents.* After dismissing non-Christian references to the historical Jesus as, by and large, inconclusive,[34] Goguel avers that the most famous of the myth-theories, that proposed by the German monist-theologian Arthur Drews, was lacking in evidence.[35] As a matter of procedure, Goguel is inclined to treat other versions of the theory (especially the work of Couchoud, which he commends as intellectually loyal, sincere and vigourous)[36] as not unreasonable but unproven. In so doing he is thrown back on the literature of the Christian movement itself as the only evidence that can count positively in favor of the existence of Jesus. Nonetheless, in one of his weaker assails, Goguel suggests that Christianity was recognized by outsiders at least from the time of Tacitus (55–120) and that none of its opponents doubted the existence of Jesus:

> The importance of this fact is considerable. . . . How is it possible to suppose that the first antagonists of the Church could have been ignorant of the fact that the entire story of Jesus, His teaching, and His death corresponded to no reality at all? That it might have been ignored in the Diaspora may be admitted, but it appears impossible at Jerusalem; and if such a thing had been known, how did the opponents of Christianity come to neglect the use of so terrible an argument, or how, supposing they made use of it, does it happen that the Christians succeeded in so completely refuting them that not a trace of the controversy has been preserved by the disputants of the second century? (p. 115)*

But in this sally Goguel does not give adequate weight to the innocence of the literary procedure through which the gospels, and thus the Jesus story, came into existence. Tacitus, even if his report (*Annals* 15.44) is authentic, is reporting on the teaching of the cult and not on historical records he is attempting to verify. In general, none of the pagan reports, nor any of the later pagan intellectual critiques of Christianity, casts doubt on the historicity of Jesus for the simple reason that after the second century—the first age of Christian apologetics—the story was regarded as a canonical record of the life and teachings of an authentic individual, thus to be refuted on the basis of its content rather than the details of its historical veracity. Furthermore, the earliest "objective" report, which most scholars consider an indubitable recognition of the existence of a Christian cult in the early second century—Pliny's letter to the emperor Trajan (111 CE)—knows nothing of a historical Jesus,

---

*Pagination in this edition.

only a cult that worships a certain Christ as a god (*quasi deo*).[37] Indeed, the *insignificance* (not the *nonexistence*) of the founder for Celsus, Porphyry, and Julian was a polemical mainstay of their war on the new religion. His historicity, therefore, was a positive advantage to their cause. This dimension of the interchange is completely overlooked by Goguel.

Goguel wrestles philologically with the possibility that the name Jesus of Nazareth is a reference not to a place of origin but to a "divine name" by which he was worshiped as Joshua the Savior or protector, after the manner of *Zeus Xenios*, *Hermes Psychopompos*, *Helios Mithras*, or *Yawheh Sabaoth*. There is no consistent spelling of the term "Nazareth" in early New Testament manuscripts,[38] and the association of Jesus with place name seems to be something the evangelists struggle with in their conflicting accounts of the nativity. In all probability, the term is, as W. B. Smith devised, related to the Semitic root *NSR*, *Nasaryu*, "God is protector," and was originally not a place name at all. The inconspicuousness of Nazareth lends credence to the myth theory, even if recent attempts to spot it as a village or tenant farm some four miles distant from the Hellenistic enclave Sepphoris have proved popular in modern scholarship. Irrespective of this, the earliest opponents of the Jesus cult were happy to think of them as disciples of a man from an inconspicuous village: as Nazarenes, or as Julian later called them, "Galileans."[39] In short, the Nazarene confusion seems embedded in ancient debate over whether to attribute geographical place or office to a figure already known as *Iesous Nazaraios*.

(b) *The Docetic heresies.* A variety of early Christian groups maintained the spiritual nature of Jesus without believing in his historical or physical reality. In general these "docetic" groups (from Greek *dokesis*, meaning "to appear") did not form a coherent movement but were widely arrayed in terms of how to understand the nature of Jesus' person. The Marcionites (second century), for example, seemed to believe that Jesus did possess a body, but (in denying his birth) maintained that it was borrowed for the purpose of imparting his revelation to humankind. Many radical Gnostic groups believed, on the other hand, that Jesus was an apparition, without physical substance (since as a manifestation of the divine, to acquire physical substance would be to degrade divinity). If these discrete groups had anything in common, it was to deny the "true" humanity of Jesus for theological reasons. The orthodox were in the complicated position, in combating them, of arguing not simply for his humanity but for a "blended reality" that affirmed both the human and divine. Goguel somewhat confusedly argues that the refutation of Docetism by orthodox Christian teachers serves as proof against the myth theory, since it is inconceivable that the church would expend so much energy in defending a Jesus it knew to be mythical. But the refutation of Docetism, which centered on the physical birth and final suffering of Jesus as human, proceeded from a need to affirm the reality of Jesus' presence in history; as Goguel rightly says, "The question discussed by the Docetists was not whether there had lived a man in the time of Pilate named Jesus who acted, suffered and died, but the problem was to determine the nature of his manifestation."[40] That is, Docetists, Marcionites, and Gnostics did not deny the reality of the manifestation of Jesus, and at least some Gnostic communities regarded it as temporally and geographically situated as well; they did, however, deny the *materiality* of the divine figure (in various degrees). Goguel does not dwell on the question of whether these pseudohistorical theories of the person and nature of Christ are vestiges of a pre-Christian Jesus myth, preferring instead to stress that the church's *response* to them would not have been so vigorous if there had been the least doubt about Jesus' historical existence.[41] The point is not acute. It is not a *myth* the church was refuting in attacking Docetism; it was the belief that Jesus was of a different order of reality than the dichotomous reality it attributed to him as both god and man. Church fathers such as Irenaeus and Tertullian will accuse the Gnostics of believing in a phantasm, an apparition, a ghost, a spirit, in order to malign their opponents' denial of the physical Jesus, but at no point do they accuse their enemies of creating a deception or myth. The heretics were not mythmakers, they simply preached bad doctrine.[42] Thus the argument against Docetism, while ingenious in its way, is misleading.

(c) *Paul and the Gospel.* As Goguel recognizes, the myth theorists made a lot to hang on the silence of Paul concerning the historical Jesus. Goguel attacks this position in predictable fashion by asserting that the silence of evidence is not evidence of silence—let alone proof of nonexistence. This conclusion is less compelling than it might be, however, since Paul was not a disinterested writer of late antiquity who might be expected to ignore the details of Jesus' life (thus Tacitus) but an apologist for a cause that had made him a zealot. Hence, it might be expected that Paul's testimony to the death and resurrection (1 Corinthians 1.23; Galatians 5.11) would include tidbits of Jesuine teaching and, plausibly, biographical detail. Goguel instead argues vigorously for the "incidental" nature of Paul's letters, not real epistles in the classical style but occasional literature, almost accidental, and nothing much more than substitutes for conversation. Their interest and purview is limited by circumstance, especially theological and moral crises in individual communities. Goguel cannot drive this point too far, however, because he is aware that much of the historicity thesis depends on a notion that the existence of Jesus would have required a certain "consensus" as to the details of this life and teaching, a unity which was being assailed on a number of scholarly fronts in the early twentieth century. If Pauline Christianity was merely one variety among many, and lacked historical grounding from the standpoint of later orthodox tradition, from what quarter did the *historical* grounding arise, and when—and for what reason? Although Goguel sticks to his belief that there was more unity than diversity in the early church, his position was soon to fall into disrepute among scholars of ancient church history who argued that early "orthodox" or a doctrinally cohesive hierarchical Christianity arose late rather than early; that early Christianity was fissiparous theologically; and that much of the success of the orthodox movement depended entirely on its use of the appeal to history—"apostolic tradition," as by Irenaeus—the presupposition for which was a historical Jesus of Nazareth and his selection of disciple successors appointed to safeguard the truth.[43] As history and authority became intertwined in the noble Roman fashion, the historical Jesus becomes all the more necessary as the *Grundpunkt* for authority.

Goguel is aware of the existence of an ancient text known to the church fathers[44] as the *Ascension of Isaiah*, a layered and significant document that in its final section (6.1–11, 43) tells the story of Isaiah's journey to heaven, where he is told the story of the Beloved Son's descent from the higher heaven to Sheol, and his reascent to the heavens. This myth appears to undergird Paul's use of a "Christ Hymn" in Philippians 2.5–11 and also the baptismal and temptation sequences in Mark 1.1–9, 13, pars. The quarrel between Jesus and the Jews as representatives of Satan, patent to John's gospel, is also expressed in the *Ascension of Isaiah* (11.19–21), where the Beloved descends to the powers of hell in order to overcome death, but is betrayed by Satan and is crucified for his attempts to despoil hell.[45] How much of this myth is pre-Christian is impossible to determine, and in view of its connections to other savior myths, such as the *Hymn of the Pearl* and the Christian apocryphal *Acts of Pilate* (*Gospel of Nicodemus*), it is equally difficult to see it as the prototype for the account of Jesus in the gospels. Goguel seems to recognize that the chief argument against so seeing it is its "conventional" dating (second century [?], but based on earlier sources) and that differences between the *Ascension* and the Pauline schema beyond that have to be argued on flimsy conceptual lines: "The relation between the myth of Satan and the Christological drama as Paul conceives it is . . . not one of simple and direct dependence." Mythologically, however, the sending of the Beloved and the sending of Jesus as a sacrifice for the sins of the world can be distinguished only nominally: The Christians tied their myth to a specific name, whereas the redeemer in the Ascension (like the Gnostic savior) is a cosmic, thus timeless, figure. Goguel senses the urgency of keeping the Pauline and gospel traditions tied together when he writes, "It is illegitimate to reduce the whole Pauline Christology [to mythology] and to pass over everything which in the Pauline epistles had reference to a historical person and to His life on earth."[46] For that reason, he spends a considerable amount of time attempting to reconcile the gospel with Paul's references, with predictable emphasis on the (few) sayings or echoes of sayings of Jesus preserved in the apostle's letters. In the long run, one would have to regard this attempt as contrived and unsuccessful.

(d) One of the remarkable features of Goguel's study is his discussion of the peculiar strata of Paul's thought. He is acutely aware of the mythological structure of the apostle's view of the world, one that would soon be brought out more emphatically by Rudolph Bultmann and his disciples in Germany. Paul's world, like that of Jesus, was one divided between God and demons, sin and evil, law and freedom, the solution to which—that is, to the disorder of the world—was redemption. The present evil age is under the dominion of evil powers; its essential character is sin, death, and impotence (Galatians 1.4; 1 Corinthians 1.20; 2.6; 3.18; 2 Corinthians 4.3). In this section Goguel struggles to maintain that *despite* the mythological strata of Paul's thought, the apostle nonetheless conceives of Jesus historically: he does not, for example, consider Jesus "preexistent" as John and the Gnostic teachers had done. "The Pauline idea is that of a divine being, the image of God (2 Corinthians 4.4; Colossians 1.15), a celestial man (1 Corinthians 15.48, 49), the first born of creation (Colossians 1.15)."[47] Unlike the Christ later refabricated by the gospel tradition, and yet again in doctrine, Paul's Jesus remains "subordinate to the father"—he is created by the father and is not a mere extrapolation of divine being. Doubtless Goguel is right in documenting, as thoroughly as he does, the angles and contours of Paul's distinctive and frustratingly undogmatic thought—which it is true differs from Gnostic, Johannine, and later expressions of the Jesus myth. What he does not suggest is equally evident from his discussion however: that Paul's imagery of the descent of the god man, the victory of Christ over the demonic spirits of this age, and his assumption to glory at God's right hand until the end of time (Romans 8.34; 1 Corinthians 15.24, 26) was already being refashioned in Paul's name before the end of the first century (Colossians 1.20, 3.1; Ephesians 4.9–13, etc.).

What Goguel in the end is unable to deny, and indeed ends up strengthening, is the case made by the myth theorists that Paul's understanding of Jesus is essentially *spiritual*. Couchoud had commented that "the history of Jesus was deduced [by Paul] from a drama of redemption." Goguel's modest reply is to say that "we know nothing . . . in the Judaism of the Diaspora which offers any real analogies with Pauline speculation on this point," unless, that is, we admit the evidence of the *Ascension of Isaiah*, and the many examples of ascending-descending gods in non-Jewish literature. His basic contention (p. 188) proves untenable, that "if Christian doctrine had come forth in its entirety from the brain of Paul as Minerva did from that of Jupiter, it would present a homogenous character."[48]

In Goguel's view, Paul was confronted with a dilemma: the life story of Jesus (which he knew) and the doctrine of redemption—and he was unsuccessful at synthesizing these elements "completely at once." In fact, Paul's theology displays only stresses in relation to the second of these elements; the first arises not in relation to the *history* of Jesus but the Jesus who overpowers history with his divine presence. History is not a literal course of events but a metaphysical process for Paul. The sinful biography of the *human race* is problematical; the literal biography of Jesus irrelevant (2 Corinthians 5.16), and even if known would remain irrelevant. Beyond this, it is highly doubtful that Paul knew many of the details being propagated by the forerunners of the gospel tradition.[49]

(e) Goguel concludes his discussion by examining other New Testament literature—the non-Pauline epistles of the New Testament, with special reference to the so-called Pastoral Epistles (1 and 2 Timothy, and Titus), and the Epistle to the Hebrews. Together with the Book of Revelation, he sees these as developing the doctrine of redemption, betraying a time period later than Paul's letters and, in various ways, dependent on the gospel traditions themselves. In the Book of Revelation, Jesus is clearly a celestial being, the Lord of Heaven, whose return is anxiously awaited by a suffering church (1.5–13; 3.11). Even the figure of the messiah "appears completely stripped of all human features. He is a being entirely ideal."[50] He grants that it is impossible to see in the idea of a newborn messiah, immediately caught up in the heavens "and transported to the throne of God the primitive form of . . . Christology." The probability that the idea is borrowed from apocalyptic Judaism, however, does not assuage the difficulty posed by the collection of mythological scenarios comprising the Book itself, especially since the "birth of the Messiah" had become a fixture of Christian lore by the end of the first or beginning of the second century as prefaces to the gospel traditions of Matthew and Luke and marking the clear attempt to historicize the prehistory of the "beloved son" of Mark's story. Inadvertently, Goguel's very precise documentation actually lends credence to the myth theory, since it shows how easily the skeletal features of the descent, appearance, and ascension motifs can be rationalized in narrative form.

(f) Goguel's purpose in his final sections is to show that the theology found in Paul's letters and in the apocalypses "presupposes" the gospel tradition—a way of saying that the historical Jesus *must* have existed to give rise to the gospels themselves. Order is everything, since the myth theory—"Christ to Jesus"—heavily depended on the belief that *historicization* of the myth *proceeded* from pre-Pauline to Pauline/paulinist and later traditions, followed ultimately by the developed form of the story recorded in the gospels. Already by the nineteenth century, the philosopher Schelling, lecturing on the philosophy of art, had observed that the history of Jesus was "completely enveloped in fables" which were taken from Hebrew prophecy.[51] With varying emphasis, both Salomon Reinach and Couchoud suggested that the whole fabric of the gospel account of Jesus is constructed from a mesh of Old Testament texts regarded as prophetic by the Jesus believers, most especially those relating to the crucifixion or "passion narrative."[52] Goguel energetically pursues this line of criticism in a way that has puzzled scholars ever since the book appeared. He spends little time arguing for the historical reliability of the gospels, choosing instead to deal, at a very technical level, with chronological and interpretative difficulties in his opponents' argument. Thus, to the familiar thesis of the myth theorists that the whole crucifixion scenario is contained in Psalm 22 and is simply "planted" as the climax of the Jesus story, Goguel objects that if this were the case, it is surprising that no writer prior to Justin Martyr referred to the connection between the Psalm and the passion of Jesus.[53] Justin was indeed the first author (1 Apology 35) to *apply* the text of Psalm 22 to the story of the passion, but his contribution is merely to recognize something within the text that would already have been consciously known by the compilers. It can as easily be argued that Justin is the first to make explicit what Christian believers of the previous generation had *mistaken* for an independent tradition—in which case Justin, in his use of typology, a standard method of Christian interpretation of Old Testament texts, becomes one of the first to discover the mythological substratum of the gospels themselves.

Whatever its argumentative shortcomings, this section of Goguel's work is especially important in setting out the assumptions and terms of the debate between the myth theorists and defenders of historicity. Goguel is by far superior to other defenders[54] of historicity because he is willing to acknowledge the serious *aporiai* of locating fugitive biographical details in a swirl of theological and mythological embellishment. He does not deny, for example, the missionary purposes of the gospel writers. He does not suggest that the reporting of "objective" fact ("natural super-naturalism") is a part of any evangelist's agenda. He recognizes that the Fourth Gospel in particular is essentially theological and religious, whereas the synoptics are essentially apologetic—neither of which characterizations precludes seeing them as essentially mythic in character. Goguel, in fact, is comfortable talking about the gospel "idea"[55] as a changing form in early Christian life and thought; from an oral message, to a composite narrative of uneven "historical, biographical, spiritual and missionary interest," to a narrative that could be used, by the start of the second century, as a sourcebook for doctrine. Goguel's most impassioned plea for historicity deserves to be quoted:

A triple interest . . . assured the preservation . . . of the gospel history: a *sentimental* interest first of all. Those who had been in contact with Jesus could not let his memory fade away in their minds and hearts; in the next place there was a *moral* interest, the words and actions of Jesus being considered as offering or inspiring the solution of the moral and practical problems which they found facing them; finally there was a *theological* interest, for it was impossible to ignore what they considered the human episode of the grand drama of redemption.[56]

But for all its passion, this sequence of reasons for the preservation of the "gospel" is flawed, as modern New Testament scholarship has shown with something approaching aggressive certainty: The theological interest is primary and causative; as the myth theorists recognized with various degrees of acuity, the theology of the early church arose from teasing out the moral and practical elements of its core myth—especially in the apologetic defense of Christianity against the praxis of other religions, Jewish and pagan. And it is out of the defense of the "whole fabric" of the story that the "sentimental" attachment arises—relatively late, and in relatively disjointed, even confused ways. Canon and liturgy were key ways of perpetuating this attachment, and also, of course, in regularizing the content of the story for purposes of day-to-day life. It is not accurate to call the theological developments reflected in the gospels ferocious confusion;[57] it is fair to say, however, that our general picture of Christian origins today is very different from the view that Goguel accepted. We no longer, for example, have the luxury of excluding from the picture of this development the apocryphal gospels or the Gnostic texts, or the satisfaction of using the canon— itself a theological decision based on the assertion of historic pedigree—as a dividing line between "early" and "late," false and true.

With chronological certainty has also gone the ability to use "orthodoxy" and "heresy" as meaningful designations in judging the reliability of the Jesus traditions presented in the gospels. I have no doubt that a book by Goguel written in 2006, rather than some eighty years ago, would reflect greater theological awareness of this loss of certainty on his part. Indeed, he concludes his study, following a consideration of the resurrection story, with a statement that hints at an alternative ending: "While the worshipers of Mithras, Attis and Adonis knew perfectly well that the redemptive history of the heroes plunged into such fabulous antiquity that all reality was lost to it, the Christians were persuaded that it was not at the beginning but at the end of the age that their Christ had lived his life for them could be fitted in a very intimate manner into the reality of history."[58] For Goguel the operant word is "mystery," which seems to possess a historical reality completely different from the facticity of birth, life, teaching, and death that he has defended in the course of his reply to Reinach, Drews, Couchoud, and others. If their view, collectively expressed, can be called "myth without mystery," myth as the fabrication of an idea, then Goguel's defense of "history" is best described as an apology for mystery as a significant category of human experience, typically— that is, historically—expressed in myth.

As it is, *Jesus the Nazarene* is a remarkable book—perhaps the best of its kind— because it poses questions that New Testament scholars must continue to ask in dealing with the newly invigorated question of the historicity of Jesus. Those questions have not yet been answered. I suspect they will never be answered with dogmatic certainty. Goguel poses real challenges to the theory that Jesus never existed, and those challenges have not yet been met with the same high seriousness he displays in his writing.

R. Joseph Hoffmann
Wells College
Feast of the Nativity, 2005

NOTES

1. Goguel himself provides an excellent and impartial introduction to the history of the myth theory in the first chapter of *Jesus the Nazarene: Myth or History* (New York: Appleton and Company, 1926), pp. 1–28 (this volume, pp. 47–70).

2. This synoptic view is possible through harmonizing details from the first three gospels: Mark, Matthew, and Luke. In general the historical markers are taken from Luke, which differs from the other synoptics in providing a quasi-historical foreground for the birth of Jesus in his first two chapters.

3. See R. J. Hoffmann, *Marcion, On the Restitution of Christianity: An Essay on the Development of Radical Paulinist Theology in the Second Century* (Atlanta: Scholars Press, 1984).

4. The Acts of the Apostles, a very late first and probably a second-century work, ends with a picaresque tale that nonetheless preserves a memory of the way in which the gospel story traveled. See especially Acts 22–28. More generally Paul's peripatetic journeys to fledgling communities in the empire support this view of the spread of early Christian propaganda.

5. The New Testament itself (Mark 13.6) asks "readers" to be on guard against claimants to the title, which would eventually range from Theudas to Shimeon Bar Kochba and Shabbatai Tzvi. Jesus is usually distinguished as being atypical of such claimants because of his advocacy of peace rather than revolt as a means of "restoring the kingdom," but many scholars see this stance as being forced upon the movement following disappointment at the leader's failure to fulfill his promise. Such a reading

presupposes the historicity of Jesus. An equally valid reading of the text, from the myth-theoretical point of view, would see messianism as something read back into the life of the community after the failure of the Jesus figure to appear.

6. Matthew 28.20; John 12.45ff., 1.29–30.

7. Romans 8.18–25, 5.1–11.

8. 1 Corinthians 15.1–58; John 12.31–32.

9. This assertion is not negated by the scattered references to the "humanity" of Jesus—e.g., Mark 10.14, John 11.35, of Matthew 26.41, which in fact are theological and not biographical in purpose.

10. John 11.26ff.

11. The theory that Matthew and Luke are derived from the Gospel of Mark, primarily, and at least one other source, labeled, for sake of convenience, "Q" (*Quelle* [= Source (German)]) because of its limitation to sayings attributed to Jesus without narrative context.

12. Equivalently, the resurrection became a fact not of world history but within the life of the community.

13. It is doubtless the case that the theological establishment's aversion to the myth theory was grounded in its acceptance of the Patristic distinction (common since the time of Irenaeus in the second century) that the historical—physical—existence of Jesus was the only refuge of the orthodox against Gnostic and docetic teachers who denied the humanity of the revealer. Strauss had shown almost complete indifference (in Hegelian fashion) to the question of historicity, preferring instead to emphasize the perdurance of a powerful moral myth initiated by early Christian belief. But Strauss did not go so far as to deny Jesus as a historical person. See *The Life of Jesus Critically Examined,* trans. Marian Evans (New York: Blanchard, 1869).

14. At the very end of the eighteenth century, Lessing reproduced fragments from the scholar Hermann Samuel Reimarus (1694–1768), who suggested that Jesus had lived, but that his "feeble life story" had been subsumed by a cult of apocalyptic enthusiasts: Following his execution in Jerusalem, where he had hoped to be enthroned as a king, they focused on a second coming of their messiah and a different kind of liberation—spiritual deliverance—through his death. The serious introduction of myth into the calculation must still be attributed to D. F. Strauss, *Das Leben Jesu* (Tuebingen, 1836).

15. I provide basic summary in my introduction to K. Jaspers and R. Bultmann, *Myth and Christianity* (Amherst, NY: Prometheus Books, 2005), pp. 9–13; more extensively, see John Robertson, *Pagan Christs: Studies in Comparative Hierology* (repr., Whitefish, MT: Kessenger, 2005). The history of the critical study of the life of Jesus is summarized brilliantly by Charles Guignebert, *Le probleme de Jesus* (Paris, 1914), who pays tribute to the work of French writers and English deists in the process of critical study.

16. Galatians, 1 Thessalonians, Romans, 1 Corinthians (composite), 2 Corinthians (composite), Philippians (arguable), and Philemon. The radical critics doubted the authenticity of most, or all, of the Pauline canon, whose origins are shrouded in a mystery extending back to the earliest collector, Marcion, in the second century.

17. The Gnostics believed that Jesus was a revealer sent from heaven to teach a form of wisdom to an elite class of aspirants in the interest of transacting the soul's journey from darkness (this world) to light (the heaven above).

18. Categorically in 1 Corinthians 15.14f., this is Paul's formulation of being "faithful" or having faith in the gospel.

19. This is the situation in Galatians 1.6–10 and 1 Corinthians 1.10–16: The letters of Paul reflect an interpretational crisis not only over who "owns" the gospel but over how the Christ myth itself is to be structured.

20. Some of the issues are examined in P. Borgen's anthology, *The New Testament and Hellenistic Judaism* (New York: Hendrickson Publishers, 1997). The most thorough remains Carl Holladay's *'Theios aner' in Hellenistic-Judaism: A Critique of the Use of this Category in New Testament Christology* (Missoula, MT: Scholars Press, 1977).

21. The birth stories in the gospels although without historical merit seem to provide insight into the conflict over particular strands of Jesuine tradition: a Bethlehem tradition which linked Jesus to Jerusalem and to the Davidic background, and a more solid tradition that located him in Galilee and thus within the history of Israel. By claiming both "Israel" and Judaea in the developed tradition, the early Christians perhaps hoped to incorporate both regions within the purview of their missionary propaganda. The greater success of the "northern" mission, together with successes in Anatolia and beyond Palestine-Syria is paralleled in the Mecca-Medina trajectories of early Islam. The "journey" to Jerusalem is the symbolic expression of this attempt at unification.

22. The story of the supper is the clearest point of contact between Paul and the gospel accounts occurring in Mark 14.12–16; Luke 22.17–13ff.; and Matthew 26.20–29 and Paul in 1 Corinthians 11.23–26. The phrase (v. 23b) "on the night he was betrayed," as usually translated, suggests that Paul knew the story of the betrayal of Jesus by Judas and thus the same scenario of trial and crucifixion as the gospels present. In fact, the Greek verb *paradidonai* typically means "to deliver" and thus can plausibly be translated "on the night he was given over." It is tempting to relate this to the Judas tradition, but Paul knows no such tradition. Paul uses exactly the same word (*paradidonai*) for "giving over" by the Father as he does to describe the working of the divine anger (Romans 1.24–32).

23. It is worth emphasizing that the connection between the Eucharistic meal and the theology of the resurrection at Corinth is made explicit by Paul: The Corinthians have no trouble in interpreting the cup and the bread as symbols of the death of Jesus; they do, however, take exception to Paul's literal interpretation of the resurrection of the dead. At no point in this long discussion does Paul attempt to win his case by reference to a received tradition concerning the manner of Jesus' death: 1 Corinthians 11.23–34.

24. There is some reason to think that the Jesus story originated in Roman Palestine; nevertheless, such historical and chronological markers as it possesses could have been manufactured in the places the gospels originated, especially the Jewish community in Rome.

25. The Creed of 325 and especially of Chalcedon as late as 451 still struggle to keep the humanity and divinity of Jesus in balance, Chalcedon against the view that his human nature had been "subsumed" in his divinity to the point of becoming all but irrelevant. A very reliable basic outline of the context is provided by Frances Young, *The Making of the Creeds* (London: SCM, 2002), though she is deficient in her estimate of the heretical imperative behind creed making.

26. See discussion and translation in W. Schneemelcher, *New Testament Apocrypha* (Philadelphia: Westminster Press, 1964), 2:428–531, esp. 498–504. The Hymn is not "Gnostic," but seems to provide a template for a scheme of redemption common to Gnostic, Jewish-sectarian, and early Christian thought.

27. See the still-classic discussion, in Franz Cumont, *The Mysteries*

of Mithra, trans. from the French by T. McCormick (Chicago: Open Court, 1904); in the year 274 CE the winter solstice fell on December 25. The Roman emperor Aurelian proclaimed the date as *"Natalis Solis Invicti*," the festival of the birth of the invincible sun.

In 320 CE, Pope Julius I specified December 25 as the official date of the birth of Jesus Christ.

28. See especially A. Schweitzer, *Geschichte der Leben-Jesu Forschung* (Tuebingen, 1913), pp. 13–26.

29. Goguel was one of the first to state this succinctly: "In reality [according to the myth theory] Jesus is not a man progressively deified; He is a God progressively humanized. He is not a founder of religion but a new God," *Jesus the Nazarene: Myth or History*, p. 60. He is basing this assertion largely on his review of P. L. Couchoud, *Le mystere de Jesus* (Paris, 1913), which saw Jesus as a typical savior figure from the mystery religions, since "at the time of Paul neither the god nor the mystery had become historical" (p. 61).

30. Martin Kaehler was one of the first (1892) to use the phrase in his book *The So-Called Historical Jesus and the Historic Biblical Christ*, trans. C. E. Braaten (Philadelphia: Fortress, 1964), from the 1896 German edition.

31. In addition to the following books by the most visible contemporary champion of the myth theory, the British scholar G. A. Wells, a number of older studies can be recommended. Of Wells's many titles, *The Jesus of the Early Christians* (London: Pemberton, 1971) is the most tightly argued; *Did Jesus Exist?* (London: Pemberton, 1986) is also worth noting, as is *The Historical Evidence for Jesus* (Amherst, NY: Prometheus Books, 1988). A "disciple" of Wells, Earl Doherty, has rehashed many of the former's views in *The Jesus Puzzle* (Age of Reason Publications, 2005), which is qualitatively and academically far inferior to anything so far written on the subject. Of older works worth consulting on the immediate context of Goguel's writing, see: Arthur Drews, *Die Leugnung der Geschichtlichkeit Jesu* in *Vergangenheit und Gegenwart* (Karlsruhe, 1926); Bruno Bauer, *Der Abschluss der neutestamentlichen Literatur*, in *Christus und die Caesaren: Der Ursprung des Christenthums aus dem römischen Griechenthum* (Berlin, 1879); and G. A. van den Bergh van Eysinga: *Hercules—Christus, Godsdienstwetenschappelijke Studiën*, vol. 1 (1947). There is now a reputable Web site devoted entirely to so-called

radical criticism of the New Testament: http://www.radikalkritik.de/Klassiker.htm.

32. It is not immediately clear that the "traditional" approach, which begins with the artificial divinizing of a historical individual is a less-fictionalizing process than the historicization of a mythic one. Nonetheless, liberal theology settled on the latter alternative, then was confronted with the erosion of those parts of the tradition it regarded as the bedrock of their historical claims, especially the "message" and the sayings of Jesus.

33. See among his many titles, Van den bergh van Eysinga, *Leeft Jezus of heeft hij allen maar geleefd? Een Studie over het dogma der historiciteit door—Kleine Bibliotheek van hedendaagsch cultuurleven.* Bijzonder Hoogleraar aan de Rijks-Universiteit te Utrecht (Arnhem, 1930).

34. See R. J. Hoffmann, *Jesus Outside the Gospels* (Amherst, NY: Prometheus Books, 1987), for a discussion of Jewish and other ancient sources.

35. Drews, *Die Christusmythe*, 2 vols. (Jena, 1909–1911).

36. Goguel, *Jesus the Nazarene*, p. 45.

37. Goguel concedes this point, p. 78.

38. *Nazarenos, Nazoraios, Nazara, Nazarat,* etc. Goguel is personally undecided about Nazareth as a provenance for Jesus, and this is reflected in his use of the phrase "Jesus the Nazarene" in the book's title.

39. See R. J. Hoffmann, *Julian's "Against the Galileans"* (Amherst, NY: Prometheus Books, 2004), p. 37.

40. Goguel, *Jesus the Nazarene*, p. 121.

41. Ibid., pp. 121–23.

42. In another sense it is true that the Gnostic heretics were in touch with an earlier stratum of belief in which the historical was not central to revelation. Argumentatively, the church fathers could not have entertained this possibility and were almost certainly unaware of it.

43. The bibliography on this subject is extensive, but the classic and pioneering work remains Walter Bauer's *Orthodoxy and Heresy in Earliest Christianity*, 2nd English translation (Philadelphia: Sigler Press, 1996). The relationship between the apologetic uses of history and the *sine qua non* of a historical Jesus are examined in my forthcoming book, *The Myth of the Historical Jesus: From God Incarnate to Jesus the Jew*.

44. Justin Martyr *Dialogue with Trypho*; Tertullian *Scorpiace* 7; Tertullian *de Patientia* 14; Origen *Commentary on Matthew* 10.18, etc.

45. Goguel, *Jesus the Nazarene*, p. 140.

46. Ibid., p. 146.

47. Ibid., p. 173.

48. Ibid., p. 188.

49. Sections of Paul's letters seem to suggest that a tradition of "dominical commands" had taken root in some Christian congregations, as in 1 Corinthians 7.10 and 1 Corinthians 7.12, where "words of the Lord" are cited as possessing certain degrees of authority. These words however are clearly suggested as words of prophetic inspiration rather than sayings of the historical Jesus and perhaps offer good evidence of how other "words" of Jesus came into existence.

50. Goguel, *Jesus the Nazarene*, p. 205.

51. W. Schelling, *Saemmliche Werke* (Stuttgart, 1856), 1:103.

52. Couchoud, *Le mystere de Jesus*, p. 49

53. Goguel, *Jesus the Nazarene*, p. 227.

54. For example, Shirley Jackson Case of the University of Chicago, in *The Historicity of Jesus: A Criticism of the Contention that Jesus Never Lived, a Statement of the Evidence for His Existence, an Estimate of His Relation to Christianity* (Chicago: University of Chicago Press, 1928).

55. Goguel, *Jesus the Nazarene*, p. 242.

56. Ibid., p. 238.

57. Thus I cannot accept the many unargued propositions of Earl Doherty's recent book, *The Jesus Puzzle: Did Christianity Begin with a Mythical Christ?* (Age of Reason Publications, 2005).

58. Goguel, *Jesus the Nazarene*, p. 315. "Christianity is not the religion of Jesus; it is that of the worshipers of Jesus."

JESUS THE NAZARENE

PREFACE

The question of the historical character of Jesus is one of present-day interest. It has once again been ably raised by Monsieur P. L. Couchoud in a small volume of considerable literary value and high spiritual inspiration.[1] Is it true that the theory of the origins of Christianity sketched out in the above work is, as announced in the programme of the collection in which it has appeared, "the synthesis of recent works on Christianity," and "the focussing that all agree in considering as indispensable"? For he who knows, even superficially, the present state of research concerning Christian origins may be permitted to doubt this. Has not one of M. Couchoud's collaborators written on the first volume of the collection: "Without Jesus, the history of Christianity would seem as inexplicable as that of Islam without Mahomet, or of Pythagorianism without Pythagoras"? The intellectual loyalty of M. Couchoud,[2] the sincerity and vigour of his thought, the loyal effort which he has made to penetrate into the spirit of primitive Christianity, are worthy of full respect, but this homage which it is a pleasure to pay him does not prevent our seeing in his book the dream of a poet rather than the work of an historian.

During the discussions which took place last winter at the

Union pour la Vérité certain criticisms were advanced and facts were cited in contradiction to his theses. It is no matter for surprise that these objections should have left him unmoved, but it is surprising that in the volume he has just published he has not attempted to answer them.

The problem of the historical character of Jesus is one of fact. It is entirely in the region of fact and by the historical method that we shall attempt its solution to decide whether modern criticism since the eighteenth century has entered a blind alley, and should admit its error, cease to see in Jesus a real personage, and in so doing enter upon a road other than that followed by Strauss, Baur, Renan, Albert and Jean Reville, Auguste Sabatier, Harnack, Lagrange, Loisy and Guignebert.[3]

NOTES

1. P. L. Couchoud, *Le Mystère de Jésus*, Paris, 1924.

2. Albert Houtin, *Courte histoire du Christianisme,* Paris, 1924.

3. Being only here concerned with the question of the historical existence of Jesus, we pass over the problem of the influence (according to certain authors) of the religions of India upon him and the Gospel tradition.

Cp. R. Seydl, *Das Evangelium von Jesus in seinen Verhaltnissen zur Buddha-Sage und Buddha Lehre,* Leipsig, 1882; *Buddha und Christus,* Breslau, 1884; *Die Buddha-Legende und das Leben Jesu nach den Evangelien,* Weimar, 1897.

CHAPTER I

NONHISTORICAL THEORIES

I. THE THEORIES OF NONHISTORICITY UP TO THE CLOSOF THE NINETEENTH CENTURY

Bayle relates that one of the greatest scholars of the Renaissance, Laurentius Valla, during a banquet, said one day to Antoine Panormita, who was as much scandalized as shocked by the remark, that he had in his quiver weapons against the Messiah Himself.[1] Did he mean by this to throw doubt upon the manner in which tradition presented the Gospel history? Or did he go so far as to question the historical reality of the person of Jesus?

The manner in which the conversation is related does not permit us to decide the point.

Up to the eighteenth century the authority of the Gospels was unquestioned. Each one contented himself by paraphrasing with more or less freedom the data of the accounts. So long as Protestants, equally with Catholics, continued to be dominated by the principle of the literal inspiration of Scripture it could not be otherwise.

The sole problem which existed was that concerning the arrangement and disposition of the parallel records. From the sixteenth up to the eighteenth century, from Osiander to Griesbach, marvelous ingenuity had been displayed to coordinate these in such a manner that, according to the very words of Osiander,[2] no word of any record should be omitted, that nothing foreign should be added, and that the order of no evangelist should be modified.[3]

If this "reconciling" was not yet a true critical study of the life of Jesus, it at all events, owing to the complexity and improbability of the hypotheses it was compelled to construct, helped to show that the problem as then presented remained insoluble, and that in consequence it was necessary to transfer it to another field.

It was during the eighteenth century that this transference took place. This revolution, the consequences of which were only gradually revealed, took place almost simultaneously in England under the influence of the Deists, in France under that of Voltaire and the Encyclopædists, in Germany under that of the School of Enlightenment (Aufklärung), which received the adhesion of Reimarus and Lessing.[4]

The first scientific essay on the life of Jesus is that published by Lessing between 1774 and 1778. It consists of seven fragments obtained from a voluminous manuscript left by Hermann Samuel Reimarus (1694–1768). The author of this had for his object the justification of natural religion in showing that Christianity had but a feeble base of support.

In the opinion of Reimarus, Jesus had never thought of founding a new religion. His preaching, exclusively eschatological and terrestrial, had solely in view His manifestation as Messiah, the son of David.

Jesus perished at Jerusalem at the time that He attempted to get Himself proclaimed King. After His death His disciples imagined the idea of a second coming of the Messiah and of a spiritual redemption through His death.

Reimarus has a double merit. He from the first recognized the importance of eschatology in the thought of Jesus, and tried to discover a natural connection of cause and effect, not only in the history of Jesus, but also in that of primitive Christianity. By the manner in which he presents the life and the teaching of Jesus, Reimarus claims to undermine traditional Christianity at the base. This intention introduces a philosophical element into his research, which is as much a disturbing factor as the dogmatic prejudices for which Reimarus reproaches his antagonists.

The same may be said of the rationalists, whose activity extends from about the middle of the eighteenth century up to about 1830. Eliminating every supernatural element, they aimed at portraying Jesus as a master of virtue whose teaching accorded with their own. Such is specially the character of the works of Herder[5] and of Paulus.[6]

The latter is particularly given to the interpretation of miracles. He sees in them real but perfectly natural facts which his contemporaries have not understood, and which they have considered as having the character of prodigies.

If, for example, it has been believed that Jesus multiplied the loaves, this is because, in the desert where the crowd had followed Him, He had given an example of distributing the few loaves at His own disposal, an example followed by those of His hearers who possessed provisions.[7] The rationalist conception of the life of Jesus does not differ in essentials from the supernatural conception. The former limits itself to the recitation of the facts recorded while combining more or less happily the Synoptic and the Johannine statements, but instead of having perpetual recourse to miracle, the rationalists display an extreme ingenuity in giving to events a natural interpretation.

The work of the French rationalists of the eighteenth century possesses a less systematic character; its import is only the greater for that. It rests upon no profound work of exegesis, and does not end in opposing a new conception of primitive Christianity to traditional opinion.

In the involved and prudent manner forced upon him, Voltaire pointed out the small documentary value of Gospels "written by

persons acquainted with nothing, full of contradictions and imposture"[8]—the improbability of the eschatological prophecies, against
which good sense rebelled. "Let each ask himself," he writes, "if he
sees the possibility of pushing imposture and the stupidity of fanaticism farther."[9] "The whole history of Jesus—only a fanatic or a
stupid knave would deny it—should be examined in the light of
reason."[10] Voltaire on several occasions draws attention to the
silence of non-Christian authors concerning the Gospel history.[11]
Obviously, Christian tradition does not inspire in him any confidence. However, he does not go so far as to maintain that it corresponds to no reality at all. He is aware that "certain followers of
Bolingbroke, more ingenious than erudite," considered themselves
authorized by the obscurities and contradictions of the Gospel tradition to deny the existence of Jesus.[12]

In so far as he is concerned, he rejects this conclusion, and it
appears that this is not entirely for reasons of prudence, as is sometimes the case when he wishes to hint at opinions which it might be
dangerous to profess openly. Indeed, Voltaire in this case gives
weighty reasons for setting aside the negations he cites. He quotes
precise cases of forged genealogies, of stories embellished and
transfigured, and as for the disproportion which appears to exist
between the humility of the person of Jesus and the importance of
the movement which He inaugurated, he relates the case of Fox, "a
very ignorant shoemaker, founder of the sect of Quakers." He concludes: "It is necessary, whilst awaiting faith, to limit oneself to
drawing this conclusion: There did exist an obscure Jew, from the
dregs of the people, named Jesus, who was crucified as a blasphemer in the time of the Emperor Tiberius, it being impossible to
determine in which year."[13]

Voltaire has not sketched any history of the origins of Christianity. His effort to place the study of the documents within the
province of reason—we should say in modern phrase the province
of history—is none the less very remarkable. In doing so he dealt
the traditional conception decisive blows.

The almost entirely negative character of the criticisms of Voltaire explains the extreme conclusions stated at the end of the eighteenth century by Volney and Dupuis. In his work called *Les Ruines ou Meditations sur les Revolutions des Empires* (Paris 1798–1808) Volney conceives a vision unfolded among the ruins of Palmyra. The representatives of the various religions explain, each in his turn, how priests have deceived mankind in inventing dogmas which obscured the real religion, spiritual in its essence. In Volney's view, the entire Gospel tradition represented an astral myth.[14]

The views of Dupuis[15] closely resemble those of Volney.[16] According to him, the philosophers who have made a man of Jesus are not less seriously in error than the theologians who have made of Him a God: "Jesus is still less man than God. He is, like all the deities that men have adored, the sun; Christianity is a solar myth. When we shall have shown," writes Dupuis, "that the pretended history of a God, who is born of a virgin in the winter solstice, who is resuscitated at Easter or at the Vernal equinox, after having descended into hell, who brings with Him a retinue of twelve apostles whose chief possesses all the attributes of Janus—a God, conqueror of the prince of darkness, who translates mankind into the empire of light, and who heals the woes of the world, is only a solar fable, . . . it will be almost as unnecessary to inquire whether there was a man called Christ as it is to inquire whether some prince is called Hercules. Provided that it be proven that the being consecrated by worship under the name of Christ is the sun, and that the miraculous element in the legend or the poem has this star for its object, then it will appear proven that the Christians are but sun worshippers, and that their priests have the same religion as those of Peru, whose throats they have cut."[17]

The year 1835 was that of the publication of the first *Life of Jesus,* by Strauss,[18] and it is a date of primary importance in the history of evangelical criticism. Strauss attacks the problem with the absolute indifference to dogma which he owed to the philosophy of Hegel. The fundamental idea of religion in his view is that of the "Gottmenschlichkeit," and it is of small import whether this idea has been realized in phenomena or not. It is the idea which is important, and not history. The first Gospel accounts, in Strauss's opinion, have not been drawn up from an historical point of view. They do not relate the event as these took place, but express certain ideas by means of images and symbols, or to employ the exact term that Strauss makes use of, by myths. What is important in the notion of the myth is not the idea of unreality, but that of a symbolical expression of a higher truth. The mythical explanation seems to Strauss the synthesis which resolves the antithesis between the naturalist and the supernatural explanations of the life of Jesus. The *Life of Jesus* of Strauss contains another novelty: it put forward as had never been done hitherto the problem of the relation between the fourth Gospel and the Synoptics.

So long as one was content, as before Strauss, to combine the statements of the four evangelists, Strauss considers that the two traditions are irreconcilable with each other, and he solves the problem offered by their coexistence in a manner unfavorable to the fourth evangelist.

The weak point of Strauss's construction was that it was not built upon a sufficiently thorough study of the sources. This omission was filled up simultaneously by the works of F. C. Baur and his disciples and by those of a series of critics who combated the theses of the Tübingen school, such as Weiss, Wilke, Reuss, Albert Reville, H. J. Holtzmann, Bernhard Weiss.[19]

The outcome of the discussions which took place on the evangelical problem was a theory whose essential points are that at the base of the evangelical literature are two principal sources: The Gospel of Mark, either under its present form or one slightly different (proto-Mark), and a collection of discourses (the Logia),[20] the fourth evangelist being considered by the majority of critics as a secondary form of the tradition, dominated by dogmatic and allegorical ideas.

The life of Jesus which would be the result of all this critical work has never been written; it is, so to speak, involved in the work of H. J. Holtzmann.[21]

To the school of Baur belong the works of Bruno Bauer,[22] who in 1841 supported the priority of the Gospel of Mark. He explained the peculiarities of the other records by what he termed the creative power of the evangelists, and clearly showed the part played in the evolution of tradition by dogmatic and theological notions. But he did not stop there, and maintained that the forces which had guided the transformation of primitive tradition explained also the genesis of Mark's record. In Bauer's view the primitive evangelist was a creator, and his work is the product of the faith of the early Christians. Christianity was born at the beginning of the second century from the meeting of the different currents of thought originating in Judea, Greece and Rome. The person of Jesus was merely a literary fiction. Jesus is the product, not the creator, of Christianity.

Bruno Bauer remained a solitary. His ideas had but little influence. When, at a later period, analogous ideas to his were expressed, either by the radical Dutch school or by certain modern mythologists, it was not under his influence, and it was only after their expression that the authors of certain theories believed to be new found out that in Bruno Bauer they had a pioneer.

The publication of the *Vie de Jésus* by Renan in 1863 marks a no less important date than that of Strauss's work on the history of criticism. This is not because the work was particularly original. Almost its entire substance was borrowed from the German criticism, but although the work of Strauss had been translated, that of Renan was the first French work on the question. It attracted all the more attention in that it was addressed to the general public. It thus produced an enormous effect.[23]

Possessing in reality but little originality, the *Vie de Jésus* of Renan is, from the literary point of view, a first-class work.[24]

Renan makes of Jesus a kind of gentle dreamer who walks through the midst of the Galilean countryside smiling at life, and as though surprised at the drama in which He takes part. When he disappears, the passion of a deluded woman gives to the world a risen God.

The work of Renan was followed in the last forty years of the nineteenth century by a large number of other "Lives," from Keim to Oskar Holtzmann.[25] They all aim at presenting the results of literary criticism, often while combining, as Renan had already done, the facts of the fourth evangelist with those of the Synoptics. The point of view as to miracles varies, but in almost all there are found attempts at the psychological explanation of the Messiahship of Jesus and of the manner in which He had concealed it from the people and revealed it to His disciples. The principal effort made is the explanation of the scene at Cæsarea Philippi (Mark viii. 27–33).

In many of these "Lives" there is an effort to diminish the importance of the eschatological element, with the preoccupation—more or less conscious—of discovering a Christ who shall not be too unfamiliar for the modern man and at the same time an ideal representative of true religion, such as is conceived by Protestantism of the liberal school.

In the neighborhood of 1890 a new period in the history of the "Lives" of Jesus begins.

Discussion was concentrated principally on the Messianic consciousness and eschatology—two problems intimately connected.

Already had Reimarus emphasized the eschatological views of Jesus, and Strauss had accorded them a certain importance. But in a general way these writers had scarcely been followed, and the aim was to give to the eschatological declarations of Jesus an interpretation which eliminated, while spiritualizing them. Attention was brought back again to this problem[26] by the progress of the study of religions in the world of antiquity and of contemporary Judaism (with Jesus), in which eschatological ideas occupy a central position; also by the success of the school of Ritschl, who assigned capital importance to the notion of the Church—more or less explicitly identified with the idea of the Kingdom of God—preached by Jesus. The examination of the Biblical base of this doctrine led

Johannes Weiss, disciple and son-in-law of Ritschl, to state conclusions of great import in a leading work dealing with the preaching of Jesus concerning the Kingdom of God.[27]

In his view Jesus preached a Kingdom of God plainly and exclusively eschatological; He considered Himself as the King of this Kingdom—that is to say, the Messiah. The thesis of Weiss was repeated and pushed to its farthest consequences by Albert Schweitzer.[28]

If the exegesis of the end of the nineteenth century has thrown light on the importance of the eschatological and Messianic element in primitive Christianity, agreement, however, was far from being complete on the interpretation of the facts noted. A whole group of scholars threw doubt on a notion of the Messiahship of Jesus being a primitive element of Christianity. This conception was formulated by William Wrede in a very acute work upon the Gospel of Mark.[29] In his view the oldest Gospel tradition suffers from a fundamental contradiction. It presents as Messianic a history which really was not Messianic. The contradiction is concealed and resolved—imperfectly it is true—by the theory of secrecy observed and imposed by Jesus. Wrede takes pains to show that the Messianic secret must not be interpreted as a kind of pedagogic proceeding employed by Jesus to prevent His followers throwing themselves into a movement of political Messianism which He would have been unable to approve, and whose control would have eluded Him. He sees in the Messianic secret a literary device, thanks to which the conceptions and beliefs of the Christian community have been inserted into the Gospel history. This theory has been discussed in the many studies devoted at the beginning of the nineteenth century to the problem of the relations between Paul and Jesus.[30]

The problem discussed is this: Who is the real founder of Christianity? Is it Jesus Himself, or is it not the apostle Paul, who introduced into the Church the notions of Messiahship and redemption foreign to the thought of Jesus and the faith of His first disciples?

The theories of Wrede did not, doubtless, go so far as to deny the historical reality of the person of Jesus; they end, nevertheless, in rendering it practically unnecessary, and they reduce the part played by Him to that of the occasional cause of the development of Christianity.[31] From the notion of a Jesus having been, if one may so put it, only the pretext for the birth of Christianity to the thesis of His nonhistorical character there is but a shade of difference. We are thus brought to examine the modern forms of the myth concept formerly stated by Volney, Dupuis and Bruno Bauer.

In the last twenty years of the nineteenth century the myth concept is only represented by an anonymous work published in London in 1887 under the title of *Antiqua Mater* and by some criticisms of the radical Dutch school,[32] which is, however, as a general rule, more occupied with the apostle Paul and his epistles than with Jesus and the Gospels.

Pierson, Matthes, Naber, Van Loon, and for some time Loman, have decided against the historicity of Jesus. The reasons which determined their conclusions are principally of the negative order. These authors insist on the uncertainty of the Gospel tradition, the absence of all external testimony, and thus consider as justified not only a skepticism regarding the possibility of reaching a positive conception of the life of Jesus, but also of His existence.

The fact that they have failed to give from their point of view a coherent explanation of the origins of Christianity and of the formation of the Gospel tradition explains the slight influence that their theories have exercised.

II. NONHISTORICAL THEORIES IN THE TWENTIETH CENTURY

That there existed in the indifference which the theories of the Dutch school met with something more than a conspiracy of silence is proved by the volume of discussion since the opening of the twentieth century upon the historical character of Jesus.

According to J. M. Robertson,[33] religions develop by a regular law, continually producing new gods, who are substituted for or added to the old ones, sometimes presenting themselves as sons of the latter. Jewish Monotheism thus gave birth to the Messianic cult. The adoration of Jesus is only the reappearance of an old religion which existed in Israel at the time when Abraham, Isaac, Moses and Joshua were still deities. Among these cults the most important was that of Joshua, the solar-deity of Ephraim, worshiped under the symbols of the lamb and the ram. This god Joshua is not unrelated to the Syrian Adonis and the Babylonian Thammuz. The new cult of Jesus-Joshua specially developed after the destruction of the Temple.

It created a whole legendary tradition, whose principal elements have a distinctly mythical character. It is possible, however, that in these developments there may have been included certain historical souvenirs relating particularly to John the Baptist and to a certain Jesus Ben-Pandera, put to death under Alexander Janneus (106–79 B.C.) Albert Kalthoff[34] considers Christianity to be a social phenomenon. The new religion was born when the proletarian masses, oppressed in the Roman world, came into contact with Jewish Messianic aspirations. The history of Jesus is only that of the idea of the Christ—it reflects the development of the community.

Jensen[35] concedes that there may be an historical element at the base of the Gospel tradition, but this fact is without import. Whatever the history of the man Jesus may have been, the Christ of the Faith was born of the transformation of the Babylonian myth of Gilgamesch. Like Jesus, Gilgamesch is a person partly human, partly divine; his history, in which Jensen finds an astral character, is that of the quest of immortality.[36]

William Benjamin Smith,[37] mathematical teacher at New Orleans, sets out with a triple observation. It is inconceivable that one simple personality could have inspired such an important religious movement as Christianity. In the second place, there are in the writings of the apostle Paul and the first Christian apologists but few allusions to the public activity of Jesus. In the third place, no man could have been so easily deified as modern theologians suppose.

In this mode Smith is led to adopt the idea of a divine pre-Christian Jesus. It is this person who was worshiped by the Naassene Gnostics, known to Hippolytus, and the Jewish sect of Nazarenes (or Nazorenes), known to Epiphanius (see later Chap. III, Section II). The name of this sect is not derived from the village of Nazareth, whose existence is very doubtful. In the name is found the root NSR, which expresses the idea of protection and salvation. In support of his theory of a pre-Christian Jesus, Smith cites a series of other proofs, such as the conjuration "by the god of the Hebrews, Jesus," in the magic papyrus of Paris, which, in truth, only dates from the fourth century after Jesus Christ; or, again, the case of Apollos and the disciples of John the Baptist at Ephesus (Acts xviii. 24–28 and xix. 1–7), who know the "things concerning Jesus" before their meeting with Paul. The magician Elymas, surnamed Bar-Jesus (Acts xiii. 6–12) and Simon (Acts viii. 9–13) were worshipers of this pre-Christian Jesus. His name (the Hellenized form of the name of Joshua) signifies deliverance, and is also related to the root of the Greek verb meaning "to heal." The history of Jesus had been created by the worshipers of the pre-Christian Jesus; it enshrines the history of the primitive community.

The theories of W. B. Smith were welcomed with enthusiasm by Arthur Drews,[38] who, in a work of religious philosophy published in 1906, maintained that the cult of Jesus was a relic of fetishism from which it was necessary to purge religion. Smith's system seemed to him adapted to bring about the religious reform he desired. He therefore adopted the theory of a pre-Christian Jesus, while combining it with an astral system, and adding to the product certain conceptions of his own devising, in particular a conjunction—unexpected, to say the least—between the Christ as lamb of God (Agnus Dei) and the Vedic lamb.

The theories, among which we have been summarizing the most characteristic, have in Germany, during the early years of the twentieth century, been made the object of an intense propaganda. The controversy was not only carried on in scientific publications, but in a large number of tracts designed for the general public, in popular lectures, sometimes as public debates, in the presence of huge audiences.[39]

The negative theses called forth a multitude of replies.[40]

In France, if one passes over certain controversialists whose work has more resemblance to an historical romance than to history,[41] the thesis of nonhistoricity has been supported, with certain reservations, by M. Salomon Reinach, and in its entirety by M. Couchoud and M. Stahl.

M. Salomon Reinach[42] does not formally give his verdict for the negative thesis, owing to the testimony of the Pauline epistles, which he is unable to consider as unauthentic. But while admitting that Jesus lived, Reinach insists upon three objections to the historicity of the Passion. The first is on the ground of the silence of non-Christian authors—particularly the absence of a report of Pontius Pilate to the Emperor Tiberius upon the condemnation and execution of the Nazarene. The second argument is that the history of the Passion fulfils certain prophecies, particularly that of verse 17 of Psa. xxii. The last argument is based upon the Docetist heresy— that is, the opinion which reduced the historical and human life of Jesus to a pure appearance. A very interesting attempt has been made by M. Couchoud[43] to present the Pauline testimony as corcerned with a Christ purely ideal, and so eliminate the difficulty which prevented M. Salomon Reinach formally supporting the thesis of nonhistoricity of Jesus. M. Couchoud differs essentially from the mythologists in that he refuses to make Jesus a mythical being, but a spiritual being—in fact, he possesses a comprehension of the spiritual value of Christianity and of the religious influence of belief in Jesus which distinguishes him radically from such theoreticians as Drews, Smith, or Robertson.

In M. Couchoud's opinion, the method in which historians, from Renan to Loisy, attempt to understand the history of Jesus and the genesis of Christianity is liable to two main difficulties. The first is that it is inconceivable that in less than a single generation a man should be deified, and this within the territory of Jewish monotheism. The second is that historically Jesus escapes us. The testimony of Josephus is an established forgery. The Talmud contains nothing about Jesus which does not come from Christian tradition. Out of three of the oldest pagan testimonies there is one—that of Suetonius—which may refer to an unknown Jewish agitator known as Chrestos. The other two—those of Pliny and Tacitus—establish only the existence of a Christian movement, but as regards its origins, they give only information borrowed from the Christians themselves.

As for the evangelists, M. Couchoud points out that these are not histories, but outlines of the good news; in other words, they are writings of an essentially mystical character. They have two sources: the inspired writings and the visions. The Gospel of Mark, the oldest, is the apocalypse of a man without eloquence; it is the creation of imaginative exegesis, not an historical document; it is a free commentary made up of Biblical texts and spiritual memoirs, on which the Christian faith is fused. One must not ask from such a book humble and commonplace historical information. Beyond the evangelists it is requisite to go back to the oldest form of the Christian faith, such as the epistles of Paul bring to our knowledge. The Christianity of Paul is neither the deification nor the cult of a man. His Christ is but a new form of the old God of Israel, Yahveh, as Messiah. When, after the fall of Jerusalem, the populace entered the Church, a kind of transformation took place in the Christian faith. The mystery of Jesus became fixed in record, and passed from the lyrical to the narrative form. The ineffable epic of Paul became an artificial legend. The bold invention of popular preachers did its work; but this secondary form of Christianity has but disguised the real nature of the Gospel.

In reality Jesus is not a man progressively deified; He is a God progressively humanized. He is not a founder of religion, but a new God.

In his article in 1924, after emphasizing the very special character of the problem of Jesus, M. Couchoud applies himself to define his theory. "At the origin of Christianity there is, if I am right," he says, "not a personal biography, but a collective mystical experience, sustaining a divine history mystically revealed."[44] At the beginning Jesus was not a man, but a Spirit which manifested itself.

Men believed in this Spirit, because of its manifestations, and because it was supposed that its existence and history could be discovered and read in Isaiah and the Psalms. And M. Couchoud aims to show that it is indeed to a spiritual being that the Pauline testimony refers. As to the origin of the tradition concerning the words of Jesus, the Pauline epistles would enable one to solve this problem in reading them. It was from the *Lord,* Paul says emphatically, that he received the account he gives of the last repast of Jesus.

Exegesis of prophetic texts, visions and revelations, projection into the past, and the attribution to Jesus of the facts of apostolic history in which the activity of the Spirit had been discerned—such are the sources from which the Gospel tradition has sprung.

Jesus must, then, have been at the beginning the God of a mystery. At the time of Paul neither the God nor the mystery had become historical. They were to become so in the period to follow the creative age, when it would be no longer possible to understand the high spirituality which had inspired the primitive faith, and when the celestial drama upon which Christianity of the first generation had lived had been transported to earth.

The two articles published by M. Couchoud in the *Mercure de France* have been almost literally reproduced, under the title *Le Mystère de Jésus,* in the third volume of the collection, *Christianity,* published under his direction. The objections which were offered in this review on the part of the Rev. Father de Grandmaison or myself, as well as those advanced in the public discussions (Union de la Vérité), have been completely ignored by M. Couchoud; they have not persuaded him to modify his views in the slightest degree; he has not even considered it advisable to state in what respect he thought them ill-founded. He contented himself by adding three chapters to his previous exposition. In the first he attempts to demonstrate that the study of the Apocalypse and the non-Pauline epistles of the New Testament confirm the conclusion to which his study of the Pauline epistles had led him; in the second he returns to what he had already said concerning the Gospel tradition; and in the last he summarizes the conclusions of his research.

We shall call attention also to an original but very paradoxical work by Monsieur R. Stahl,[45] which has the somewhat enigmatical title *The Document 70*. This "document 70" is the fragment of the Jewish Apocalypse which Wellhausen has disentangled from Chap. xii of the Johannine Apocalypse. In this is found the idea of a Messiah transported to heaven immediately after His birth.

While Wellhausen sees in the Apocalypse of the year 70 a Jewish fragment made use of by the Christian author of our Apocalypse, M. Stahl thinks he can recognize in it the oldest Christian document— one might almost call it the birth certificate of Christianity.

The Apocalyptic Messiah referred to must have been first presented as an actual individual, in a symbolic manner, in the fourth Gospel, and later in a more material way in the Synoptic Gospels, which would be younger than the Gospel of John. The letters of Paul are all unauthentic. Paul is not, however, a completely imaginary individual, but the real person, whose portrait has been somewhat modified, has been preserved for us in the book of Acts. He was merely a Pharisee missionary who had some quarrels with the Sadducees concerning the resurrection of the dead. M. Stahl has tried to sketch the development of Christianity as he represents it. It might be summarized in the following series: *Document 70—Apocalypse—Fourth Gospel—Synoptics*. He has no explanation of the first manifestations of Christianity in Rome, and particularly of the persecution by Nero. To get rid of this it would be necessary to overthrow the accepted ideas on Latin literature as well as those which appear the best established upon the books of the New Testament.

III. THE PROBLEM

The review which we have presented to the principal theories, which (while utilizing the critical work of the nineteenth century) have during the last twenty years opposed the traditional acceptance of the historicity of Jesus, gives occasion to make several observations. The difficulty of the problem consists not only in the complexity and obscurity of its data, but also in the fact that in a certain sense it is a unique problem without analogy in the whole history of religion. M. Couchoud has much insisted on this fact.[46] "The problem of Jesus," he writes, "is no ordinary historical difficulty. The case of Jesus is unique. For the historian, unique cases are enigmas." But history, even in contemplating less exceptional cases, is nevertheless not exclusively a science of the particular. The wish to remove from its jurisdiction everything which does not present the character of collective fact is simply to prohibit it dealing with great personalities, and to exclude from its domain a Julius Caesar, a Mahomet, a Luther, and a Napoleon, and thus to suppress one of the most important factors on human evolution. So also, when it is claimed that the problem of Jesus is no historical problem, it is nevertheless (and here M. Couchoud is no exception) by the methods of historical criticism that it is attempted to solve it.

It is important, we think, to distinguish carefully the observation of facts from their interpretation. If in this second part of historical research there is more or less a philosophical element, it is not the same thing for the first part.

To carry the work out properly it is necessary to make an effort to reach impartiality, to free oneself from all preconceived ideas, and to see the texts as they are, to extract from them what they contain, and not what one would like them to say.

But is perfect objectivity possible in a question whose solution cannot fail to have a very direct bearing upon our philosophical and religious concepts? The objection is a grave one; it does not seem to us decisive if only we consent to admit as the first premise of every religious philosophy that it is not the facts which must be adapted to our theories, but rather that it is our theories which must, if necessary, be corrected and rectified to put them in harmony with the facts.

It is in the religious domain more than in any other that the principle proclaimed by Paul holds most truly. "We can do nothing contrary to the truth; we have no strength except in the truth" (2 Cor. xiii. 8). This principle was also proclaimed by one of the most eminent representatives of German theology, Herrmann, at the beginning of this century, who delighted to repeat: "Die erste Pflicht der Religion ist Wahrhaftigkeit." It is a question of fact which is before us: Are there historical proofs of value for the actual existence of Jesus? We shall therefore leave on one side the discussion of the more or less complicated theories offered to explain (other than by the existence and activity of Jesus) the appearance and development of Christianity. It would be easy to show how much there enters of the conjectural, of superficial resemblances, of debatable interpretation into the systems of the Drews, the Robertsons, the W. B. Smiths, the Couchouds, or the Stahls. We shall not linger on the way to do it. We shall not discuss theories which to a greater or less extent are inspired by considerations depending neither on history nor on criticism, but upon religious philosophy.[47]

If there are sufficient proofs of the historical existence of Jesus, it is above all things necessary that the theory offered of the origin of Christianity should accommodate itself to them. And even if there were no proofs, it might still happen that the explanation of the genesis of Christianity as due to the work and teaching of the prophet of Nazareth would be less conjectural than the theories which bring in the epic of Gilgamesch, the astral system, the pre-Christian cult of Joshua-Jesus, a collective mental representation, or the "document 70."

NOTES

1. Bayle, *Dictionnaire historique et critique,* article "Valla."
2. See his *Harmonie,* published in Basle in 1537.
3. Concerning *L'Harmonistique,* see M. Goguel, Introd., i. pp. 49, *et seq.*
4. Concerning the beginnings of the critical history of the life of Jesus, see Albert Schweitzer, *Geschichte der Leben Jesu-Forschung,* Tübingen, 1913, pp. 23–26; also Chas. Guignebert, *Le Problème de Jésus,* Paris, 1914, pp. 7–21. The part played by English Deists and French writers, completely ignored by Schweitzer, has been well emphasized by Guignebert.
5. Herder, *Vom Erlöser der Menschen nach unsern drei ersten Evangelien: Vom Gottessohn der Welt Heiland nach Johannesevangelium,* Riga, 1797.
6. Paulus, *Das leben Jesu als Grundlage einer reinen Gesch. des Urchristentums,* Heidelberg, 1828.
7. With rationalism may be connected the works of Bahrdt (*Ausführung des Plans und Zwecks Jesu,* 1784–92), Venturini (*Natürliche Gesch. des grossen Propheten von Nazareth,* 1800–1802), which represent Jesus as an agent of the sect of the Essenes. Concerning these authors see Schweitzer (*Gesch.,* pp. 38–48).
8. Voltaire, *Examen important de Milord Bolingbroke* (Edition Kehl), xxxiii, pp. 44–60. Cp. *Sermon des cinquant,* xxxii, pp. 399–400; *Hist. de l'étabt. du christianisme,* xxxv, pp. 274–93.
9. *Id., Ex. de Milord Bolingbroke,* xxxiii, p. 68.
10. *Id., Dieu et les Hommes,* xxxiii, p. 271.
11. *Id., ib.,* p. 272; *Sermon des cinquant,* xxxii, p. 401; *Hist. de l'étabt. du christianisme,* xxxv, p. 274.
12. *Id., Dieu et les Hommes,* xxxiii, p. 273.
13. Voltaire, *Dieu et les Hommes,* xxxiii, p. 279. Further to what has been quoted it is necessary to read *L'Essai sur les mœrs* (especially Chap. ix); *Les Homelies prononcées à Londres,* 1765, xxxii; *Conseils raisonnables à M. Bergier,* xxxiii; *Questions de Zapata,* xxxiii; *Epitre aux Romains,* xxxiii, many articles in the *Dictionnaire philosophique,* xxxvii to xliii. With the ideas of Voltaire may be compared those of Hol-

bach, *Système de nature, Londres,* 1770; under the name of Mirabeau, *Le bons sens du curé Meslier, Londres,* 1772.

14. Napoleon I was under the influence of Volney when, in a conversation that he had with Wieland at Weimar, in 1808, he said it was a great question to decide whether Jesus had existed (Schweitzer, *Gesch.,* p. 445).

15. Dupuis, *L'Origine de tous les cultes ou la religion universelle,* Paris, anno III (1794); *Abrégé de l'origine de tous les cultes,* Paris, anno VII (1798). These two works have been reprinted several times.

16. It was during a conversation with Dupuis that Volney conceived the project of his book.

17. Dupuis, *Abrégé,* p. 251. The views of Dupuis have been wittily criticized by J. B. Perès, librarian of the town of Agen, in a curious booklet in which he applied the method of Dupuis to the *History of Napoleon* to prove the latter had never existed.

18. Strauss, *Das Leben Jesu,* Tübingen, 1835, 1836, 1840. Concerning Strauss see Schweitzer, *Gesch.,* p. 69; also A. Levy, *David Frederick Strauss,* Paris, 1910; Guignebert, pp. xxii *seq.*

19. Concerning these works see Maurice Goguel, *Introd.,* i, p. 67, and ii, p. 27.

20. Usually referred to in England and Germany by the letter Q (Quelle).

21. Schweitzer, *Gesch.,* pp. 124–40.

22. Bruno Bauer, *Kritik des Evangelischen Gesch. des Johannes,* Bremen, 1840; *Kritik der Evangelischen Gesch. der Synoptiker,* Leipzig, 1841–42; *Kritik der Evangelien,* Berlin, 1850–51; *Christus und die Cäsaren,* Berlin, 1877. Concerning Bruno Bauer see M. Kegel, *Bruno Bauer und seine Theorie über die Entstehung des Christentums,* 1908.

23. See Schweitzer (*Gesch.,* pp. 647–51) for a list of eighty-five books and pamphlets published in 1863–64 concerning Renan's work.

24. There are, however, in Renan's work certain errors in taste. "There is no work," writes Schweitzer, "which swarms with so many and such grave errors in taste as the *Vie de Jésus.* It is Christian art in the worst sense of the word—an art of waxen figures. The gentle Jesus, the pretty Maries, the refined Galileans who make up the retinue of the charming carpenter have been taken from the windows of a shop in the Place St. Sulpice." See also opinion of Marcel Proust on the style of the work—"A sort of Lovely Helen of Christianity" (*Revue de Paris,* Nov. 15, 1920).

25. Schweitzer, *Gesch.,* pp. 193–221.

26. Sometimes these were simply declared unauthentic, particularly by Colani, *Jésus Christ et les croyances messianiques de son temps,* Strasbourg, 1864.

27. Johannes Weiss, *Die Predigt Jesu vom Reiche Gottes,* Göttingen, 1892.

28. A. Schweitzer, *Das Leidens- und Messiasgeheimniss,* Tübingen, Leipzig, 1901; *Gesch.,* pp. 390–443; *Die psychiatrische Beurteilung Jesu,* Tübingen, 1913.

29. W. Wrede, *Das Messiasgeheimniss in den Evangelien,* Göttingen, 1901; *Paulus,* Halle, 1904.

30. Concerning this literature see Schweitzer, *Gesch. der Paulinischen Forschung,* 1911, pp. 119–40.

31. Such appears to be the point of view reached by M. Loisy. Under the influence of the sociological school, many critics in recent years insist upon the part played by the community, and specially of worship, in the development of Christianity and of the evangelical tradition. As characteristic of this tendency we cite the work of Bertram, *Die Leidensgeschichte Jesu und der Christuskult,* Göttingen, 1922.

32. On this school, see a book, somewhat one-sided, by G. Van den Bergh van Eysinga, *Die holländische radikale Kritik des Neuen Testaments,* Jena, 1912.

33. Robertson, *Christianity and Mythology,* London, 1900, 1910; *Short History of Christianity,* 1902; *Pagan Christs, Studies in Comparative Theology,* 1902–11; *The Jesus Problem—Restatement of the Myth Theory,* 1917. Concerning Robertson, see Schweitzer (*Gesch.*), Guignebert (p. 88). Some ideas of Robertson resemble the astral theories developed by Niemojewski (*Gott Jesu im Lichte fremder,* etc., München, 1910; *Das werwende Dogma vom Leben Jesu,* Jena, 1910); and by C. P. Fuhrmann (*Der Astralmythus von Christus,* 1912). The idea of a pre-Christian cult of Jesus-Joshua is also admitted by Bolland (*De Evangelische Jozua—Het Evangelien*), Leiden, 1907–10. Cp. also W. Erbt, *Von Jerusalem nach Rome, Untersuchungen zur Geschichte des Urchristentums,* Leipzig, 1912.

34. Kalthoff, *Das Christusproblem, Grundlinien zu einer Sozialtheologie,* Leipzig, 1902–3; *Die Entstehung des Christentums,* Leipzig, 1904; *Was wissen wir von Jesus?* Berlin, 1904. Concerning Kalthoff see Schweitzer (*Gesch.,* p. 345) and Guignebert, p. 78.

35. P. Jensen, *Das Gilgamesch-Epos in der Weltlitteratur,* Strasbourg, 1906; *Moses, Jesus, Paulus, Drei Varianten des Babylonischen Gottmenschen Gilgamesch—Eine Anklage wider die Theologie ein Appel an die Laien,* Frankfurt-a.-M., 1906–9; *Hat der Jesus der Evangelien wirklich gelebt?* On Jensen see Schweitzer (*Gesch.,* p. 466) and Guignebert, p. 85.

36. H. Zimmern (*Zum Streit um den Christusmythe, Das Babylonische Material in seinen Hauptpunkten dargestellt,* 1910) admits, in addition to the influence of Gilgamesch, that of the cults of Marduk, Mithra and Thammuz.

37. W. B. Smith, *Der vorchristliche Jesus* (Giessen, 1906); *Ecce Deus; The pre-Christian Jesus* (*American Journal of Theology,* 1911). Resembling the ideas of W. B. Smith are those of G. T. Sadler, *Behind the New Testament,* London, 1921.

38. A. Drews, *Die Christusmythe,* Jena, 1909–11; *Die Petruslegende,* Frankfurt, 1910; *Das Markusevangelium als Zeugnis gegen die Geschichtlichkeit Jesu,* Jena; *Die Entstehung des Christentums aus dem Gnostizismus.* Concerning Drews see Schweitzer (*Gesch.,* p. 483), Guignebert (p. 107).

39. See particularly the public debates in Berlin in 1910, published by the German Monist Union and translated into French by A. Lipman, *Jésus—a-t-il existé?* (Paris, 1912).

40. Among all this literature we shall only cite: Bousset, *Was wissen wir von Jesu?*; L. C. Fillion, *L'Existence historique de Jésus et le rationalisme contemporain*; Jülicher, *Hat Jesus gelebt?* H. von Soden, *Hat Jesus gelebt?* 1910; Weinel, *Ist das "liberale" Jesus-bild widerlegt?* 1910; Joh. Weiss, *Jesus von Nazareth, Mythus oder Geschichte?* 1910; Dunkmann, *Der historische Jesus, der mythologische Christus,* 1910; S. J. Case, *Historicity of Jesus,* 1912; Guignebert, *Le Problème de Jésus,* 1914. The method employed by Pérès against Dupuis (see Section I) has been turned against the modern mythologists by J. Naumann (see *Die Bismarcksmythe*) and by an anonymous writer to show that Martin Luther never existed (*Beweis dass Docktor M. Luther nie existiert hat*).

41. The most prolific of these authors is Arthur Heulhard (*le Mensonge chrétien, Jésus Christ n'a pas existé,* Paris, 1908–10, 11 vol.; *la Vérité Barabbas, le Mensonge Jésus; Tu est Petrus l'histoire et la legende,* Paris, 1913–14). Heulhard sums up his theory in the two following theses:—

"1. It was the Jew known as John the Baptist who said he was Christ and Bar Abba (son of the father), and he was certainly not beheaded."

"2. It was Barabbas who, condemned to death for his public crimes—such as assassination, robbery and treason—was crucified at Guol Golta by Pilate. The evangelists are a mystification invented more than a century after the execution of this scoundrel. It is Barabbas that the Church worships under the name of Jesus, an imaginary personage substituted by the evangelists for the crucified, and invented by them to impart the hue of innocence to the individual by whose invention they exploited lucratively the remission of sins by baptism."

42. Salomon Reinach, *Orpheus*, 1909; *Le Verset 17 du Psaume xxii; A tropos de la curiosité de Tibère; Bossuet et l'argument des propheties; Simon de Cyrène; Une source biblique du Docétisme*.

43. Couchoud, *L'Enigme de Jésus* (translated into English by Mrs. G. Whale); *Enigma of Jesus*, with introduction by Sir J. G. Fraser; *Le Mystère de Jésus* (*Mercure de France*).

The first article in the *Mercure de France* by M. Couchoud was discussed by me. Under the pretext that it was not a review of religious history, the *Mercure* refused to insert an article in which I discussed the second article of M. Couchoud. On the other hand, M. Couchoud has explained his views in a series of informal discussions at the Union *pour la Vérité* (Jan.–April, 1924). The development of the objections made by me on these occasions will be found in the present volume.

44. See Couchoud, *Le Mystère de Jésus,* p. 117.

45. R. Stahl, *Le Document 70,* Paris and Strasbourg, 1923. On this book see the observations of M. Alfaric, *Revue d'histoire,* 1924.

46. See Couchoud, *Le Mystère de Jésus* and *Mercure de France* (March 1924).

47. This has been well noted by Guignebert (p. 23). Let us recall only, for example, the case which Drews has pointed out (p. 25, French edition). There is something similar with M. Couchoud, who, pointing out how the concept formed about Jesus was transformed according to the particular epoch, foresees that this evolution will continue and that in "about 1940 Jesus in His entirety will have passed from the historical stage to that of collective mental representations" (*Le Mystère de Jésus*). Have we not here a theory upon the essence of religious facts? The same author supposes that if Christianity had really arisen from the deification

of an historical personage it would be something very mean, a religion of a low type, on the commonplace level of the Imperial Roman Cult, in any case quite inferior to Judaism and Islamism, which have taken great care that neither Moses nor Mahomet should be taken for gods. For him this is an objection to the historicity of Jesus, at any rate, "because he has a vague idea that Christianity is not there." We can hardly fail to recognize in this an a priori opinion calculated to hinder historical inquiry.

CHAPTER II

THE NONCHRISTIAN TESTIMONY[1]

I. FLAVIUS JOSEPHUS

The most ancient non-Christian testimony concerning Jesus is—or rather would be, if it were authentic—that of Josephus. In his works, as we read them, Jesus is mentioned twice,[2] in the eighteenth and the twentieth book of *Jewish Antiquities.*

The first of these reads thus: "At this time Jesus appeared—a wise man, if He can be called man. For He accomplished marvelous things, was the Master of those who received with joy the truth, and led away many Jews and also many Greeks. He was the Christ. Upon the denunciation of the leaders of our nation, Pilate condemned Him to the cross; but those who had loved Him from the first ceased not to revere Him, for He appeared to them on the third day, raised again from the dead, as had announced the divine prophets, as well as a thousand other marvelous things concerning Him. There still exists to-day the sect which, after Him, received the name of 'Christians.'"[3]

This text is given by three known manuscripts, of which none, it must be admitted, goes farther back than the eleventh century. Eusebius (*H.*, i, p. 11, and *Dem. ev.*) knew of it. But Origen seems

71

to ignore it, for upon two occasions he quotes the praise given by Josephus to James, while remarking that nevertheless Josephus did not admit Jesus to be the Christ (*Comm. in Matt. x.*, c. 17, also *Contra Celsius,* i, 47).

From the point of view of external criticism, the passage is therefore strongly *suspected,* at least, to be an interpolation.[4]

The arguments from internal criticism appear to be still more convincing. If Josephus had said of Jesus, "if He can be called a man" and "He was the Christ," if he had spoken of resurrection, of miracles, the fulfillment of prophecies, he would have been a Christian.

From the sixteenth century the authenticity of this passage has been questioned, specially by Osiander; one feels a certain diffi-culty in understanding how such a critic as Harnack has been able to defend it.[5]

The passage that we read betrays with evidence a Christian hand, but has not the interpolator confined himself to retouching that which Josephus had written?[6] And if this hypothesis be accepted, is it possible to reconstruct the original text? Or is one simply to maintain that he spoke of Jesus, which in itself would be a fact of importance? Schürer has observed that if the expressions and phrases whose origin is certainly Christian are put aside, the remainder is very insignificant. But the interpolator could easily have mutilated the primitive passage at the same time as he exag-gerated it. Norden remarks that the account of Pilate's government in the eighteenth book of the *Antiquities* consists of a series of episodes presented as troubles which arose among the Jews, the word θόρυβος (noise, clamor, disturbance) being the *leit* motif of the account.

The general plan is interrupted by paragraphs 63 and 64, which speak of Jesus. If these are removed, paragraphs 62 and 65 are in perfect connection with each other. The bond between them is broken by what is said to Jesus. Norden therefore considers this fragment to be quite unauthentic. But Corssen replies against this that the general plan of the account is artificial. The events related are not all, in the strict sense of the word, troubles. There is, for instance, in paragraph 62 a reference to an incident which happened in Rome and in which the Jews were not implicated, and in paragraph 65 it is not a question of troubles among the Jews, but of measures directed against them. It might therefore be supposed, if the original passage had contained anything about Jesus, that His history would equally have been presented as that of an agitation. The reasoning which Corssen uses against Norden's theory seems to us decisive, but still it only establishes a mere possibility. Is it possible to go farther? In the retouching of a passage there very often appear certain peculiarities of the primitive form. According to Corssen this is the case in the passage we are concerned with. The expression "receive with pleasure" is a formula that Josephus is very fond of, and which he uses no less than seven times in the eighteenth book of the *Antiquities*. The words, "the chief among us" are also quite his style. It would be possible to say as much of the epithet "wise man," as applied to Jesus; it would be difficult to understand from the pen of a Christian, while it accords well with the tendency of Josephus to class as philosophical schools such Jewish movements, essentially religious, as those of the Pharisees, Sadducees and Essenes. The idea of the Greeks allying themselves with Jesus is also very characteristic. It may be that the Christian editor of our passage took pains to imitate the style of Josephus; it is nevertheless difficult to suppose that he succeeded so well in it. The passage might therefore be the retouching of one written by Josephus himself. This conclusion seems confirmed by the fact that in the passage in the twentieth book, where the death of James is referred to, the latter is presented as "the brother of Jesus, surnamed the Christ," which would seem to indicate that this Jesus was a personage already known to the readers, of whom therefore Josephus must have made mention.

Is it possible to reconstruct, by surmise, the original passage of Josephus? Theodore Reinach thinks it is, and, eliminating that coming from a Christian hand, he restores the following passage: "At this time there appeared Jesus, called Christ, an able man (for He was a worker of miracles) who preached to those eager for novelties, and He led away many Jews and also many Greeks. Albeit that Pilate upon the denunciation of the leaders among us, condemned Him to the cross, those who had loved Him from the beginning (or those whom He had deceived from the beginning) ceased not to be attached to Him, and to-day there still exists the sect which from Him had taken the name of Christians." Here is nothing more than a conjecture, for if it is easy to recognize in the actual text that which comes from a Christian hand, it is not so easy to guess at what the portions suppressed by the interpolator might have contained.

In the twentieth book of the *Antiquities* (paragraph 200) there is another mention of Jesus. It is found in the account of the death of James whom the high priest Annas caused to be tried, and put to death by stoning, during the period between the death of Festus and the arrival of his successor, Albinus. At this time Roman authority seemed to be somewhat lax at Jerusalem. "Annas," says the text, "called the Sanhedrin together, and summoned to appear before it the brother of Jesus, surnamed Christ, and certain others under the charge of illegality, and caused them to be stoned to death." Eusebius cites this passage (*H.*, II, xxiii, pars. 21–24), but Origen, who on three occasions[7] establishes (following Josephus) a relation between the death of James and the destruction of the Temple, has read the passage in a text retouched by a Christian.

Schürer (*Gesch.*, i, p. 581) concludes from this that the existing text is also to be suspected of interpolation. This conclusion goes too far.

Admitting that this passage is among those that the Christians might have been tempted to exaggerate, it does not at all follow that they did it. Besides, between the expression "Jesus, surnamed Christ," and the categorical declaration "He was the Christ" of the eighteenth book there is a great difference. The words *may* then be authentic.[8] Mgr. Batiffol[9] has believed it possible to deduce from this passage an important conclusion. The accusation brought against James and his associates is couched in ambiguous terms which may just as well refer to the violation of Roman laws as to that of the Jewish Law. In order to admit that the ground of the charge against James was revolt against Roman law, it would be necessary to attribute to the high priest and the Sanhedrin a scrupulous loyalty to the Roman power which seems very far from likely to have been the case. On this hypothesis it would be difficult to understand why (as Josephus says) they were accused of this before the Governor by the Jews.[10]

What, asks Mgr. Batiffol, would constitute a revolt against religion if it were not the Christianity of the accused? This argument is in conflict with a difficulty, for tradition presents James as a very strict observer of the "Law."

The text of Josephus seems to us too concise to allow us to maintain that there could have been no other motive of opposition between the high priest and James other than Christianity.[11]

Even if it be recognized that the silence of Josephus concerning Jesus and Christianity is not so complete as was formerly said, the extremely brief character of the allusions found in his work (under even the most favorable hypothesis) is none the less striking. How explain it, seeing that the work of Josephus deals precisely with the environment and the epoch in which Christianity was born and began to develop? Is it not surprising that an author who spoke of the Pharisees, the Sadducees, the Essenes and the Samaritans has said nothing, or has said so little, about the Christians? So complete a silence is perhaps more embarrassing for the mythologists than for their opponents. By what right, indeed, should it be permissible to conclude from it that Jesus never existed, and not permissible to deny that a Christian movement existed in Palestine prior to the year 70? Since Josephus has been silent not only concerning Jesus, but also concerning Christianity, how is his silence to be explained? Uniquely by his character and the object of his work. The writer desired to flatter the Romans and gain their good graces. To do this he expunged from the picture he drew everything likely to offend or excite their apprehension. Thus it is that he has scarcely at all spoken of the Messianic cult which nevertheless constituted the center of Jewish thought in the first century. That he did so was because this cult was a menace to Rome, for the Kingdom of the Messiah could only be built upon the ruins of the Empire.

Josephus portrays John the Baptist as a moral preacher, and passes by unnoticed everything which presented him as the prophet of the Messiah, the one to announce the baptism of fire (*Antiquities,* xviii. pp. 116–19). The preaching of repentance is thus deprived by him of everything lending its support and giving it any significa-tion. The little that Josephus preserves of Messianism is used by him to flatter basely authority in connecting the Messianic prophe-cies with Vespasian.[12] It was not possible to speak of Christianity while amputating it from Messianism. Josephus therefore main-tained silence on the subject.

It might besides have been determined by another reason. At the time he wrote—and at least since the persecution by Nero—Chris-tianity was separated from Judaism. Josephus could thus consider it as outside the history that he wished to write.[13] Doubtless the same thing was not the case as regards Palestine Christianity, but Jose-phus could not have spoken of it without exposing Judaism to the accusation of a compromising solidarity with a dangerous move-ment, odious to the governing class, and to which, it has been sup-posed, he had contributed to draw the attention of the court of Nero.[14] The silence of Josephus is not therefore the silence of igno-rance; it is the silence of prudence and fear—a silence actuated by interest. Far from proving that Jesus and the Christian movement did not exist in Palestine in the first century, it only proves that Josephus did not wish, by speaking of it, to compromise himself, and with himself the Jewish people.[15]

The reasons which explain the silence or the discretion of Jose-phus account also for the fact that, according to Photius (Codex 13),

Justus of Tiberiade (author of a chronicle and a history of the Jewish war, written at the same time and in the same spirit as the work of Josephus) has not mentioned Jesus or Christianity either.

As regards Philo, astonishment is sometimes expressed that in his works no mention is found of the Gospel. But it suffices to remember that he died shortly after the year 40,[16] and there is nothing to prove that Christianity had reached Alexandria before this date. That the Talmud and other Jewish sources[17] say nothing about Jesus which is not the distortion of Christian tradition is sufficiently explained by the date of these documents and the fact that those who compiled them were governed by entirely polemical considerations. Their sole object was to combat the Christians; they were not interested in writing the history of their religion. The first mention of the Christians in this Jewish literature is the curse contained in the "Schemonè Esrè," the daily prayer of the Jews (at close of the first century), "May the Nazarenes and the Minim perish!"

II. THE LATIN AUTHORS

The first Latin text to mention the name of Christ is dated A.D. 110. It is the letter from Pliny to Trajan concerning the conduct to be observed toward the Christians.[18] He recounts his methods of action, punishing those for obstinacy, who, after two or three interrogations, persisted in the confession of Christianity, releasing those, who denounced as being Christians, denied the charge, and who in the Governor's presence invoked the gods, offered wine and incense before the statue of the emperor, and cursed the name of Christ. The case of those who confessed they were formerly Christians, but declared they were so no longer, caused Pliny some embarrassment; he had questioned them and compared their replies with information obtained by putting two deaconesses to the torture. He had only discovered, he declares, a coarse and exaggerated superstition. From what he states concerning Christian practices one point may be noted: The Christians were in the habit of meeting upon a certain day and singing a hymn (*carmen dicere*), or, in other words, invoking Christ as a God.

This text is evidence of the cult of Christ, but it does not say explicitly whether He was conceived to be a personage having lived on earth or a being of entirely spiritual nature. The expression "Christo quasi Deo" appears to mean, however, that for Pliny, Christ was not a God like unto others. Was not the fact that He had lived on earth, that which distinguished Him from others? The testimony of Tacitus in the *Annales,* written between 115 and 117, is more explicit: "To destroy the rumor [which accused him as guilty of the burning of Rome] Nero invented some culprits, and inflicted on them the most excruciating punishments; they were those who, detested for their infamies, were called by the populace, Christians. The author of this name, Christ, had under the reign of Tiberius been condemned to death by the Procurator Pontius Pilate. This execrable superstition, held in check for a time, broke out anew, not only in Judea, the birthplace of this evil, but also in the city in which all atrocities congregate and flourish."[19]

There are two remarks in this passage whose authenticity is certain.[20] The first concerns the burning of Rome and the persecution of the Christians; the second concerns the Christ.[21] The first reflects the point of view of the contemporaries of Tacitus. It is a question of the hatred and contempt excited by the Christians and the infamies with which they were reproached, whilst it is precisely the accusation launched by Nero against them which seems to have unchained this hatred and contempt. The second must originate in some documentary source, since it contains no such word as "*dicunt*" or "*ferunt*," which would authorize us to suppose that Tacitus is only relating gossip. There is in this remark a characteristic idea—namely, that Christianity had been crushed out by the death of Christ, and had only reappeared about the year 64, simultaneously in Rome and in Judea. This resurrection of the execrable superstition in Judea can only be understood if we suppose that

Tacitus does not make any distinction between the two manifestations of Messianism—Christianity and Judaism.

The words "not only in Judea" would imply, then, the sudden outbreak of nationalism which caused the revolt and the Jewish war.[22]

We can here form an idea of the character of the source: it was not Christian, since it presumed an eclipse of Christianity after the death of Jesus;[23] neither was it Jewish, for no Jewish document would have called Jesus "Christ," nor would it have presented Judaism as solidary with Christianity.[24]

The hypothesis which asserts that Tacitus could have consulted official documents preserved in the imperial archives can only be mentioned to be passed by, seeing that these archives were secret, and there is nothing to authorize our supposing that any exception to a general rule was made in the historian's favor. The dependence of Tacitus upon Josephus, as supposed by Harnack, has generally been discarded, particularly by Goetz, Norden and Corssen.

The fact that in the account which he gives of the Jewish war, Tacitus has utilized the *De Bello Judaico* of Josephus[25] is hardly conclusive, because if it were difficult for Tacitus to ignore so important a document as Josephus' account of the war, there is no reason at all to suppose that Tacitus, for whom Judaism was an object of the most profound contempt, had read the *Antiquities of the Jews,* and that he had sought therein any information to complete his account of the burning of Rome. Between the text of Tacitus and the passages of Josephus there are, besides, appreciable differences. The text of Josephus states that Jesus' death was not the cause of a cessation of faith among his disciples; Tacitus, on the contrary, supposes that Christianity temporarily disappeared after the death of its founder. The judgment of Josephus upon Christianity is upon the whole a favorable one; that of Tacitus was one of supreme contempt. Finally, Tacitus appears to accept the word Christ as the name of the founder of the sect, while Josephus is aware that this founder was called Jesus, and that the word Christ designates the dignity to which he laid claim.

Goetz[26] has surmised that Tacitus obtained his information concerning Christianity from his friend, Pliny the Younger. The two writers certainly contemplate Christianity from the same point of view—that of the police—but this fact is characteristic of all the Romans. On the other hand, between Pliny and Tacitus there is an important difference. If they are in agreement in only seeing in Christianity a superstition, the first considers it an innocent one, the second calls it execrable, and appears to endorse the infamous accusations brought against the Christians. Mgr. Batiffol,[27] dwelling on the fact that Tacitus made use of the history of Pliny the Elder, has surmised that he borrowed from it his notes about the Christians. That is a supposition which in its nature one is unable to verify. But one fact is certain, and that is, Tacitus knew of a document, which was neither Jewish nor Christian, which connected Christianity with the Christ crucified by Pontius Pilate. The importance of this observation does not require to be emphasized.

In his *Life of Nero* (Chap. xvi) Suetonius mentions the persecution of the Christians, but he says nothing concerning their teachings. In the *Life of Claudius* (xxv, p. 4) he refers in passing to the expulsion of the Jews from Rome, to which the book of Acts also makes allusion (xviii. 2): "Judæos, impulsore Chresto assidue tumultuantes, Roma expulit" (He expelled from Rome the Jews, who under the impulsion of Christ did not cease to make tumult).[28]

Is one obliged to see in "Chrestos"[29] an unknown Jewish agitator, as do certain critics,[30] and thence conclude that the text does not relate to the Christians? Or, stressing the fact that at Rome the Christians seem to have been called "Chresitanoi" and not "Christianoi,"[31] must we suppose that it is Christ who is referred to, and that it was the disputes concerning Him which stirred up the Jewry of Rome and provoked the action of Claudius? The fact that Suetonius mentions Chrestos as a known personage without joining to his name *quodam* or *aliquo*[32] is favorable to the second interpretation, and it is also the one generally accepted.[33] The text of Suetonius tells us only that Christianity had reached Rome under the reign of Claudius, and that it was considered to have connection with a personage of the name of Chrestos. But Suetonius could have believed that Chrestos had come to Rome in the time of Claudius,[34] and this proves how slightly the Romans interested themselves at the beginning of the second century in the traditions which the Christians invoked.

What the Roman authors say about Jesus and Christianity amounts to very little indeed. Only the testimony of Tacitus is plainly incompatible with the theory of a Christ entirely ideal. The rarity of the details furnished by the Latin authors is, however, striking. One is aware how prudent one must be in handling the "argument from silence" (*ex silentio*). To make it convincing it requires two conditions which are not satisfied in the case before us. In the first place the silence must be complete, which it is not, without taking any account of what the portion not preserved of contemporary literature might contain. In the second place the silence must have a real signification; in other words, the authors considered *must* have been obliged to mention, had they known them, the facts of which they say nothing. Now this second condition has not been satisfied either. Pliny, Tacitus and Suetonius agree in seeing in Christianity only a contemptible superstition. It only interested them just so far as it was a cause of social disturbance. They only mention it to relate the measures directed against it, not to inquire into its origin, and still less to write the history of its real or supposed founder.

The importance that Christianity eventually reached leads many modern minds to commit a strange error in perspective. Because the birth of Christianity appears to them as the most pregnant fact in the whole of first-century history, they find it difficult to understand that the ancients did not see things from the same point of view, and only paid any attention to Christianity at the happening of certain events which had no essential importance for its development.

III. "ACTA PILATI" (THE ACTS OF PILATE)

There is no reason to suppose that there has ever existed in Rome any official document which refers to the condemnation of Jesus by Pontius Pilate.[35]

It is true that in two passages in his *Apology,* addressed (toward the middle of the second century) to Antoninus the Pious, to Marcus Aurelius, to Lucius Verus, to the Senate and all the Roman people, Justin Martyr invokes (to confirm the account he gives of the Passion and miracles of Jesus) the "Acts of Pontius Pilate" (I *Apol.,* xxxv, 48).

Tertullian also in his *Apologeticum,* dating from 197, mentions a report that Pontius Pilate, already a Christian in his inner conscience ("jam pro sua conscientia christianus"), had sent to Tiberius.

Eusebius, who cites Chapter v of the *Apologeticum,* does not appear to know the document of which he speaks, while in another passage he refers to the "Acts of Pilate" as forged by the pagans as an arm against Christianity. There has existed a whole literature of "Acts of Pilate," which (particularly in the form it has assumed in the Gospel of Nicodemus) enjoyed great favor in the Middle Ages.[36] Critics are in agreement in considering this literature, in the form in which we know it, to be of a later age, and in any case not older than the fifth century, but it is not certain that its primitive element does not go farther back, since Epiphanius (fourth century) knew of the "Acta Pilati" (*Hær.,* 50–51).

The narratives for which Justin and Tertullian invoke the authority of the "Acta Pilati," or of a report sent by the Procurator to the Emperor, rest on evangelical tradition, and merely accentuate its tendency to portray Pilate as well disposed toward Jesus and convinced of His innocence.[37] The documents designated by them would therefore be of Christian editing, but is it certain that they were acquainted with them or had done anything more than suppose their existence?

Justin would not have expressed himself other than he does if he had merely heard the "Acts of Pilate" spoken of or had presumed their existence.

Many writers have therefore considered that these "Acts" did not exist in his time,[38] and the fact that in another passage of the *Apology* (I, xxiv, p. 2) he quotes in the same way the census registers of Quirinius confirms this opinion. It has been objected that Justin cited the "Acts" not only to support his narration of the Passion, but also to support the account he gives of the miracles of Jesus. He must, therefore, it is thought, have known this document, or at any rate something about its contents.[39] But the first hypothesis is excluded by the somewhat vague way in which the "Acts" are cited; the second is not without some difficulties. If such an important document had existed, how is it that Justin should only have known it by hearsay? It is doubtless by mere conjecture that he supposed the "Acta Pilati" must have narrated both the trial and the career of Jesus.

Certain authors, however, following H. von Schubert,[40] have thought that a trace of the primary elements of the "Acta Pilati" was to be found prior to Justin's period.

They rest their case upon the fact that the Gospel of Peter and Justin (I *Apol.,* xxxv) state that, to mock Him, Jesus was made to seat Himself in a chair, and invited to act as a Judge.[41] Seeing that the hypothesis of a direct connection between the Gospel of Peter and Justin encounters certain difficulties, it has been supposed that both were dependent upon a common source. But even if this were so, there is nothing to prove that this source was anything other than a mere extra-canonical tradition.

As regards Tertullian, Harnack considers that he has simply made use of what he found in Justin, and that it is his work which suggested the composition of the letter from Pilate to the Emperor which is found in Chapters xl–xlii of the Acts of Peter and Paul.[42] The last words of this letter reveal, indeed, its polemical character, and show that it must have been compiled to combat the pagan Acts spoken of by Eusebius.

Nevertheless, Justin and Tertullian do not invoke the testimony of Pilate in reference to the same facts, and the document is presented by Justin as the acts, and by Tertullian as a letter of Pilate to the Emperor. Tertullian, for his part, only makes one allusion, somewhat vague, to the document, and he does not know it at first-hand. At the most he has heard it spoken of, if he does not altogether guess at its existence.

As neither Origen nor Eusebius make any allusion to the "Acts of Pilate,"[43] it may be considered that the work did not exist in their time.

What is the interpretation of this absence of testimony from Pilate concerning the punishment of Jesus?

For M. Salomon Reinach it is decisive:

"There was no official report, while there ought to have been one," he says. "The conclusion which is forced upon one is assuredly not favorable to the historicity of the Passion."[44]

So radical a conclusion appears to us unwarranted. From the fact that spurious "Acta Pilati" have been fabricated as well by Christians as by their opponents, it does not follow that an authentic work never existed. The conclusion is simply that these "Acts," if they existed, were not at the disposal of those whose interest it was to consult them. We know that the archives of the emperors were not accessible to the Senate. Tacitus himself, notwithstanding his relations with Neva and Trajan, seems to have been unable to obtain access to them.[45] Still less reason existed to permit access to them by private persons, and Christian apologists could make no examination of them. If their opponents had been more favored and authorized to make researches which remained fruitless, they would have made a point about it in their polemic. Because an official document has not been produced, no one is authorized to conclude that it could not have existed. But, even if it were proved that no report was made by Pilate to Tiberius, what would be the significance of this fact? Justin, who had presumed the existence of a report, says M. Salomon Reinach, was in a better position than we are to estimate the obligations of a Procurator. But the death of

Jesus was in his eyes an event of such capital importance that it was difficult for him to see that for Pilate it may only have been an incident without importance. Besides, Justin is influenced by the tendency to make of Pilate a witness favorable to Jesus and opposed to the Jews. Everything that we know concerning Pilate shows him to us as a cruel and unscrupulous man, for whom the lives of those under his jurisdiction had but little importance; he had no hesitation in sending to execution whosoever resisted him or became a pretext for agitation. Jesus was certainly not the sole victim of his procedure of summary justice. To condemn to death was for him merely an act of administrative routine. Is it to be supposed that in each particular case he considered it necessary to send a report to the Emperor, and in so doing furnish arms to his enemies by allowing them to accuse him of cruelty and injustice?

No more than the almost complete silence of Josephus, or the rarity and paucity of the details furnished by the Latin historians, does the absence of any report from Pilate to the Emperor constitute an objection against the historical character of Jesus.

NOTES

1. K. Linck, *De antiquissimis quæ ad Jesum Nazarenum spectant testimoniis,* Giessen, 1913.

2. The best edition of Josephus' works is that of Niese (Berlin, 1885–95) in six volumes. A French translation is appearing under the direction of Th. Reinach (Paris, 1900). Concerning Josephus see Schürer (*Gesch.,* i, pp. 74–106), with very complete bibliography.

3. *Ant. Jud.,* xviii, pp. 63–64.

To the bibliography given by Schürer must be added the following: Burkitt (*Josephus and Christ*), Harnack (*Der jüdische Geschichtschreiber Josephus und Jesus Christus*), Smith (*De Katholieck,* as regards authenticity), Batiffol (*Orpheus et l'Evangile*), K. Linck (*op. cit.*), Norden (*Josephus und Tacitus über Jesus Christus und Messianische Prophetie*), Seitz (*Das Christuszeugniss des Josephus Flavius*), Jacoby (*Jesus bei Jose-*

phus), Ed. Meyer (*Ursprung und Anfänge des Christentums,* for authenticity), Goetz (*Die Ursprüngliche Fassung des Stelle Ant.*), Corssen (*Die Zeugnisse des Tacitus und Pseudo-Josephus über Christus*), Goethals (*Mélanges d'histoire chrétienne*), Brüne (*St. u. Kr.,* unauthentic text, but substituted for a text in which Josephus spoke of Jesus), R. Laqueur (*Josephus,* passage added afterwards by Josephus himself).

4. The text of Josephus seems to have existed under another form, for in an Apocryphal dialogue concerning a religious discussion at the court of Sassanides we read: "Josephus spoke of the Christ as a just and good man manifested by Divine Grace by means of signs and miracles, and who did good to many." (Bratke, *Das sogenannte Religionsgespräch am Hofe der Sassaniden*).

5. Among the most recent defenders of authenticity we may cite Bole (*Flavius Josephus über Christus und die Christen in den jüdischen Altertümern*), Kneller (*Flavius Josephus über Christus, Stimmen aus Maria Laach*), Burkitt, Harnack, etc.

6. The thesis of unauthenticity is admitted, besides authors quoted, by Schürer, Niese (*De testimonio christiano quod est apud Josephum*); that of interpolation by Reinach (*Josephe sur Jésus*), etc.

7. Origen, *Comm. in Matt.* 17 and *Contra Celsum,* i, 47; ii, 13.

8. This, for instance, is the opinion of K. Linck.

9. Batiffol, *Orpheus et l'Evangile.*

10. Mgr. Batiffol adds that the punishment inflicted—stoning to death—presupposes a crime of a religious character. This is not convincing, for it does not appear that blasphemers alone were stoned to death.

11. A Slavonic version of the *De Bello Judaico* contains various additions to the Greek text in which Jesus is referred to. It will suffice to establish its character of secondary importance to summarize what is said of the death of Jesus in the first portion: Jesus remains on the Mount of Olives and refuses to humble Himself as He is ordered by Pilate and the Roman authorities. The Jews accuse Him then of fomenting a conspiracy, in the presence of the Procurator. The latter, after having massacred many innocent persons, seizes Jesus, and finding that He is no malefactor sets Him free, after having obtained from Him the healing of his wife. The Jews, jealous of this success, give thirty pieces of silver to Pilate, and so obtain the right to crucify Jesus. It is difficult to understand how the first

editor, A. Berendts (*Die Zeugnisse von Christo im Slavischen De Bello Judaico des Josephus*) has been able to find in such accounts the authentic elements that Josephus made away with in translating his work from Aramaic into Greek.

12. *De Bello Jud.*, vi, pp. 310–14. The same thing is found in Tacitus (*History*, v., p. 13), and in Suetonius (*Vesp.*, p. 4), who have probably borrowed in this matter from Josephus.

13. Ed. Meyer, *Ursprung und Anf.* i, p. 211.

14. So Corssen thinks (*Z.N.T.W.*, xv, p. 135), who points out that Josephus was in Rome at the time of the fire, and that he was in relation with the empress Poppœa.

15. Joh. Weiss, *Jesus von Nazareth, Mythus oder Geschichte*, p. 89.

16. Philo was one of an embassy sent to Rome by the Jews of Alexandria in A.D. 40, and he was then very old. He speaks of himself as an old man (*Leg. ad Gaium*, par. 28). The account of the embassy was written immediately after.

17. Concerning this literature see H. Laible (*Jesus Christus im Thalmud*), an English edition published in Cambridge (1893), with additions of Dalman and Streeter (*Jesus Christ in the Talmud*, etc.). See also R. T. Herford (*Christianity in Talmud*), A. Meyer (*Jesus im Talmud*), H. L. Strack (*Jesus die Häreteker*, Leipzig, 1910).

18. X, p. 96. The authenticity of this text has often been challenged since Semler. It is, however, generally admitted. See E. C. Babut (*Remarques sur les deux lettres de Pline et de Trajan relatives aux Chrétiens de Bithynie*), Linck (pp. 33–60), Reinach (*Orpheus*, p. 371), Couchoud (*Le Mystère de Jésus*). There may be in Pliny's letter some Christian interpolations (cp. Guignebert, *Tertullien*, pp. 77 *et seq.*), M. Goguel (*L'Eucharistie des origens à Justin Martyr*, pp. 259 *et seq.*). From our present point of view we may neglect them.

19. *Annales*, xv, 44. See further certain studies cited respecting Josephus, Linck, pp. 61–103; also Batiffol (*Orpheus et l'Evangile*, pp. 44–47).

20. It is admitted without any reserve by S. Reinach (*Orpheus*). Hochart, after discovering in this passage an interpolation (*Etudes au sujet de la persecution des Chrétiens sous Neron*), maintains that the entire work of Tacitus was an invention of the fifteenth century (*De l'authenticité des annales et des histoires de Tacite*). Hochart's theory has only been admitted by Drews (*Die Christusmythe*).

21. Corssen, *Z.N.T.W.,* xiv, 1913, p. 135 (*Zeitschrift für die Neutes-tamentliche Wissenschaft*).

22. Corssen, *Z.N.T.W.,* xiv, 1913, p. 123.

23. In this argument the hypothesis of Meyer (who thinks the details made use of by Tacitus relate to a form of confession of the Christian faith) is invalidated. Meyer thinks that Tacitus was obliged to occupy himself with the Christians during his government of Asia, and that he had made an inquiry into the origin of their movement. Meyer thinks he can recognize an affinity between the phrase of Tacitus, "*per procuratorem Pontium Pilatum supplicio adfectus,*" and that found in Timothy, "He bore witness before Pontius Pilate." He also supposes that Tacitus became acquainted with the Christian faith by his exami-nation of those who were persecuted. Besides what has already been said, it must be replied against Meyer's opinion that on one side it is merely a question of a condemnation pronounced by the Procurator, and on the other side the profession of faith of Jesus. The two things are far from being equivalent.

24. These two points have been well emphasized by Batiffol.

25. *History,* v, 13, depends upon *De Bello Jud.,* vi, 310–14.

26. Goetz, *Z.N.T.W.,* xiv, 1913, p. 295.

27. Batiffol, Orpheus et l'Evangile, p. 46.

28. Here again Hochart has in a very arbitrary way suspected a Christian interpolation. This thesis is indefensible, for no Christian would ever have expressed himself as Suetonius does.

29. Linck gives a list of more than eighty inscriptions at Rome in which the name of Chrestos is found.

30. Linck, also Reinach and Couchoud, consider this interpretation possible.

31. Tacitus, *Annales,* v (Codex Mediceus), has the form "Chres-tianos." In the three passages only in the New Testament where the word "Christians" is found (Acts xi. 26, xxvi. 28; I Pet. iv. 16), the first copy of the Sinaiticus has χρηστιανοί. The MS. (B) Vaticanus has χρειστιανοέ. Compare with Justin (I *Apol.* 4), Tertulian (*Apol.* 3). The form "Chres-tianoi" is frequent in the inscriptions. Compare with Linck.

32. Batiffol, *Orpheus et l'Evangile,* p. 43.

33. Meyer, *Ursprung und Anf.,* iii, 463.

34. Preuschen (*Chresto impulsore*) supposed that some connection

existed between the details given by Suetonius and the tradition that Jesus died under Claudius. (See Chap. X, Section III.)

35. Concerning an examination of documents and archives which, according to S. Reinach, was made at Antioch in the time of Ignatius, see later (Chap. IV).

36. Concerning this literature consult R. A. Lipsius (*Die Pilatusakten*), Harnack (*Gesch. des altchristlichen Litt. bis Eusebius*), Bardenhewer (*Gesch. des Altkirchlichen Litt.*), A. Stuelken (*Pilatusakten*) in Hennecke (*Handbuch Neutestamentischen Apokryphen*).

37. Concerning this tendency see M. Goguel, *Les Chrétiens et l'Empire Romain à l'Epoque du N.T.; Juifs et Romains dans l'histoire de la Passion.*

38. This is the opinion of Lipsius, Harnack, Bardenhewer, and also of Mgr. Batiffol.

39. Stuelken (*Handbuch*).

40. H. von Schubert, *Die Komposition des pseudopetrinischen Evangelienfragments.*

41. There is no trace of any such episode in the canonical Gospels unless, perhaps, in John xix. 13, if there is given to the verb a transitive sense. But even thus the scene would have quite another character than in Justin and the Gospel of Peter.

42. *Acta Apostolorum Apocrypha* (edition Lipsius and Bonnet, 1891).

43. The silence of these two men is important owing to their vast erudition. That of Eusebius is particularly significant. There are at least three passages in his *Ecclesiastical History* where it was difficult to avoid mention of the "Acta Pilati"—had he known the work. These are: i, 9 (concerning Pilate), ii, 2 (quoting Tertullian's *Apology*), ix. 5–7 (quoting the pagan "Acta Pilati").

44. S. Reinach, *A propos de la curiosité de Tibère.*

45. Ph. Fabia, *Les Sources de Tacite,* p. 324.

CHAPTER III

HYPOTHESIS OF A PRE-CHRISTIANITY

I. JESUS THE NAZARENE

Does the name of Jesus the Nazarene—or rather do the two names associated in this expression—designate an historical person or the hero of a cult? Does the term Nazarene signify "Saviour Protector," and should it be considered as a divine name of similar character to Zeus Xenios, Hermes Psychopompos, or Jahveh Sabaoth? "There is every reason to think," writes Drews, "that the name of Joshua or Jesus was that under which the expected Messiah was worshiped in certain Jewish sects."[1] Upon examination the arguments offered in support of this opinion seem somewhat shallow. Robertson[2] finds in the worship of Jesus a new form of the old Ephraim cult of Joshua, a solar divinity. A trace of this cult is to be found in a passage in the book of the prophet Zechariah, where the high priest Joshua appears before the Angel of the Eternal, who causes him to take off his soiled garments and put on festal clothing. He receives this promise: "If thou wilt walk in My ways, and if thou wilt keep My charge, then shalt thou also judge My house and shalt also keep My courts" (Zech. iii. 7). Jesus was a divine name, Jesus the Lord was God, considered in His essential character as liberator, healer, guardian, and saviour. Is it not said, indeed, in Matt. i. 21: "Thou shalt call His name Jesus, for He shall save His people from their sins?"[3]

It is unnecessary to inquire if Joshua, at a certain period, was a solar divinity; it suffices to note that at the epoch with which we are concerned, the Jews who read his history in the sixth book of the Bible saw in him a national hero, the successor of Moses, and the continuator of his work. He was one of the most popular heroes in Israelitish history, as is proved by the number of persons named after him, and of whom there is no temptation to make a mythical being or a divine hero. The high priest Joshua, mentioned by Zechariah, is also an historical personage; so little is he to be identified with Messiah that he receives the promise of the coming of the latter (Zech. iii. 9).

Robertson and Drews also find mention of a pre-Christian Jesus in the magic papyrus of the *Bibliothèque Nationale,* where occurs the formula, "I adjure thee by the God of the Hebrews, Jesus." This papyrus, which is not earlier than the fourth century of our era, may doubtless reproduce a more ancient formula; there is nothing, however, to authorize us to date it so far back as the mythologists would like. The form of words must doubtless be attributed to a pagan. It merely proves that the name of Jesus was considered to have great power, a thing which is explained by the great part played by exorcism in primitive Christianity.[4] The magical pagan formulas have readily adopted Jewish and Christian names.[5] That does not prove as Reitzenstein remarks,[6] that their authors were really acquainted with and understood Judaism or Christianity. This is proved, for instance, in a text cited by Dieterich,[7] in which Abraham, Isaac and Jacob are taken to be names for the God of Israel.

If there is nothing to authorize us to consider the name of Jesus as a divine name, is the same the case with the designation "Nazarene" which accompanies it? Outside the New Testament, no text attests the existence in Galilee of a village called Nazareth. Neither the Old Testament, nor Josephus, nor the Talmud mention it, but it is not legitimate to conclude from this silence, as Cheyne[8] does, and as the mythologists willingly suppose as proved, that Nazareth is only a geographical fiction. We know from Josephus that Galilee was densely populated, and that it boasted 204 villages and 15 fortified towns.[9] We only know a small part of these 219 localities, and even if the figures given by Josephus were exaggerated, many Galilean townships would not be mentioned in any text.[10] There is nothing astonishing in the supposition that Nazareth[11] a village of very trifling importance, should be among the number.[12]

The fact that evangelical tradition represents Jesus as coming from Nazareth[13] is far from being without significance. According to Messianic dogma the Messiah was to be born at Bethlehem, and the Gospels of Matthew and Luke in different ways, which are mutually irreconcilable, strive to keep to this postulate.[14] Christian tradition would not have created the fact destined to cause it so much embarrassment, that of the birth of Jesus at Nazareth.[15]

The explanations of the term Nazarene offered by the mythologists scarcely seem probable either. This term, which constitutes the most ancient designation of the Christians, is derived, according to W. B. Smith, from the root NSR, which is found sixty-three times in the Old Testament in the sense of protector and guardian. It is even more ancient still, for the Babylonian term Na-Sa-Ru is met with seven times in the code of Hammurabi. The Syrian form Nasaryu, in which is to be recognized the divine name Yah, signifies "God is Protector." It is not a term of geographical origin, but a cultural name. This hypothesis could only be entertained if there were some real proofs of the existence of a pre-Christian sect of Nazarenes. The indications which the mythologists invoke cannot take the place of these. There is in the Gospel of Matthew a passage which puzzles interpreters. After the death of Herod, Joseph and Mary leave Egypt to settle in Nazareth of Galilee.

The evangelist says that this was "that it might be fulfilled which was spoken by the prophets—he shall be called a Nazarene"

(Matt. ii. 23). It is impossible to identify with certitude the prophecy here alluded to, and if it be desired to avoid recourse to the gratuitous hypothesis of the use of some apocryphal work which has not been preserved, it is necessary to suppose that the evangelist connects the word Nazarene with some passage of Scripture containing a word from the same root or having some assonance with it.[16] There would be here a play on the words which we should (owing to its obscurity) be unable to understand. One cannot suppose that this is the true origin of the word Nazarene. Rather would it be incumbent to suppose an assimilation worked out by Matthew, who always aims at showing in the Gospel history the fulfillment of prophecy.

The word Nazarene contains perhaps an allusion to John the Baptist and his disciples, with whom Jesus was certainly in relation at the beginning of His ministry. It is well-known that the Mandæan tradition represents Jesus as an apostate from the Baptist community. Thus would be explained the fact that the Christians were also called Nazarenes, while it would not be at all natural to have designated them as people of Nazareth because their master was a native of this village.[17]

But the problem of Nazareth is still not solved in this way. There occur in the New Testament the two forms, Nazarenos and Nazoraios.[18] W. B. Smith[19] considers these equivalent, and supports his opinion by the coexistence of the two forms, Essenes and Essenians.

The analogy is not conclusive, for the two forms do not only differ in their termination, but also in the quantity of the second syllable. If the form Nazarenos can be philologically derived from Nazareth,[20] the same does not hold for Nazoraios, which must have another origin.

The simplest explanation is that, as applied to Jesus, the term Nazarenos related to his native village, and that the association with the word Nazoraios, by which name the disciples of John the Baptist were called, caused the Christians to be called Nazarenes. In this it was desired to emphasize that they were only apostates from the Baptist community.

It seems very likely indeed that at first the Christians called themselves "disciples" or "brothers," and later on "saints," and that the names Nazarene and Christian were given to them by their opponents.

II. THE HYPOTHESIS OF A SECT OF PRE-CHRISTIAN NAZARENES, WORSHIPERS OF JESUS

The explanation which we propose of the words Nazarene and Nazarenian would have no import if it were possible to prove the existence of a pre-Christian sect of Nazarenes, worshipers of Jesus, as is maintained, in particular by W. B. Smith, who entitles one of his books *The pre-Christian Jesus.*

The first proof alleged in favor of the existence of this sect is based upon the hymn of the Naasseni,[21] who date back to the most remote antiquity and attest the cult of a celestial Jesus.[22]

The subject is the Soul who has quitted the Kingdom of Light and groans in suffering and tears. Lost in a labyrinth, vainly escape is sought.[23]

"Then Jesus said: 'Behold, O Father! this tempted being who, far from Thy influence, wanders miserably on earth. He longs to fly from bitter chaos, but he knows not how to ascend. For his salvation, O Father! send Me; that I may descend with the seals[24] in My hands, that I may traverse the æons, that I may open the mysteries, that I may reveal unto him the essence of God, and announce unto him the mystery of the holy life which is called the gnosis.'"

According to the mythologists, the Jesus of this hymn had no contact with Christianity, and was a Being entirely celestial. Their conclusion seems to have been drawn with some precipitation. Nothing authorizes us to date the Naasseni hymn before the Christian era. Hilgenfeld[25] has shown that the Naassenes had made use of the epistles of Paul and of the fourth Gospel. In the form known to us, and whatever its distant origins may be, the Naasseni doctrine betrays the influence of Christianity.[26] It would therefore be unable to prove the existence of a pre-Christian cult of Jesus. This argument is strengthened by the consideration that, following a very judicious remark of Bousset, it is not certain that in the hymn preserved by Hippolytus the name of Jesus may not proceed from a retouching of a corruption of the text. For at the beginning of the hymn there is presented the "Nous" along with Chaos, and the Soul to be saved. In these conditions the decisive argument that the mythologists thought they possessed disappears.

Epiphanius (*Hær.,* xviii) mentions among the Jewish heresies a sect of Nazarenes, and what he says about it does not permit him to attribute a Christian character to it. As he does not state that it was developed only after Christianity, this would prove, according to Smith, that the Nazarenes were a pre-Christian sect from which Christianity doubtless adopted much.[27] And against this conclusion, according to him, it would not be possible to urge as argument the silence of other students of heresy, who, being less honest and less naïve than Epiphanius, saw how dangerous to the official Church doctrine was the existence of these Nazarenes, and kept a discreet silence concerning them.[28] There is a singular lack of proportion between the statements of Epiphanius and the conclusions which he claims to deduce from them. An entire historical construction of the greatest importance, which would overthrow many facts apparently solidly established, rests upon one single testimony—that of a man who does not always show himself well informed, and who frequently has not made the most judicious use of the information at his disposal.[29] If we scrutinize closely the testimony of Epiphanius, we find that concerning these Nazarenes he appears to know nothing more than the name; it is noteworthy that he says nothing which attributes to them a worship of Jesus.[30] All that there is in common between them and the Christians is a name only. To permit any conclusion to be drawn from this fact it would be necessary to show that it cannot be a simple coincidence, or, what would be still more probable, some confusion made either by Epiphanius or by the author of whom he makes use. Now this proof has not been furnished. On the contrary, two scholars, Schmidtke and Bousset, have proposed a simple and plausible explanation of the testimony of Epiphanius. There might, perhaps, be certain reservations to make on some details of their theories, but in their main outlines it does not appear a matter of doubt that they are well founded, and that they have consequently caused the disappearance of the pre-Christian Nazarenes from history.

In the course of his research in Judeo-Christianity and the Jewish Christians,[31] Schmidtke has proved that all the narratives found in the writings of the Fathers of the Church concerning a Judeo-Christian sect going under the name of Nazarenes and not under the usual name of Ebionites originate with Appollinarius of Laodicea (310–90). The Nazarene sect really existed at Beroé in Syria; it was strictly Judeo-Christian, and used an Aramaic gospel, some fragments of which are preserved, and which seems to have been a translation of the Gospel of Matthew slightly revised. Concerning these Nazarene Christians, Epiphanius speaks in the twenty-ninth chapter, according to Appollinarius. The details he gives concerning them seem worthy of belief. It is in the eighteenth chapter that he speaks of the pre-Christian Nazarenes. Schmidtke says that here he depends both upon Hippolytus and a list of heretical Jewish sects.[32] He believes that Epiphanius has substituted the Nazarenes for the Ebionites.[33] He even believes that in his work, as first sketched out, Epiphanius had called them Ebionites.

The peculiarities of those which he describes in Chapter xxx correspond exactly, in fact, with the account given of the Nazarenes in Chapter xviii. Epiphanius was misled in taking for a Jewish sect the Nazarenes, whom the Jews in their daily prayer cursed under the name of Nozrim simultaneously with the heretics (Minim).[34]

Bousset,[35] who accepts the argument of Schmidtke in its generality, and who believes that he has definitely found the key to the enigma, supposes that in the source of which he makes use concerning the Nazarenes, Epiphanius had only found some geographical details about the place in which the sect was met with, and that in order to write his account he had utilized, from what he knew about the Judeo-Christian groups, everything which had not a Christian character. Bousset supposes that the Nazarenes were mentioned in the list of Jewish heresies utilized by different Fathers. The Jewish author who had furnished it mentioned in fact Christianity as among the heresies to be rejected.

In these circumstances one has no choice but to endorse the conclusion reached by Bousset in these terms: "The pre-Christian Nazarenes of Epiphanius are definitely consigned to the domain of error and misunderstanding, and it is to be hoped that they will forever disappear from the arsenal of proofs invoked in support of a pre-Christian cult of Jesus."[36]

But even when deprived of the hymn of the Naasseni and the Nazarene sect the mythologists are not disarmed; there remain for them the positive indications of the existence of a pre-Christian Jesus which they think they find in the New Testament itself.

The first of these is the passage in the book of Acts which refers to Apollos. For Smith this text is the most valuable of ancient Christian literature.[37] We read in Acts xviii. 24–26: "And a certain Jew named Apollos, born at Alexandria, an eloquent man and mighty in the Scriptures, came to Ephesus. This man was instructed in the way of the Lord, and being fervent in spirit[38] he spake and taught diligently the things concerning Jesus, knowing only the baptism of John. And he began to speak boldly in the synagogue, whom, when Aquila and Priscilla had heard, they took him unto them and expounded unto him the way of God more perfectly."

It follows from this text, thinks Smith, that Apollos knew nothing about Jesus, otherwise he ought to have known everything, including the doctrine of baptism. This ignorance did not hinder his preaching "that which concerned Jesus."

"It is therefore," writes Smith, "as clear as the noon-day sun that this form of words can have no relation to the history of Jesus." It must mean the doctrine concerning Jesus—a doctrine which a man who knew nothing about an historical Jesus could not only profess, but preach. This text is therefore for the mythologists (the expression is again Smith's) "an inestimable diamond."[39]

But, when closely examined, the passage may not perhaps have all the significance attributed to it, or, to put it more precisely, its value and significance may have a quite other character. Whatever the origin of the reference used by the editor of the Acts may be, we are not certain we know its original purport. It is possible, indeed, that the form "that which concerned Jesus" may be put to the account of the editor,[40] and that it merely expresses the belief that the religious attitude of Apollos, when he arrived at Ephesus, fitted him to become a Christian. Priscilla and Aquila doubtless recognized in the ardent and eloquent Messianist a man who would be able to render eminent service to their faith, and they succeeded in gaining him over to their cause. But we have no wish to insist on this interpretation, which to a certain extent is conjecture.

The exegesis of Smith rests upon a postulate which is in contradiction with certain historical data. This postulate is that the doctrine of Christian baptism, opposed to that of John the Baptist, is an essential element in the history of Jesus in that he who ignores the Christian baptism must perforce ignore all the evangelical history. If at the opening of His ministry Jesus (as shown in John iii. 22 and iv. 1) may have administered a baptism in every way identical with that of John the Baptist, He seems to have relinquished it in the sequel.[41] No text attributes the institution of baptism to Jesus during His ministry, and when account is taken of the interest the Church had in covering with the Master's own authority her rites, it is impossible to pass over this extremely significant silence. Matthew alone (xxviii. 19, 20) relates that Jesus, risen again, said to His disciples at the moment he was to leave them: "All power has been given to Me in the heavens and in earth. Go ye therefore and teach" (literally "make disciples") "all nations, baptizing them in the name of the Father, the Son, and the Holy Spirit."

Neither Luke nor John[42] contains any equivalent of this narrative, which thus appears as relatively recent. The passage in Matthew has for its object to support, upon the authority of the resurrected Christ (that is, Christ as Spirit), the institution of baptism as practised by the Church. This reveals nothing as to the real origin of the rite, but merely shows that it has no place in the historical mission of Jesus.[43] In these circumstances it is easily understood that it was not immediately introduced in all the Christian communities. The fact that Paul (1 Cor. vii. 14), without making any allusion to baptism, admits that the children of Christians are saints— that is, belong to God, uniquely because they are born of parents themselves saints—shows that the baptism of children was unknown in the Pauline communities, and it allows us to suppose that the rite was only practised for those who entered the Church, not for those born in it. It may not have been in use at the beginning in the Jerusalem community. Doubtless the accounts in the Acts on several occasions speak of baptism,[44] but their testimony is not conclusive, for the editor of this book has naïvely projected into the primitive community the situation which existed in the Church of *his* time. The use of baptism might have arisen, as Bousset supposes, not in the midst of the Palestine community, but perhaps in the Diaspora at Antioch, in analogy with the Jewish baptism for proselytes. A teaching which was intimately connected with the historical ministry of Jesus, and based upon memoirs of this ministry, might very easily have only known of the baptism of John.

The exegesis of Smith evokes another objection. It is in no way proved that the expression "that which concerned Jesus" must be understood in the sense of "the doctrine concerning Jesus." Smith himself recognizes that the Greek words used may signify[45] "the story told concerning someone," but he considers that the three passages of the New Testament (outside of the Acts) where this form of words is found refer to the doctrine and not to the story of Jesus, or at least they originally did so. According to Acts xxviii. 31, during his two years of captivity passed in Rome, in his own hired house, Paul taught freely "that which concerned the Lord Jesus Christ." Paul did not tell histories to the Romans; he preached the Gospel to them. But to lay it down as a principle that the Pauline Gospel is a doctrine concerning Jesus which contains no historical element is to suppose, as resolved in favor of the mythological theories, the very question in dispute. In the teaching imparted to the Romans, as in that which had been given to the Galatians (iii. 1), the crucifixion of an historical personage was the starting-point of the Pauline preaching.

The two passages in which is found the phrase "that which concerned Jesus" are characteristic. In the story of the woman with the issue of blood Mark has it: "Having heard the things concerning Jesus, she came in the crowd behind and touched His garment; for, said she, if I but touch His garment I shall be made whole."

"The things concerning Jesus" could only mean the story of His miracles, which made the sufferer hope that she also would be cured. Smith is certainly compelled to recognize that such is indeed the meaning of the passage, but he attempts to put aside its evidence by maintaining that it must be attributed to some reviser of Mark.[46] If it had been primarily a question of healing, he thinks, the woman would not have said "I shall be saved," but "I shall be cured." This observation takes no account of the fact that in many passages "to be saved" has exactly the same meaning as "to be healed" (Mark v. 23, vi. 56; Luke viii. 36–50).

There is here no impropriety of expression, since, according to the current conception of the period, the disease was caused by the action of a demon, from whom the sufferer must be delivered in order to be healed. The phrase attributed to the woman "I shall be saved" does not therefore prove that it was originally a question of anything other than healing.

Smith also supposes that the words "having learned that which concerned Jesus" cannot belong to the primitive text because they have no equivalent either in Matthew or Luke. But these two evangelists give a recension of the passage considerably briefer than that of Mark.

The comparison of the three narratives leads one to think that (as is fairly often the case) there is an abbreviation of the account by Matthew and Luke, and not a development by Mark. That which is found, indeed, only in his narrative is too insignificant to induce us to find a reason for its addition, while the single desire to condense a narrative fairly lengthy suffices to explain the form *they* have adopted. It is therefore not possible to attribute to a subordinate editor the phrase "that which concerned Jesus" as interpreted in the sense "that which Jesus had done."

The passage in Luke xxiv. 19 is not less significant. The story is well known of the two disciples who the day after the death of Jesus reach Emmaus while talking over what had just taken place.

Jesus, whom they do not recognize as yet, comes up to them and takes the same road. He asks them what they have been talking about. One of them replies: "You must indeed be a stranger in Jerusalem not to be aware of what has happened in these last few days . . . the matter concerning Jesus of Nazareth."

The matter concerning Jesus of Nazareth can only be the condemnation and execution of the prophet in whom they had placed their hopes. To understand the phrase as referring to some doctrine about Jesus, a divine Being, would be to give it no meaning at all, so Smith is obliged to suppose that the passage has undergone a radical revision. But this is a conjecture which rests upon nothing, and is only put forward for the exigencies of the case.

The expression "that which concerns Jesus" refers, then, to the story, or certain portions of the story, of Jesus. There is no reason to give to this expression any other meaning than in Acts xviii. 25. We must not, then, see in Apollos a Jew who teaches a form of doctrine concerning Jesus which ignores the Gospel history, but a Christian who knows nothing of baptism.

If Smith is thus deprived of the "diamond of inestimable value," the stones which he has attempted to group around it to make a tiara lose very much of their value. We are not, however, for that reason excused from examining them.[47]

There is in the first place the case of Simon the Magician. It is narrated in Acts viii. 9–13 that when Philip came to evangelize Samaria, he met a magician named Simon, enjoying great authority over the population, who considered him the "great power of God." Like other Samaritans, Simon was converted by the preaching of Philip. A little further on it is narrated that when, after the arrival of Peter and John, Simon learned that by the laying on of hands the apostles conferred the Holy Spirit, he offered money to Peter to receive the same power. Peter rejected his proposal with indignation, and pronounces a malediction upon him. Simon then asks the apostles to pray for him, so that his sin may be pardoned (viii. 18–24). The rapidity of the conversion of Simon and the Samaritans is explained, for Smith, by the fact that they were already won over to ideas very similar to those preached by Philip. They were therefore Christians, although they were strangers to the tradition which it is claimed is connected with an historical Jesus.[48] Smith deduces here from the text something quite other than what it contains. The point is the conversion of Simon and the Samaritans to the gospel preached by Philip,[49] and not the fusion of a group of Simon's followers with the Church which Philip represented—a fusion which would have been determined by recognition of the fact that at bottom the ideas professed by each side were the same.

There are in the second portion of the narrative about Simon many suspicious elements. In it is found a theory concerning the apostolate and the laying on of hands which is not a primitive one, and it is possible to discern, with M. Meyer and M. Alfaric,[50] an apologetic fiction which shows how the Christian missionaries anticipated the conversion of the Simonian community and prefaced it by that of Simon himself. The first portion of the narrative has quite another value. It reveals the existence in Samaria, at the time of the first mission, of a pre-Christian Gnosticism which perhaps was not without sensible influence on the development of Christian thought.[51] But this Simonian Gnosticism, so far as we can form an idea of it, is not the pre-Christian doctrine that the mythologists imagine, which consisted in worship paid to a divine personage. All that we know concerning the Simonian Gnosticism is its idea of the incarnation in a man, Simon, of the "great power of God."[52] This shows—and it is an extremely valuable indication certain theorists ought not to lose sight of—that the idea of a human being in whom a divine principle incarnated was not in any way a strange idea in the environment in which Christianity was born.

Neither do we recognize an adept of pre-Christianity in the magician Elymas, or Bar-Jesus, a Jewish false prophet whom Paul met at Paphos in the coterie which surrounded Sergius Paulus (Acts xiii. 6–12). Smith interprets the name Bar-Jesus in the sense of "servant or worshiper of Jesus"[53]—a sense which would be plausible if the name of Jesus was not attested as one in current use. It is only by an argument in a vicious circle, in postulating a priori that "Bar-Jesus" is formed from a divine name, that it is possible to find in the episode an argument to support a pre-Christian worship of Jesus.

Smith[54] also lays emphasis on the fact that the proconsul, not yet initiated into the preaching of the apostles, asks to hear from them "the word of God" (Acts xiii. 7). It is very evident that the terms of the narrative must be put to the editor's credit. If the proconsul really expressed the wish to hear Paul and Barnabas, it was not because he saw in them the preachers of a doctrine already known to him, but because they presented themselves as bearers of a divine message.

The case of the exorcists of Ephesus (Acts xix. 13–20), on which the mythologists also lay stress, has not the significance they attribute to it. Impressed by the miracles of Paul at Ephesus, seven Jewish exorcists, sons of a priest named Skeuas, attempted to make use of the same formula used successfully by the apostle, and adjured the spirits saying: "I adjure you by Jesus, whom Paul preaches." But the spirit answered them: "Jesus I know, and Paul I know, but who are ye?" And the one possessed fell upon the exorcists and maltreated them.[55] The fact is without significance as regards the existence of a pre-Christian cult of Jesus. It is merely a case of the imitation by outsiders of a formula of exorcism whose efficacy has been observed. This, at any rate, is so in the text as we read it, and nothing authorizes us to suppose that it was otherwise in the original. According to the mythologists, Christianity had no unique source from which it was spread, as Jerusalem. It had several simultaneous sources. Afterwards the memory of this fact was lost, and Christianity was connected with the preaching of Jesus. However, it may still be recognized that Cyprus and Cyrenaica were centers from which Christianity was spread, entirely independent of Jerusalem. According to Acts xi. 20 it was the men of Cyprus and Cyrene who were the first (at Antioch) to preach the gospel to the pagans.[56] But we know (see Acts iv. 36) that a Cypriote, destined later to play an important part at Antioch, was converted to the gospel at Jerusalem, and we learn in the book of Acts (vi. 9) that persons belonging to the synagogue of the Freedmen,[57] and people from Cyrene, Alexandria and Asia, raised violent opposition against Stephen, which proves that the gospel had been preached by him in this synagogue. There is therefore no reason to suppose that it was anywhere other than in Jerusalem, or in the communities which grew out of that of Jerusalem, that the Cypriotes and the Cyrenians who played an active part in the early missions were converted to Christianity. This equally applies to a certain Mnason, "a Cypriote and old disciple," who received Paul in his house on the latter's arrival in Jerusalem (Acts xxi. 16), and in whom some have tried to also see an adept of the pre-Christian cult of Jesus.[58] Although he was a Cypriote, he lived in Jerusalem, and in stating that he was an "old disciple" (we are between the years 56 and 58), the editor only desired to indicate that he had long been a Christian.

III. CHRISTIANITY AND THE
DISCIPLES OF JOHN THE BAPTIST

At the beginning of Chapter xix of the book of Acts it is stated that, after his arrival at Ephesus, Paul met with a group of a dozen disciples who had never heard of the Holy Spirit. "What baptism have ye then received?" he asked. They replied: "That of John." "John," he answered, "baptized with the baptism of repentance in speaking of Him who was to come after, in order that they should believe, that is to say, in Jesus." He then conferred on these disciples the baptism in the name of the Lord Jesus; he laid his hands upon them; they received the Holy Spirit, and began to speak in different tongues and to prophesy (xix. 1–7). In the view of the mythologists these twelve men were, like Apollos himself, pre-Christians, and the facility of their conversion shows how closely their point of view resembled that of Paul himself.[59]

Many critics[60] see in them the disciples of John the Baptist.[61] But the word "disciples," by which these men are designated, is that commonly employed in the Acts for the Christians, and it is not stated that these twelve men received instructions along with baptism. This leads us to suppose that the position of these men must have been similar to that of Apollos. But even if they were really disciples of John the Baptist, no very important conclusions can be drawn from their story.

There are serious reasons for thinking that neither during the life of Jesus nor after His death did the group of His disciples remain out of contact with the Baptist community. The two movements combated and influenced each other reciprocally.

The preaching of Jesus Himself was very strongly influenced at the beginning by John the Baptist. The Gospels present John as the forerunner. According to them, his duty was to announce the arrival of one "greater than himself," whose work would be to impart the baptism of the spirit and of fire (Matt. iii. 11). This last word opens out already an interesting perspective in showing that the thought of the Baptist had already broken through the limits within which it was sought to imprison it. Wellhausen[62] has recognized one source emanating from a group of the Baptist's disciples in the statement about his Messianic teaching which belongs peculiarly to Matthew (iii. 11, 12) and to Luke (iii. 16, 17). Where Mark merely says, "He shall baptize you with the Holy Spirit," Matthew and Luke add "and with fire. He has His fan in His hand, and He shall thoroughly purge His floor. The wheat He shall store in His granary; the chaff He shall burn in everlasting fire." The personage that John the Baptist announces in these words is an Apocalyptic Messiah who pronounces judgment, and it is in view of this judgment that repentance is preached and baptism is administered. Jesus had been in contact with John the Baptist. His first sermon, as it is given by Mark (i. 15) and Matthew (iv. 17) is almost word for word identical with that of John (Matt. iii. 2). Christian tradition, so jealous to maintain the originality and the independence of Jesus, would not have arbitrarily imagined Him as merely reëchoing the teaching of one in whom it only saw a forerunner.

The point upon which Christian teaching, even in the lifetime of Jesus, separated itself from the Baptist's teaching is of capital importance. While for John and his followers "He who is to come" (Matt. xi. 3 and Luke vii. 19)—the Son of man (the idea, if not the word, is at the heart of John's thought)—belongs to the future, for the Christians He has come, although He may not have had all the attributes of power. The fourth Gospel clearly shows this contrast in the way it affirms that John was not the light (i. 8), and makes him declare that he was not the Christ (i. 20), while it states, not less categorically, that Jesus is the light (i. 9, iii. 19, viii. 12, xii. 46), and that He is the divine Logos (i. 14), the Son of God (i. 18 and 34, iii. 16, xx. 31, etc.), the Christ (xi. 27, xx. 31).

Reitzenstein[63] has extracted from Mandæan writings an Apocalypse which appears to him slightly posterior[64] to the yar 70,[65] and which he believes to originate from John's disciples. A passage of this Apocalypse presents at once an analogy and a striking contrast with the reply of Jesus to the messengers of John, who asked: "Art thou He who should come, or do we look for another?" "Go," declares Jesus, "and tell unto John that which ye see and hear; the blind see, the lame walk, the lepers are cleansed, the deaf hear, the dead are raised, and to the poor the gospel is preached" (Matt. xi. 4, 5; Luke vii. 22). In other words, the Messianic program of Isaiah (xxxv. 5) is fulfilled.

In the Mandæan Apocalypse the same program is announced as destined to be fulfilled by the expected Messiah: "Enoch Uthra enters into Jerusalem clothed with clouds; he walks in bodily form, but he has no material clothing. He comes in the years of Paltus [Pilate]. Enoch Uthra comes into the world with the power of the great king of light. He heals the sick, he causes the blind to see, he cleanses the lepers, he straightens those who are bowed, he causes the impotent to walk and the dumb to speak. With the power of the great king of light he brings back the dead to life. Among the Jews he wins over believers and shows unto them there is life, and there is death, there is error and there is truth. He converts the Jews in the name of the great king of light. Three hundred and sixty prophets go out from Jerusalem; they testify in the name of the Lord of might. Enoch Uthra ascends on high, and places himself near unto Meshumè Kushtra. All the Uthras are hid from the eyes of men. Then shall Jerusalem be laid waste. The Jews shall go forth into exile, and shall be dispersed in all cities."

As thus presented this text does not appear to be homogeneous; if must have been, in certain points, influenced by Christian tradition. It suffices, however, to show that the disciples of John taught as necessary to be fulfilled by the Apocalyptic Messiah the program that the Christians said had been accomplished by Jesus.

Here is the great difference between the ideas of John the Baptist and those of the Christians. For the first named the coming of the Messiah is in the future; for the second it is in the past, and only His second coming is expected. The difference is a capital one, and suffices to prove that if the two movements were born on the same soil the second cannot be reduced to the first, but appears with reference to it, as though it were an original creation.

NOTES

1. Drews, *Die Christusmythe,* i. p. 23.
2. Robertson, *A Short History of Christianity,* p. 8.
3. "Jesus" signifies "Jahveh aids."
4. Joh. Weiss, *Jesus von Nazareth,* p. 19.
5. Deissmann, *Licht vom Osten,* Tübingen, 1909.
6. Reitzenstein, *Poimandres,* Leipzig, 1904.
7. Dieterich, *Abraxas,* Leipzig, 1891.
8. Cheyne, article in *Encyclop. Biblica,* iii, "Nazareth."
9. Josephus, *Vita,* par. 235.
10. Meyer, *Ursprung und Anf.,* iii.
11. Wellhausen has suggested that the word Nazareth designates Galilee in the form Gennesar (Garden of Nesar), met with in 1 Macc. ii. 67, Matt. xiv. 34, Mark vi. 53. The similarity of Matt. xxvi. 69 and 71 proves the equivalence of Galilean and Nazarene. This ingenious hypothesis collides with the fact that if Galilee was commonly designated by the word Nazar or Nazareth, it is very strange that it is nowhere clearly found.
12. The fact that later tradition was acquainted with Nazareth proves nothing. So soon as one was persuaded that the place has existed, failure to find it again was impossible.
13. Matt. xxi. 11, Mark i. 9, John i. 45, Acts x. 38. The comparison between Mark vi. 1 and Luke iv. 16 shows that Nazareth was considered to be the birthplace of Jesus.
14. Matt. ii. 13–23 states that the family of Jesus was originally settled at Bethlehem, and returned after the flight to Egypt to live in Nazareth to escape the jurisdiction of Archelaus, grandson of Herod. Luke ii. 1–7 states that Jesus was born during a journey of his parents to Jerusalem on the occasion of the census made by Quirinius.
15. The birth of Jesus in Galilee constituted one of the Jewish objections to his Messiahship. Cp. John vii. 41.
16. H. J. Holtzmann (*Die Synoptiker*) and F. Nicolardot (*Procédés de*

redaction des trois premiers evangelistes) think of Es. xi. 1, in which the Messiah is called "Nèzer" (offspring). It is impossible to connect the word Nazarene with the notion of the sect for the Christian tradition (Matt. xi. 18, 19; Luke vii. 33, 34; Mark ii. 18–20, etc.) has preserved a clear memory that Jesus was not an ascetic like John the Baptist.

17. Wetter, *L'Arrière plan hist. du Christianisme primitif; R.H.L.R.,* 1922; Wellhausen, *Das Evangelium Matthaei,* Berlin, 1904, p. 142.

18. The first is found in Mark i. 24, x. 47, xiv. 67, xvi. 6; Luke iv. 34 and xxiv. 29. The second in Mark ii. 23; Luke xviii. 37; John xviii. 5–7 and xix. 19; and Acts ii. 22, iii. 6, iv. 10, vi. 14, xxii. 8, xxiv. 5, xxvi. 9. There is a certain variation in the manuscripts. The duality of form is, however, certain, and the testimony of the book of Acts proves that it is the form "Nazarene" which prevailed.

19. Smith, *D. vorchr. Jesus,* p. 53.

20. The correctness of the derivation (Nazarenos) is admitted by Meyer, who cites the opinion of Lidzbarski. In the New Testament are to be found the forms, widely divergent, as follows: Nazara, Nazarat, Nazaret, Nazareth, etc. In the oldest manuscript there is no consistent spelling.

21. Preserved by Hippolytus, *Philosophoumena,* v. 10. 2.

22. Smith and Drews.

23. The text is not absolutely certain.

24. It is often a question of seals with the Gnostics, particularly in the Pistis Sophia.

25. Hilgenfeld, *Die Ketzergesch. des Urchristentums.*

26. Reitzenstein, *Poimandres,* p. 81.

27. Smith, *D. vorchr. Jesus,* pp. 56, 57.

28. Smith, *D. vorchr. Jesus,* p. 64.

29. "His criticism is not sound. . . . The moment he leaves the region of contemporary facts his information should be checked; it is confused and lacks precision. He had a relatively uncritical temperament without intellectual acuteness."—Tixeront, *Patrologie,* 1918, p. 253.

30. Joh. Weiss, *Jesus von Nazareth;* Windisch, *Der geschichtliche Jesus* (Th. R.).

31. Schmidtke, *Neue Fragmente und Untersuchungen zu der Juden-christlichen Evangelien,* xxxvii, 1911, Leipzig.

32. *Id., ib.,* p. 199.

33. He writes their name with a sigma and not with a zeta, to distinguish them from the Nazarene Christians, just as he distinguishes between the Essenians and the Ossenians.

34. The twelfth request of the "Schemonè Esrè" is given in the text discovered in the synagogue of Cairo and published in 1897: "May there be no hope for the apostates! Mayest Thou, in our time, annihilate the domination of the insolent! May the Christians (Nozrim) and the heretics (Minim) be suddenly annihilated! May they be no longer written in the book of life! Praised be Jahveh, who brings low the insolent!" (Strack, *Jesus die Hæretiker,* etc.)

35. Bousset, *Th. Rundschau,* xiv, 1911.

36. Bousset, *Th. Rundschau,* xiv, 1911, p. 381.

37. Smith, *D. vorchr. Jesus,* p. 7.

38. The text is translatable in two different ways.

39. Smith, *D. vorchr. Jesus,* pp. 7–9.

40. Meyer, *Ursprung und Anf.,* iii, p. 112.

41. Tradition has so little belief that baptism goes back to Jesus, that the fourth Gospel after quoting a statement that Jesus had baptized, itself corrects this (John iv. 2).

42. The testimony of Mark is lacking on this point, owing to the mutilation of the end of his book. The nonauthentic end of Mark, which appears not to be anterior to the second century, gives (xvi. 16) something equivalent, with this particularity, that the practice of baptism is only supposed, but not directly attributed to institution.

43. Meyer, *Ursprung und Anf.,* iii, p. 245.

44. Acts ii. 38–41; viii. 12, 13, 16, 36, 38; ix. 18; x. 48.

45. This is evidently the meaning of the phrase in Acts xxviii. 15.

46. Smith, *D. vorchr. Jesus.*

47. We pass over for the moment the case of the disciples of Ephesus, and shall deal with it further on.

48. Smith, *D. vorchr. Jesus,* p. 11.

49. There is nothing to show that this conversion was more rapid than that of pagans unacquainted with any ideas analogous to those of the Christians.

50. Meyer, *Ursprung und Anf.,* iii; Prosper Alfaric, *Christianisme et Gnosticisme (Rev. Hist.,* 1924).

51. Alfaric, *Rev. Hist.,* cxlv, 1924.

52. It seems to us not possible to admit, as some have supposed, that Simon could have been influenced by the teaching of Jesus, as Meyer thinks, and still less that of Paulinism, as Harnack admits.

53. Smith, *D. vorchr. Jesus*, p. 16.

54. *Id., ib.*, p. 22.

55. There are certain incoherences in the account. Sometimes it is a question of one demoniac, sometimes of several. This appears to arise from the fusion of two parallel accounts, and is without importance.

56. Smith, *D. vorchr. Jesus.*

57. Certain critics think that instead of "Freedmen" the phrase should read, "the people of Lybia." In Greek the confusion between the two words is, from the paleographical point of view, very easy.

58. Smith, *D. vorchr. Jesus.*

59. *Id., ib.*

60. Reitzenstein, *Das iranische Erlösungsmysterium,* 1921.

61. As Reitzenstein shows well in the above work, no objection can be raised against the presence of disciples of John at Ephesus. The fact is that we know nothing about the conditions in which the doctrine of John was spread outside Palestine. We know nothing either of the conditions under which Christianity was carried to Rome. We can especially urge in support of the existence of the disciples of John the Baptist at Ephesus the fact that the fourth Gospel in its present form originates at Ephesus, and is a direct polemic against the disciples of John the Baptist. Cp. Baldensperger, *Der prolog des vierten Evangeliums;* Maurice Goguel, *Introd. au N.T.,* ii, p. 508.

62. Wellhausen, *Einleitung in die drei ersten Evangelien,* 1911.

63. Reitzenstein, *Das Mandaische Buch des Herrn der Gross und der Evangelienüberlieferung.*

64. It is known that the Mandæan religion, whose character is markedly syncretist, is related to the tradition of the Baptist's disciples.

65. This date should be received with reservations. See those stated by M. Loisy. From our present point of view, it suffices that the Apocalypse reflects the ideas of John the Baptist, which seems hardly contestable.

CHAPTER IV

TWO PRELIMINARY OBJECTIONS TO THE NONHISTORICAL THESIS

I. THE POLEMICS OF THE OPPONENTS OF CHRISTIANITY

From the earliest period of its existence Christianity was an object of the liveliest attacks, both on the part of Jew and pagan, in Jerusalem and Palestine, as also in the Greco-Roman world through which it spread at an early date.

We are familiar enough with the anti-Christian polemics from the second to the fourth century; that of Lucian by the witticisms of *De morte Peregrini;* that of Celsus (in his *True Discourse,* composed in the year 180) by the quotations which Origen makes from it[1]; that of the unknown philosopher and of Porphyry (233–304) by the refutation of Macanus of Magnesia (about 410); that of Julian the Apostate (331–63) by the refutation of Cyril of Alexandria. By means of the various apologies of the second century (those of Justin Martyr, Tatien, Aristides), and by the dialogues of Justin with the Jew Tryphon, we can gain a fairly accurate conception of the doctrines which were opposed to the Christians in the course of the second century. Just as there was an apologetic tradition, so was there a polemical one. They are always the same critical ideas, characterized with more or less of ability and penetration, which flow from the pens of the opponents of Christianity.

The pagan polemic did not present a physiognomy very different from that of the Jews. One philosopher, Celsus, sought in the Jewish arsenal for weapons to wield against Christianity.[2] For everything which concerned evangelical history the discussion had to depend upon Christian tradition. It was upon the ground of the Gospels that the opponents of Christianity took up their position. They called attention to the lack of culture of the evangelists, pointed out in their narratives incoherences, contradictions, and improbabilities, but they never stigmatized them as purely and simply fictions.[3] They only attempted to give to the story of Jesus an interpretation which eliminated from it the miraculous and the supernatural; they did not contest its veracity.[4]

Doubtless it is not possible to extend to the first century the conclusion which holds for the period which followed it. Is it not, however, improbable that the disputants of the second century would have neglected an efficient weapon which they found had been used by their predecessors? Already, from this point of view, there are strong presumptions that the nonhistorical thesis was not supported in the primitive period.

M. Salomon Reinach thinks that if we have no work of the first century in which the historical character of Jesus is questioned,[5] the reason is that if such very subversive documents had existed the Church would not have permitted them to survive.[6] It may be admitted that the Church would have eliminated them from the canonical books and in a more general way from orthodox literature, but its power was limited to that, and it is not easy to see how the Church would have succeeded in completely prohibiting them. If the work of Lucian is excepted—is it not striking that all we know about the polemical literature of Jews and pagans has been preserved for us by Christian apologists?—how would the central question of the existence of Jesus have been treated otherwise than for other controverted questions? Would not opponents have made capital out of this attitude, which would have been an avowal? Although no polemical anti-Christian document belonging to the first century has come down to us, it is possible to form an idea of its quality by the influence which it exerted upon Christian tradition. The comparative study of the four evangelists shows that solicitude for apologetics was one of the factors which most directly influenced the form into which they were cast.[7]

It could not be otherwise, for the Gospels were not written to satisfy the curiosity of historians, but to gain men to the faith and to strengthen the convictions of those already won.[8]

The editors therefore had to present the facts in the way the most likely to answer the objections of opponents in advance. Now in none of the four Gospels is there to be found anything which directly or indirectly is directed against the thesis that the person Jesus had no historical reality. There are in several accounts of apparitions, remarks to emphasize the reality of the body of Jesus, *resurrected,*[9] but never does any evangelist feel the need to affirm the reality of the body of Jesus during His ministry. This is because they were not engaged with opponents who denied it.

The importance of this fact is considerable, for it was on the morrow of His birth that Christianity was confronted with Jewish opposition. How is it possible to suppose that the first antagonists of the Church could have been ignorant of the fact that the entire story of Jesus, His teaching, and His death corresponded to no reality at all? That it might have been ignored in the Diaspora may be admitted, but it appears impossible at Jerusalem; and if such a thing had been known, how did the opponents of Christianity come to neglect the use of so terrible an argument, or how, supposing they made use of it, does it happen that the Christians succeeded in so completely refuting them that not a trace of the controversy has been preserved by the disputants of the second century?

Against this argument the opponents of the historical thesis may be tempted to rejoin that no decisive case can be based upon our Gospels, since under the most favorable hypothesis the oldest among them was not compiled less than forty years after the events which they relate or are supposed to relate. In a period of intense religious ferment, forty years suffice for exact memories to disappear or undergo profound transformation, or for the birth of a legend ready made. But our Gospels are not the first narrations which saw the light; and before their compilation had begun there existed an oral tradition capable of preserving the facts with remarkable fidelity.[10] The Gospel tradition in its essential elements goes much farther back than the compilation of the first written Gospels. We shall attempt in a later chapter to prove that the theology of Paul implies this fact.

II. DOCETISM

Docetism is the opinion of those who believed that in the person of Jesus the human element was only an appearance. Such as we find this belief, for instance in Marcion and in many second-century Gnostics, Docetism is not an affirmation of historical order: it is an interpretation of the history on which the Christian faith was based. Among the second-century theologians, and even those of the first century, there are found side by side these two theses: Jesus is a man and He is God. Herein was presented a problem for Christian thought: How define in the person of the Christ the relation between the human element and the divine? The most diverse attempts were made in ancient Christianity to solve this problem up to the time when the orthodox doctrine was fixed. There were attempts which sacrificed one of the terms of the problem, either in making of the Christ a mere man raised to the heavens by His resurrection, or, on the contrary, by reducing the humanity in Him to but a mere appearance.

That which the Docetists of the second century denied, was not that the story narrated by the evangelists was real, but that the humanity of the person to whom the story referred was anything more than a mere appearance or a garment worn by a divine

Being.[11] Docetism is a theological opinion; it is not an historical affirmation.[12]

Such is particularly the character of Marcion's system,[13] that deep and daring thinker who in the first half of the second century gave, concerning the Christianity which he sought to free from every link with Judaism, an interpretation so original and so fertile, and which Harnack compares to those of the apostle Paul and St. Augustine. In Marcion's view Christ had not been begotten; He had nothing of the human about Him; He was and remains a Spirit. He appeared in human form (*in hominis forma*); His body was but an appearance.[14] It is necessary to conceive Him as like the angels who appeared to Abraham, who ate and drank and performed all the actions of human life[15] (Gen. xviii. 2–8). Harnack writes: "The Christ of Marcion is a God who appears in human form, feels, acts and suffers like a man, although the identification with a carnal body, naturally begotten, is in His case merely an appearance. It is incorrect, then, to assert that according to Marcion Christ did not suffer, and only died in appearance. This is the opinion His adversaries attributed to Him, but He only predicated appearance to the substance of the flesh of Christ."[16]

Marcion was so far from denying the Gospel history that he accepted a Gospel (that of Luke) which he had only purged of what he considered Judaising additions. This he adapted to his ideas, particularly in suppressing the narration of the birth of Jesus and in making His history begin at the baptism.

The Gnostic Cerinthe also believed that Christ was only united with the man Jesus at the time of baptism, and separated from Him at the time of the Passion, so that Christ Himself had not suffered.[17]

This solicitude to preserve the full divinity of Christ by discarding the idea of suffering gave rise to rather strange interpretations of the story of the Passion. Irenæus, for instance, states that Basilides[18] taught that Simon of Cyrene not only carried the cross of Jesus, but that he had been miraculously substituted for the latter, been crucified in His stead, while Jesus, lost in the crowd, looked on, laughing at the punishment of his double.[19] In the *Acta Johannis* (Chap. xcvii) there may be read how at the moment of the crucifixion Jesus appeared unto John, who had fled, and said to him: "John, for the people who are there, at Jerusalem, I am crucified; I am pierced with thrusts of lance, I have vinegar and honey to drink, but to thee I speak; harken to what I tell thee." All these legends do not deny the story of the Passion; they develop upon the basis of the Gospel tradition an interpretation of the facts which eliminates the idea of the suffering and the death of a God.

If such was the Docetism of the second century, it would be surprising if there had been previously a Docetism of an entirely different character. That Docetism is met with at the beginning of the second century, and perhaps earlier, there is no room to doubt. Jerome attests its high antiquity when he says that the blood of Christ was still fresh in Judea, and the apostles were still living when men could be found to affirm that the body of the Lord was merely a phantom.[20]

M. Loisy has with justice pointed out, as is shown in the context, that there is in the passage from St. Jerome an oratorical exaggeration in which hyperbole and inaccuracy abound. The phrase about the blood of Christ has no more significance than the statement concerning the apostles. As regards the latter, its sole origin is in the fact that Docetism was combated in the Johannine Epistles (1, iv. 2 and 2, 7).

The formula in the first Epistle of John about the confession of Jesus Christ having come in the flesh (1, iv. 2) is not sufficiently precise to enable the thesis to which it is opposed to be reconstructed. This might just as well have been a negation of the Messianic character of the personality of Jesus as of the reality of His body. It is doubtless in the second sense that the testimony of the Johannine Epistle should be interpreted, because of an analogous, although more precise, controversy found in the Epistles of Ignatius. The Bishop of Antioch insists upon the reality of the facts of the Gospel history. To show this it suffices to quote a passage from the Epistle to the Christians of Tralles. It refers to Jesus Christ, "who had really been begotten, who had eaten and drunk, who had really been judged under Pontius Pilate, really crucified and put to death . . . who had really been raised from the dead." And Ignatius in his next chapter formally opposes the opinion thus stated to those of the unbelievers, who maintained that He only appeared to suffer.[21] The Docetism attacked by Ignatius may have been associated with Judaising tendencies combated in Philadelphians ix. 1.[22] The evidence of Jerome on the Palestinian origin of Docetism is favorable to this interpretation.

According to M. Salomon Reinach,[23] Docetism is far older than Ignatius; already it is found attacked in the Gospels, particularly in the episode concerning Simon of Cyrene, who at the time when Jesus was led to Calvary was forced by the soldiers to carry the cross (Mark xv. 21; Matt. xxvii. 32; Luke xxiii. 26). Mark alone states that this Simon was the father of Alexander and Rufus.[24] In Reinach's view the historical character of this episode is inadmissible, in the first place because there is no instance of any requisition similar to that of which Simon was the object, and in the next place because the condemned was obliged to carry the *patibulum* himself, and lastly because the whole episode is only the illustration of the words of Jesus, "Whosoever will come after Me, let him take up his cross and follow Me." None of these three arguments is convincing. The requisition of Simon the Cyrenian was certainly not legal; one must see in it one of the thousand daily annoyances the Romans did not hesitate to inflict on the Jews. It must not be explained by the compassion that Jesus would have inspired in the soldiers, but by the physical impossibility for Him, after flagellation, to carry the cross. Lastly, it is inconceivable that the episode should have been suggested by words in which it is a question not of carrying Jesus' cross, but one's own cross.

There is therefore no reason to recognize in the account the remains of a tradition analogous to the conception of the Gnostic Docetists concerning the crucifixion of Simon of Cyrene. If the

evangelist had substituted Jesus for Simon, who really was crucified, it is not comprehensible why they should not have pushed the
substitution to the end, but instead have preserved the details of the
carrying of the cross by Simon.

As for the names Alexander and Rufus, which are found only in
Mark, these are generally explained by saying that these persons
must have been known in the community in which the second
Gospel was composed.[25]

Matthew and Luke neglected this detail, which had no interest
for them or their readers. M. Reinach, on the contrary, considers
that the names Alexander and Rufus were added afterwards in
Mark because of a tradition which represented them as associates
of Peter.[26] But this tradition is only supported by a text of very
recent date, "The Acts of Peter and Andrew"; and if Alexander and
Rufus had been persons sufficiently known to make it worth while
to invoke their testimony (which, moreover, is only done in Mark
in a very indirect way), it would not be intelligible that their names
should have been omitted in the Gospels of Matthew and Luke. It
is not legitimate, therefore, to dispute the authenticity of the incident of Simon carrying the cross of Jesus.

The system which boldly dates back to the period which preceded the composition of the Gospels—a form of Docetism for
which Irenæus is the first witness—and claims to explain the origin
of the episode of Simon as a reaction against it, must be considered
an arbitrary construction. The conclusion to which we are thus led
is that there is no evidence for the existence of Docetism older than
is to be found in the Epistles of John and Ignatius.

The Docetism at the beginning of the second century must have
arisen from the same beliefs which inspired the theories of Gnostic
Docetism. It is necessary, therefore, to see in it, not a negation of
the Gospel history, but an attempt to interpret it, which in no degree
compromises the transcendent character of the Saviour by representing Him as accomplishing His work on humanity without par-
taking of the frailty of human nature.

A different interpretation has been proposed by M. Salomon Reinach,[27] who finds in Docetism an attempt to reconcile the Christian affirmations about Christ with a Jewish "X" who is the negation of the whole Gospel history.

The Christians, incapable of opposing to this negation positive proofs based upon authentic documents, replied that Jesus was a kind of divine phantom, a Being ethereal and entirely spiritual, that human eyes had seen, and whose voice human ears had heard, but who could not be touched.

To this theory M. Couissin[28] rightly objects that the answer to the Jewish negation would have been without efficacy, since the Jews denied precisely that which the Docetists affirmed, namely that Jesus had been seen and heard, either as an illusion or otherwise. M. Loisy observes that the answer of the Docetists would have been a "masterpiece of human stupidity," and that "we are here in the domain of pure phantasy, of stark improbability, of conjecture based upon nothing."

Indeed, the question discussed by the Docetists was not whether there had lived a man in the time of Pilate named Jesus, who acted, suffered and died, but the problem was to determine the nature of His manifestation. Here it is that M. Reinach[29] thinks he finds a decisive argument in favor of his theory in the Epistle of Ignatius to the Philadelphians.[30] "I have heard certain men say," writes Ignatius, "if I do not find (a certain thing) in the archives, I do not believe in the Gospel. And as I replied to them: It is written (in the Old Testament), they answered: 'That is the very question.' But for me the archives are Jesus Christ, His cross, His death, His resurrection, and the faith which comes from Him."

It is generally understood that Ignatius in this passage replies to those who demanded proofs drawn from the Old Testament before they accepted the affirmations of the Christian faith. He declares that these proofs exist, and as his adversaries dispute their value, he appeals to what is for him the supreme demonstration, Jesus Christ. In M. Reinach's view the archives referred to in the first part of the phrase are those of Cæsarea, the capital of Palestine. Ignatius had to deal with "a critical school, which, demanding documents concerning the terrestrial life of Jesus, and seeking these vainly among the archives, annoyed Ignatius with its negations." These critics are also aimed at in Ephesians (xix) where Ignatius says that the prince of this world had no knowledge either of the virginity of Mary or of the death of the Lord.

If this critical school of Antioch had existed, it would be inexplicable that its arguments have not been used again by later controversialists. But that is not all. If the word "archives" can be rigorously applied to the archives of Cæsarea, it holds none the less that Ignatius thinks he replies to the demands of his opponents in proving that the facts referred to are attested by the Old Testament, for the words "It is written" cannot, as M. Reinach recognizes, refer to anything except the Old Testament. His opponents do not deny that the proof offered by Ignatius, if it were really furnished, would be convincing. They only doubt that it is really given. If they had insisted on documents from archives, why should they have been able to content themselves with scriptural proofs? There must be some correspondence between the demand and the answer. If Ignatius were dealing with persons requiring documentary proofs of the Gospel history, why should he not have attempted to give them? In ignoring the question he would have given his opponents a manifest proof of feebleness. It appears, as M. Loisy admits, that it was not the Docetists, but the Judaising Christians who, while admitting in their generality the evangelical facts, disputed the interpretation that Ignatius gave of them. The conclusion we reach is therefore quite clear: The Docetists did not contest the Gospel history. They were Christian idealists, attached above all to the notion of the divinity of Christ and the celestial character of His person, who attempted to give it an interpretation harmonizing with their ideas. So understood, Docetism was only able to develop in the soil of evangelical tradition. If the Docetists had had the slightest reason to think that Christ was no more than an ideal person without historical reality, they would not have expended such treasures of ingenuity to give an interpretation of His story which cut Him off completely from too intimate contact with humanity. The Docetists thus appear as witness to Gospel tradition.

NOTES

1. In his *Contra Celsum,* written about 248. Concerning this work of Celsus and its refutation by Origen consult Neumann and De Faye.

2. This has been well shown by W. Bauer. Bauer gives a table showing the life of Jesus according to Jewish and pagan opponents of Christianity. This table shows the fundamental agreement of the two sides.

3. Bauer, *Das Leben Jesu,* etc. Tübingen, 1909.

4. Lucian, *De morte Peregrini;* Celsus (in Origen's work); Cæcilius reproaches the Christians with worshiping a man punished with death.

5. Exception is made of opponents whom Ignatius combated in the Epistle to the Philadelphians. We shall return to this passage when treating of Docetism.

6. S. Reinach, *Questions sur le Docetisme.*

7. Baldensperger, *L'apologetique de la primitive Eglise; Urchristliche Apologie.*

8. This is evident from the express declaration of Luke (i. 4) and John (xx. 31).

9. Luke xxiv. 39–42; John xx. 25–29.

10. M. Hubert Pernot (*Etudes de litterature grecque moderne*) has quoted a very curious case of the fidelity of oral tradition. It refers to a Cretan poem (*La Belle Bergère*). "In 1890," writes M. Pernot, "an inhabitant of Chio, Constantine Kaneallakis, gave, without knowing its ancient origin, a version of it, which is a guarantee of authenticity so complete that I supposed it to be a revised copy of one of the Venetian editions, until one day this conscientious worker told me that he had picked it up at Nenita, his native village, from an old peasant woman. The women of middle life being all illiterate in these places, the latter had only been able to hear the poem read. This is a characteristic example of the astonishing

facility with which people, whose memory has not yet been enfeebled by the use of writing, are capable of retaining works of considerable length."

11. Justin, *De resurrectione,* ii; *Tractatus Origensis;* Origen, *Contra Celsum,* ii, 16.

12. Concerning the character of Docetism, see Harnack, *Lehrbuch der Dogmengeschichte.*

13. Concerning the Doceticism of Marcion, see De Faye, *Gnostiques et Gnosticisme;* also Harnack, *Marcion, Das Evangelium vom fremden Gott.*

14. Irenæus, *Adv. Hær.,* iii, 16, 1.

15. Tertullian, *Adv. Marcionem,* iii, 9.

16. Harnack, *Marcion.*

17. Irenæus, *Adv. Hær.,* i, 26.

18. De Faye (*Gnostiques et Gnosticisme*) thinks that if Clement of Alexandria had known of this theory of Basilides, he would not have failed to attack it, and for this reason it should be only attributed to later adepts of the sect.

19. If one may judge by the formula of abjuration imposed upon them, the Manicheans seem to have had the same opinion (Kessler). The same thing is found, according to Photius, in the "Acts of John" (Leucius Charinus). There is also a legend which has it that it was Judas who was crucified in the place of Jesus (Liepsius).

20. Jerome, *Adv. Luciferum,* 23.

21. Cp. Eph. vii. 18; Smyrn. i, 2; Polycarpe, *Phil.,* vii, p. 1. A trace of Docetism is also found in the Gospel of Peter, where it is said that Jesus, when crucified, kept silent, as though He felt no pain. M. Reinach (*Source biblique du docetisme*) has with justice proposed to seek the origin of this idea in the passage in Isa. 1. 7: "I have made my face like unto a rock."

22. This is admitted, for instance, by W. Bauer (*Die Briefe des Ignatius von Antioch,* etc.).

23. Reinach, *Simon de Cyrene.* The criticism of Reinach by Loisy should be read (*Revue d'Histoire et de litterature religieuses,* 1913).

24. This episode is not found in the fourth Gospel. Some authors, such as Jean Réville (*Quatrième évangile*), consider that the evangelist has omitted it in the interest of anti-Docetism; others, like Holtzmann-Bauer, believe that he was influenced by the words of Jesus on the necessity of

carrying one's cross, or by the story of Isaac, who himself carried the wood for the burnt-offering. The fact that John has allowed other details of the Passion to be passed over leads us to consider it a simplification of the narrative, designed to concentrate all attention upon Jesus. The incident is wanting also in the Gospel of Peter. (M. Goguel, *Introd. au N.T.,* ii.)

25. This community was probably Roman. (See M. Goguel, *Introd. au N.T.,* i.)

26. Reinach.

27. *Id., Questions sur le docetisme (Revue Moderniste).*

28. P. L. Couissin, *Quelques reflexions sur la lettre de M. Reinach, Revue Moderniste,* reproduced by Reinach.

29. Reinach, *St. Ignace et le Docetisme.*

30. M. Reinach's translation is given. The text of the passage is not certain. For basis of discussion we accept that of M. Reinach.

CHAPTER V

THE APOSTLE PAUL AND GOSPEL TRADITION

I. THE EPISTLES OF PAUL[1]

The canon of Muratori, a Roman document of the second half of the second century, states that what the apostle Paul wrote to the Christians of a particular church is meant for all (*omnibus dicit*). This is the conception which inspired the canonization of the Epistles, and which has prevailed, but it was certainly not with the idea that his letters would become elements of a sacred collection that the apostle wrote them. It is only by a kind of transposition—at times not without prejudice to their true spirit—that these letters, which spring spontaneously from a sensitive personality, whose emotions, enthusiasms and indignation they reveal, have been changed into encyclicals or dogmatic treatises and interpreted in the style of a code.

Deissmann has maintained that it is a radical mistake to consider the Epistles of Paul as literary works, for they were only written as substitutes for conversations which distance rendered impossible. They are not in the technical sense of the word "Epistles"—that is, works which in an epistolary form are intended for a larger public in time and space than those to whom they are addressed, and treat of questions which might just as well be the object of a dissertation or a book. To thoroughly understand the Epistles of Paul it is necessary to forget the halo which for eighteen centuries has surrounded them, but which, while glorifying, distorts them. They are writings adapted to circumstances, improvised hastily between two journeys, dictated in the evening after a day devoted to manual work or to preaching, to meet some unforeseen circumstance, to solve some difficulty, to give instruction or warning, or to prevent a misunderstanding. Each one of them answers to some complex situation, which, having disappeared, the main reason for its existence has disappeared also. Further, there appears no trace of any custom on the part of the churches of the apostolic age of regularly reading the Epistles of Paul. They were communicated to the assembly when they were received; perhaps they were read again as it happened, so long as the question which had dictated their composition was not settled, but afterwards they were simply preserved in the archives, and that, it appears, with but little care. Many of these letters have disappeared, and among those preserved to us several seem to have undergone various alterations. When in Thessalonians (1, v. 27) Paul writes, "I charge you in the name of the Lord that this epistle be read unto all the Brethren," he merely requests that all may be informed of his message, and in no wise thinks of a second reading. To the Colossians Paul writes: "When this letter is read among you, cause that it be read also in the church of the Laodiceans, and that ye likewise read the epistle from the Laodiceans" (Col. iv. 16). The apostle is so far from the idea of a regular reading that he speaks of the dispatch, not of a copy, but of the original itself. There is nothing more unsound than to see in the Pauline Epistles theological treatises. Therefore complete expositions of the faith or system of thought of the apostle must not be sought in them. Written for those who had received his teaching, they lay stress upon what these persons knew, and proceed very often by allusions to what he had taught and the common tradition of Christianity. The fundamental doctrines are not more systematically treated than the facts upon which they rest. The initiates to whom they were addressed knew both, and had no need to have them recalled.

II. PAUL, BEFORE HIS CONVERSION, A WITNESS TO THE CROSS

Through the narratives in the book of Acts (vii. 58, viii. 1–3, ix. 1, 2), and particularly through the narrative of Paul himself (1 Cor. xv. 9; Gal. i. 13, 23; Phil. iii. 6), we know that before his conversion Paul was a bitter persecutor of the Christians. It is scarcely probable that the future apostle ever saw Jesus Himself, in spite of the passage in which he says: "If even we have known Christ after the flesh, we know Him no more" (2 Cor. v. 16). The words "after the flesh" may as well belong to "we know Him no more" as to "Christ." It is therefore possible to understand this as "we have known Jesus during His earthly life," or "we have had a carnal and Judaic conception of the Messiah." Even if the first of these two interpretations is to be preferred, account must be taken of the hypothetical element contained in the phrase. Paul appears to allude, in order to contest its value, to a privilege of which certain of his opponents boasted. In this passage merely an hypothesis is outlined. It must be added that if Paul had known Jesus he would have been among His enemies. Why should he who accuses himself of persecuting the disciples not have said that he had fought against the Master Himself?[2]

It was in the period which immediately followed the drama of Calvary that Paul must have come into contact with Christianity.[3] Even if it be supposed that the disciples of Jesus had only seen in Him, during His ministry, a prophet or a doctor, it is impossible to hold that after the Passion they remained grouped together in His name without attributing to His personality a quite peculiar value. They must have been led to see in His death the realization of a plan conceived by God for the salvation of humanity. We do not know how far Christology had developed before the conversion of Paul. It suffices to explain his sentiments and the attitude which they imposed upon him to know that the Christians continued to invoke Jesus, and to consider Him as one sent from God.

Saul of Tarsus—to give him the name by which he seems to have been known in the Jewish world—was then a young Rabbi, full of fanaticism and zeal for the Law. He must have been profoundly scandalized by the attitude of men who proclaimed themselves disciples of a madman whose pretensions had been condemned by the Sanhedrin, the supreme Jewish tribunal, and who had perished at the hands of the Roman authorities. The attitude of Paul is characterized by the phrase he was to employ later on: "Christ crucified, a scandal to the Jews" (1 Cor. i. 23; cp. Gal. v. 11). It epitomizes at once his experiences as a missionary to the Jews and his personal feelings before he was yet a Christian. His thought was dominated by the principle of the Law, which he recalls in his Epistle to the Galatians, "Cursed is everyone that hangeth on a tree" (Gal. iii. 13; cp. with Deut. xxi. 23). In permitting Him to die this infamous death, God Himself had pronounced against Jesus, and declared Him accursed. Those therefore who declared that this accursed one was the Son of God, the promised Messiah of Israel, were guilty of an appalling blasphemy. Wellhausen has supposed that, taught wisdom by hatred, Paul from this time recognized in Christianity a doctrine whose development would ruin Judaism. To admit this would be to misunderstand Paul's fanaticism and the depth of his faith in the destiny of Israel. It is still more rash to suppose, as does Pfleiderer, that the things which Paul knew and heard concerning Jesus exercised upon him a secret attraction, and that he was impressed by the spectacle of the lives of the Christians.

That would have been the spur for him to kick against,[4] the secret anxiety which he would have wished to silence by persecuting the Christians. That Paul, unknown to himself, may have been influenced by Christianity in the Jewish period of his life is, a priori, very plausible, but that he was at all conscious of it appears less likely. The testimony which he gives of himself when speaking of the persecutions directed by him against the Christians does not permit any doubt of the sincerity of his motives. The explanation of his attitude is more simple. Paul considered the Christians blasphemers and sacrilegious. Now blasphemy and sacrilege, in antiquity, were not sins which it belonged alone to God to judge; they were crimes which exposed the nation to the risk of divine anger. In this respect the judicial authorities had to take cognizance of them, and it was part of the duty of every one to aid them, and if need be to stimulate their zeal. An important consequence flows from this fact; it is that the cross had dominated the period of Paul's antagonism to Christianity, just as later it was to dominate his Christian thought. Paul the persecutor—and not only Paul the Christian—thus appears to us as a witness to the cross, and this also within the few months which followed the day of its erection on Calvary.

Here is a decisive objection against the doctrine that the entire Gospel history has been deduced from a theory or from a preëxisting myth and, if the word is allowed, from the supernatural life of an ideal Christ of whom the experiences of Peter and the primitive Christians were the initial manifestations.

III. PAUL AND THE UNITY OF PRIMITIVE CHRISTIANITY

Notwithstanding the opposition (exaggerated by the Tübingen school, nevertheless real) which existed between the apostle Paul and the Jerusalem Christians, who remained more attached to Judaism and its traditional ritual than he was himself, there existed within primitive Christianity a fundamental unity. Paul was conscious of it when summing up the essentials of Christian teaching. He said: "Therefore whether it were I or they (the apostles at

Jerusalem) so we preach and so ye believed" (1 Cor. xv. 11). Upon their side the Jerusalemites had confirmed this unity in offering Paul the hand of fellowship and in recognizing that he had received the mission to preach the gospel to the pagans (Gal. ii. 7–10). How is it possible to explain this fundamental unity of Christianity if at its origin there only existed conceptions relating to an ideal Christ and to His spiritual manifestations? Paul insists in the most formal way that his conversion took place without direct contact with the Jerusalem church. He declares himself "Paul, an apostle, not of men, neither by man, but by Jesus Christ and God the Father, who raised him from the dead" (Gal. i. 1). How is it possible to reconcile this absolute independence of Christianity and the apostleship of Paul with the unity of primitive Christianity unless by the fact that the apostle recognized in the activity of the celestial Christ, to whom he attributed the birth of his faith, the continuation and consequence of the historical ministry of Jesus to which the Christianity of the Twelve and the Jerusalem church owed its origin?

IV. THE BROTHERS OF JESUS AND THE JERUSALEM APOSTLES

Before examining the testimony that the apostle Paul renders directly to the evangelical tradition, it will be convenient to point out two facts which prove that the Pauline Christ is indeed a real human personality. On two occasions the apostle speaks incidentally of James and other brothers of the Lord (Gal. i. 19; 1 Cor. ix. 5). In neither of these two passages is it possible unless the text be distorted in an inadmissible manner,[5] to give to the word "brothers" any other interpretation than that which belongs to it in its natural sense.[6] There were then in the Jerusalem church (Paul knew it, and the churches of the Diaspora were not ignorant of it) men who passed for being the brothers of Jesus according to the flesh.

How can this well-established fact be reconciled with the

theory that the Christ preached by Paul was a purely ideal personage?[7] Drews,[8] it is true, has maintained that the phrase "brother of the Lord" meant simply member of the community, but to designate the faithful the apostle merely said "the brothers" or "the brethren in the Lord," and in the passages in which the brothers of Jesus are referred to Paul names them besides other Christians, the apostles and Cephas, and he does not confuse them with these. In 1 Cor. ix. 5, in particular, it is remarkable that Paul, in speaking of the wife that he might have, says quite simply "sister," while he says "brethren of the Lord" concerning the persons to whom he compares himself.[9]

One other fact imposes a similar conclusion. Paul assimilates his apostleship entirely to that of the Twelve; he obtained, not without difficulty, the recognition of the validity of his vocation by the Jerusalem church (Gal. ii. 1–10). He connects his apostleship, like that of the Twelve, with an apparition of the risen Christ,[10] but he must have been obliged to fight a hard and persevering battle to establish that he was in nothing inferior to those whom in derision he called the archapostles (2 Cor. xi. 5 and xii. 11). The latter, or at any rate their partisans, must have maintained that Paul lacked a qualification of which his rivals could boast. It was impossible to question either the qualifications of Paul from the Judaic point of view (Phil. iii. 4–6; 2 Cor. xi. 21, 22) or his services to the cause of the Gospel and the sufferings accepted by him for it[11] (1 Cor. xv. 10; 2 Cor. xi. 23–33; Gal. i. 17) or the signs accomplished and visions obtained by him (2 Cor. xii. 1–12). A text in the epistle to the Galatians enables us to understand the nature of the objection raised against the Pauline apostleship. Concerning the apostles at Jerusalem Paul said:[12] "But of these who seemed to be somewhat (whatsoever they were it maketh no matter to me: God accepteth no man's person)—for they who seemed to be somewhat in conference added nothing to me" (Gal. ii. 6).

The qualification on which the Jerusalem apostles prided themselves and which Paul lacked, referred to the past. The Twelve could boast of having been Christians and apostles before Paul, but he in no wise attempted to hide the fact that he had formerly persecuted the church and that he was a late recruit for the Gospel.[13] On the contrary, he boasted of it as something to be proud of (1 Cor. xv. 8–10), because he considered it a manifest proof of the intervention of God in his life.

What could this former qualification of which the Jerusalem apostles boasted be, other than that they had been witnesses and associates of the historical ministry of Jesus? The controversies between Paul and Jerusalem apostles thus establish that the latter boasted of having been witnesses of the life of Jesus—a fact which Paul did not contest.

V. EXAMINATION OF TEXTS SUPPOSED TO CONTAIN ALLUSIONS TO A CHRIST MYTH

In the opening salutation of the Epistle to the Romans Paul speaks of "Christ Jesus, born of the seed of David according to the flesh, as God had announced in advance by the prophets in the holy scriptures" (Rom. i. 2, 3). In M. Couchoud's view[14] it follows from this passage that the human (or apparently human) life of Jesus was not told, but revealed to Paul, and that by prophecies. The fact that the apostle thought he recognized concordance between the history of Jesus and certain prophecies does not prove that the history has been deduced from the prophecy.[15] But this is not all. Two announcements are made in the phrase before us—one is the existence of Jesus, the other asserts His descent from David. The Davidic origin asserted by Paul on the faith of prophecies gives Jesus a human lineage. The notion of the Davidic origin of Jesus appears to have a theological source. The Gospels record no word of Jesus which supports it. It is merely implied in certain episodes to which no great importance can be attached.[16] The blind man, Bartimeus, addressed Jesus once as "Jesus, Son of David," and on another occasion as "Son of David," according to Mark (x. 47, 48) and Luke (xviii. 38, 39), while Matthew has on both occasions simply "Son of David."[17] In the narrative of the entry into Jerusalem, organized to fulfill the prophecy of Zechariah (ix. 9), the mention of David in the popular welcome does not occupy the same place in Mark (xi. 9) and in Matthew (xxi. 9), and is lacking in Luke (xix. 38), which requires us, at any rate, to consider its authenticity as not certain.[18] One single idea remains from study of these texts, and that is, considering Jesus in a more or less vague manner as the Messiah, He was sometimes spoken of as the Son of David. But there is nothing to show that Jesus Himself accepted it, and still less that He claimed this title. On the contrary, in a remark whose authenticity is beyond question,[19] Jesus appears to oppose the notions of the Messiahship and the Davidic origin one against the other. In the Temple Jesus asks: "How is it the scribes say that Christ is the Son of David? David himself, inspired by the Holy Spirit, says, 'The Lord said unto my Lord, Sit Thou upon My right hand until I make Thine enemies Thy footstool.' David himself calls Him his Lord—how then can He be his son?" (Mark xii. 35–37, Matt. xxii. 41–46, Luke xx. 41–44).

In the context, as we read it, this question appears to be a subtle problem propounded by Jesus to the Scribes, and which they were not prepared to solve. It is to some extent an argument *ad hominem.* But it is doubtful, in spite of the opinion of some exegetists,[20] that we have here only a flash of wit. The text has a wider implication. It establishes an antinomy between the true Messiahship that Jesus invoked and the popular and current notion of the Messiah, Son of David.[21] The idea of the Davidic origin of Jesus has therefore a secondary character. It is a theological creation made under the influence of prophecies and popular beliefs. This tends to restrict the affirmation concerning the prophecies in Rom. i. 2–3 principally, if not exclusively, to the words "born of the seed of David."

The fact that, either by Paul or by others before him, the notion of the Davidic origin had been introduced into Christology is not without importance. The Jewish Messianic conception oscillated between two poles: the idea of a transcendent and celestial Messiah to come with power to execute the judgments of God, and that of a human Messiah, a king of the race of David, for whom and by whom the national monarchy of Israel would be restored. The first conception is found specially in the books of Daniel and Enoch, the second in the Songs of Solomon. These two conceptions have sometimes been combined; they are constantly so in the Christology of the primitive Church. The two currents of the Messianic conception are none the less distinct. If the Jesus of the most primitive Christianity and of Paul himself had been a purely spiritual and celestial Being with no connection with humanity except an external and unreal form, why should the apostle have contradicted himself in connecting his Messiah to a human lineage?

In another passage M. Couchoud thinks he also understands the inner significance of the debt of Paul to the prophecy of what is supposed to be an historical tradition. The reference is to the passage in which the apostle, summing up the essentials of Christian teaching, expresses himself thus: "For I delivered unto you first of all that which I also received—how that Christ died for our sins according to the Scriptures, and that He was buried, and rose again the third day according to the Scriptures" (1 Cor. xv. 3, 4). Then follows an enumeration of apparitions (xv. 3–8). In the opinion of M. Couchoud, the words "according to the Scriptures" mark the source of the knowledge. It follows therefore from this passage that faith in Jesus rests partly on the Scriptures and partly on the apparitions. The faith in Jesus is possible, but not the knowledge of Jesus implied in this faith. The apostle draws a parallel between "I have transmitted" and "I have received."

They are facts of the same class, therefore, which lead us to suppose that the apostle presents himself as witness of a tradition. The teaching given and the teaching received could not be thus assimilated if on the one side there had been supernatural revelation or exegetical deduction, and on the other didactic teaching; the examination of the context confirms this first impression. It may be admitted with reason that the passage in question is, so to speak, the first rudiment of a confession of faith. It is unnecessary to bring in the narrative of the visions, which belongs to the affirmation of the resurrection, and which in its amplitude contrasts with the brevity of the phrase preceding. The account of the apparitions is added to the epitome of the faith as a confirmation of the point on which Paul makes his entire argument depend. While three facts are named in the Pauline formula, the words "according to the Scriptures" are only found twice in it, and these are with reference to two facts—the death and the resurrection—which possess in Paul's thought a redemptive character. The words are wanting in respect of the burial, which has no importance in the Pauline theory of salvation, and which is only incidentally touched upon in the symbol of baptism (Rom. vi. 4 and Col. ii. 12). This proves that the formula "according to the Scriptures" has no bearing upon the facts, but upon their interpretation. What Paul knew from the Scriptures was not that Christ died, but that He died for our sins. Paul, even when he persecuted the Christians, knew perfectly well that their Master was dead; he either did not know or refused to believe that He died for sins. It was the Scriptures which, once he had the certitude of the living Christ in his inner consciousness, enabled him to understand the meaning of Christ's death. Similarly, if Paul believed in the resurrection, it was not because of the prophecies, but because of the apparition he had seen. Besides, he had read the prophecies long before he was a Christian, but he only discovered the resurrection when, in an entirely different way, the faith in the Christ still living, in spite of death, had developed within him.

M. Couchoud[22] can only see a mystical, almost Gnostic, idea in the passage of the Epistle to the Galatians, in which Paul says that in the fulfillment of time "God had sent His Son, born of a woman" (Gal. iv. 4). In his view there is no historical reference. Taken alone, this text would constitute, in fact, but a very short and insufficient biography—not even the outline of a life of Jesus. But does it not contain, at least, the idea of the historical life of Jesus? And by what right besides is this affirmation isolated? The Galatians do not separate it from the teaching in which the apostle retraced the story of the crucifixion in so vivid a manner that they had the feeling of contemplating it with their own eyes (iii. 1). Paul does not return to this part of his teaching because it was not contradicted by the missionaries of his opponents. Besides, the expression "born of a woman" was not invented by Paul. He borrowed it from the Old Testament,[23] where it is used to designate man under the ordinary conditions of his birth and existence. The declaration of Galatians (iv. 4) would be unintelligible if, in Paul's view, Jesus had not lived under the ordinary conditions of humanity.

A very special importance attaches to the long passage of the Epistle to the Philippians, in which, in a way otherwise accidental, Paul epitomizes his whole thought concerning Christ and His work. The apostle writes: "Who, being in the form of God, thought it not robbery to be equal with God,[24] but made Himself of no reputation, and took upon Him the form of a servant, and was made in the likeness of men. And being found in fashion as a man, He humbled Himself and became obedient unto death—even the death of the cross. Wherefore God also hath highly exalted Him and given Him a name which is above every name. That at the name of Jesus every knee should bow of things in heaven and things on earth and things under the earth, and that every tongue should confess that Jesus is Lord, to the glory of the Father" (Phil. ii. 5–11).

M. Couchoud thinks that in this passage is found the most ancient epitome we possess of the story of Jesus. It appears to him to include two elements—firstly, the descent of the divine Being into humanity and His death; and secondly, His ascension and glorification.

M. Couchoud considers that a less lyrical version of this myth, but one containing more details, is found in the Ascension of Isaiah. The prophet was caught up and carried away from world to world up to the seventh heaven. In this region he was a spectator of the mysterious drama which will mark the end of time. God commands a Being who is called the Well-Beloved, the Chosen One, or the Son, to descend through the seven heavens, the firmament, the air, and the earth down to Sheol, where He is to bind the angel of death. That His descent shall not be perceived by the angels inhabiting the successive worlds, the Son receives the power to take to Himself in each of them a form resembling that of the beings who dwell therein. His mission accomplished, the Son ascends, this time in His own form, up to the seventh heaven. While looking upon His glorious ascension the angels are astounded. They ask how the descent of the Son of God could have escaped their perception, and they are obliged to glorify Him. The celestial Being then seats Himself at the right hand of the Supreme Glory.

There are two questions to be successively examined: Is the passage from the Epistle to the Philippians an Apocalyptic element, and is the myth it expresses quite identical to that we find in the Ascension of Isaiah? Seeing that the thesis of the affinity between the Ascension of Isaiah and the Epistle of the Philippians only enters in a subordinate manner into the reasoning of M. Couchoud, we shall first of all examine this point.

What is the Ascension of Isaiah? In the form in which we know it, it is a fairly complex whole in which three principal portions are easily distinguished:

1. A purely Jewish narrative of the martyrdom of the prophet Isaiah sawn asunder by order of Manasseh (i. 1, 2, 12, and v. 1–16). It appears once to have had an independent existence, and to have been known in this form to Justin Martyr, Tertullian and Origen.[25]

2. An Apocalyptic vision about Antichrist, the decadence of the Church, and the return of the Lord. In its present form this portion, whose Christian origin is not doubtful, betrays a certain dependence as regards the Ascension, properly so called. It seems that this may be owing to editorial work, for the conception of the work of Christ found in the vision differs from that in the Ascension, and can neither be considered as the germ of it nor a development from it (ii. 13–iv. 22).

3. The Ascension, in the exact sense of the word (vi. 1–11, 43), is the portion which specially interests us. Isaiah was carried away by an angel up to the seventh heaven; he received an explanation of the descent of the Well-Beloved from the higher heaven down to Sheol, whence He was to reascend to the heaven. The prophet is afterwards a witness of the events which had been announced to him.

The date of the compilation of the Ascension of Isaiah, in its completeness as well as in each of the portions which constitute it, cannot be determined with absolute precision. Critics are almost agreed in considering that the Ascension (in the exact sense) cannot be older than the middle of the second century. It is even possible that it may be necessary to bring the date of its composition considerably later. The fact that Origen mentions the martyrdom as a Jewish book proves that he did not know the Ascension in its present form. True, it might have had an independent existence before its incorporation into the book as we read it. The amount of Christian retouching which it has undergone (especially the eleventh chapter) is favorable to this hypothesis.

But even supposing the Ascension not anterior to the middle of the second century, the ideas which are developed in it might date back to an older period. Indeed, it appears necessary to distinguish in the Ascension between a fundamental myth—that concerning the descent of the celestial Being and a Christian interpretation given of it. This compound of two elements explains certain peculiarities of the book. For instance, the Well-Beloved receives the command to transform His image into that of the beings inhabiting various spheres of the universe, so that He may arrive without difficulty at Sheol, where He is to despoil the angel of death (ix. 16), but He does not pursue His descent in a straight line (if it may be so expressed), and when He arrives on earth[26] He has need of the intervention of Satan in order that He may reach Sheol. Satan raises the jealousy of the Jews against Him, and causes them to put Him to death (xi. 19–21).[27] This compound of two dissimilar elements is to be noted in another matter. The triumph of the Well-Beloved is attained through the power He receives to transform Himself while traversing the different spheres of the universe. It is not stated that, having reached Sheol, He wages battle with the angel of death. It appears that the latter is incapable of resisting the Chosen One, and is conquered at the instant the Lord reaches Him. After this victory the Well-Beloved, recognized by all the angels, judges and annihilates the princes, angels and gods of this world and the world over which they have dominion. He ascends in glory, and sits down at the right hand of God (x. 12–15). The triumph of the Chosen One is therefore attained by his ascension. This idea is quite different from the Christian conception, according to which the judgment and annihilation of the powers hostile to God is the work of Christ returning from the heavens to His second coming, and not of the Lord ascending to heaven after the resurrection. There is thus recognizable behind the Christian interpretation which dominates the present form of the Ascension of Isaiah a myth of the reëstablishment of the sovereignty of God by a divine being who descends into Sheol to despoil the angel of death, and afterwards ascends gloriously to the heavens. It is possible that the myth may be older than Christianity.[28]

There is a certain affinity between this myth and the idea dominating the Christological development of the Epistle to the Philippians, but while in Paul's thought Christ divests Himself of something, in the Ascension of Isaiah He merely transforms Himself. The development of the Epistle to the Philippians cannot have been from the myth, because (the negative determination in which the development of the myth begins is a proof of it) the work of Christ is described by Paul in opposition to another myth, in which there is recognizable the story of Satan, who desired to raise himself to supreme power and to claim for himself the adoration of men and angels, and who as a consequence of this rebellion must be annihilated. The correspondence between the work of Satan and that of Christ is not, however, complete, since to Jewish thought the idea of an incarnation of Satan was unknown.

The relation between the myth of Satan and the Christological drama as Paul conceives it is therefore not one of simple and direct dependence. Paul has simply interpreted the story of Jesus by a doctrine formulated in opposition to the Satanic myth.

It would only be possible to see in the Christological development of the Epistle to the Philippians the oldest form of the history of Jesus if this portion had been written to make the Church known to persons who had never heard it spoken of—which is certainly not the case.

The incidental manner in which the development proceeds would alone suffice to prove it, even if we did not already know that the Epistle is addressed to Christians to whom it may perhaps be necessary to explain the importance of the work of Christ, but superfluous to rehearse its history. Replaced in its historical setting, the text of Paul is an attempt to epitomize the history of Jesus in one grand drama of redemption. That it contains dogmatic elements— or, if you prefer it, mythical elements—is undeniable, but these elements do not make up the substance of the story; they serve as comments on it, and supply the materials for the speculative construction erected upon the foundation thus furnished.

Attention must be called to an idea borrowed from Judaism by Paul, and which in his eyes possesses capital importance—that of preëxistence. The conception of the preëxistence of souls is found distinctly in certain Jewish texts,[29] but more distinctly still that of the preëxistence of the Messiah.[30] Paul affirms the preëxistence of Christ not only when, in the Epistle to the Colossians (i. 15), he speaks of Christ's part in creation, but also when he uses such terms as the "man from heaven" (1 Cor. xv. 47, etc.), or again, when in a portion of rabbinical exegesis he identifies Christ with the rock which accompanied the Israelites in the desert (1 Cor. x. 4). These affirmations do not contradict the human and earthly personality of Jesus; they merely imply that humanity is unable to explain to its roots this personality and activity. Weinel observes in this connection that these ideas must only be judged by those of antiquity, when it was habitual to explain the mysterious in a personality by forces belonging to another world.[31] Just as Paul felt that the spiritual Christ dwelt and lived in him (Gal. ii. 20), without for that reason losing consciousness of his own human personality, so also was he able to see in Christ a celestial and preëxisting Being without thereby forcibly depriving humanity of Him. One is forced to cultivate the mentality of antiquity in order to understand the conceptions in virtue of which the theology of primitive Christianity (and especially that of Paul) attempted to explain in the person and work of Jesus that which surpassed the common standard of humanity. The notion of the Messiah furnished the idea of preëxistence; that of divine Sonship tended to identify Jesus with the hypostasis of "Wisdom" and the "Word." In this manner, starting from soteriology, the mind was quickly led to attribute a cosmological character to Christ. But the movement of Pauline Christology, if so it may be called, progresses from humanity to divinity, and not from divinity to humanity. If in the Epistle to the Colossians Paul develops the theme of the cosmological character of Christ and the idea of His sovereignty over all celestial beings, it is because those whom he addressed were fascinated by speculations concerning angels, and it was of moment to show them that the worship of Christ attained the realities of the celestial world in a manner more complete and efficacious than devotion paid to angels. The whole of this side of Pauline Christology thus appears to be the development of a doctrine elaborated on other grounds.

The distinctly theological element of Pauline Christology is not the point from which he sets out in thought. It is the conclusion of it. It is the result of an effort imposed on him in the interest of practical apologetics, rather than of speculative curiosity, to give an interpretation of the person and work of Jesus harmonizing with conceptions about spiritual beings current in his time, and with the position assigned to Jesus by the faith. At times Paul's thought assumes a character distinctly philosophic. In certain passages we have the impression of being in presence of a cosmological theory instead of a human history. Such, for example, is the character presented by the portion of the Epistle to the Colossians (i. 13–20) where God is referred to as He "who has delivered us from the power of darkness and brought us into the Kingdom of His well-beloved Son." Then follows a lyrical description of what this Son is like, "in Him we have redemption, the remission of sins." "For Christ is the very image of the Invisible God—the first-born and head of all creation; for in Him was created all that is in heaven and on earth, the visible and the invisible—angels, archangels, and all the powers of heaven. All has been created through Him and for Him. He was before all things, and all things unite in Him; and He is the head of the Church, which is His body. The first-born from the dead, He is to the Church the source of its life, that He in all things may stand first. For it pleased the Father that in Him the divine nature in all its fullness should dwell, and through Him to reconcile all things to Himself (making peace by the shedding of Christ's blood offered upon the cross)—whether on earth or in Heaven."[32]

The conception developed in this passage, where Christ appears as a divine Being, almost an hypostasis, closely resembles that found in Philo, and is certainly related to it. Are we to conclude that the Christ of Paul is an ideal Being like the Logos of Philo? It does not seem necessary, for the ancient mentality saw no contradiction between the human character of a person and his divine character. One example of the association of the two concepts is given us by the fourth evangelist, who means to relate the story of a man who has lived on earth, and whom he identifies with the creative Logos.

The case of the Epistle to the Colossians is quite analogous; and if the historical side of the person of Jesus is only touched upon by the mention of the cross, this is explained entirely by the character of the Epistle. M. Couchoud considers as quite decisive in favor of the nonhistorical theory the passage in which Paul speaks of the wisdom of God, "that none of the great ones of this world had known, for if they had known it, they would not have crucified the glorified Lord" (1 Cor. ii. 8). M. Couchoud[33] finds that it follows from this text that those who crucified Jesus were mythical beings, not persons of flesh and bone, and that the drama consequently took place between heaven and earth, in an Apocalyptic atmosphere. And to prove that we are certainly dealing here with a mythical theory, M. Couchoud points to the analogy that exists between our passage and the Ascension of Isaiah, where it appears that if the angels had perceived the descent of the Son of God, they would have opposed it, and would have hindered the accomplishment of His work. They, however, did not collaborate in any way. The part played by them was entirely negative and unconscious.[34] But, on the contrary, according to Paul, when the archons crucified the Lord, they were not ignorant that He was the Savior,[35] but they did not know the divine plan, nor did they realize that the death of Christ would cause their own annihilation. The two concepts differ so much that one cannot have been deduced from the other; they have only a very general theme in common, that of the demon deluded. It is consequently illegitimate to interpret the indication given by Paul in an incidental way by the theory developed in the Ascension of Isaiah. But there is more than this. It is doubtful if Paul attributes to the archons anything more than responsibility for the death of Christ. There is easily to be recognized in them the seventy angels to whom, according to an idea particularly developed in the book of Enoch, God has confided the government of the world.[36] They direct the nations and inspire their actions.[37] In saying that they had crucified the Lord, Paul does not appear to have thought of anything other than the crucifixion of Jesus by men, but by men whom he considers as agents of demoniacal powers. This conception is in all points similar to that found in the fourth Gospel, where Jesus is arrested by the cohort and tribune (guided by Judas, into whom Satan had entered), judged, and condemned by Pilate at the instigation of the Jews, and finally crucified by soldiers. The whole drama is explained by the action of "the prince of this world"—in other words, Satan (see John xiv. 30).[38] There is therefore, as Dibelius justly remarks, no contradiction between 1 Cor. ii. 8 (which holds the archons responsible for the death of Jesus) and 1 Thess. ii. 15, where it is stated that the Jews put Jesus to death.

We have thus passed in review the principal passages of the Pauline Epistles where allusions to a Christ myth are supposed to be found. In Paul's writings these reveal a Christological doctrine in which are incorporated elements borrowed from the dogmatic tradition of Judaism, and even fragments of myths, but it is illegitimate to reduce the whole Pauline Christology to these, and to pass over everything which in the Pauline Epistles and teaching had reference to the historical person of Jesus and to His life on earth. In another chapter we shall return to the subject of the relation between these two elements. Let us only note here that this relation appears to be that between admitted fact and its interpretation. Far from contradicting the historical personality of Jesus, the Pauline Christology would be incomprehensible if it had not made the historical facts its starting point.

VI. THE GOSPEL TRADITION IN PAUL[39]

The Epistles of Paul contain but few allusions to the Gospel history, but when these are closely examined it is found that the apostle was much more familiar with the life of Jesus than a superficial reading of the Epistles would lead one to think.

Paul presents Jesus as a man born of woman (1 Cor. xv. 21; Rom. v. 15; Gal. iv. 4), belonging to the race of Abraham (Gal. iii. 16; Rom. ix. 5), and descending from the family of David (Rom. i. 3). He lived under the Jewish Law (Gal. iv. 4; Rom. xv. 8). The Epistles say neither when nor where, but importance need not be attached to this, since it was only at a relatively secondary stage in the evolution of the tradition that it was considered necessary to establish synchronism in the history of Jesus (Luke iii. 1).[40] Paul places himself at a point of view similar to that of Mark. If Paul does not know the parents of Jesus,[41] he mentions His brothers, and gives the name of one of them, James (1 Cor. ix. 5; Gal. i. 19 and ii. 9; cp. 1 Cor. xv. 7).

It is impossible to decide how Paul conceived the character and moral physiognomy of the Lord. It is, in fact, not always possible to recognize whether the passages dealing with this order of ideas apply to Jesus or the Christ in His preëxistence or His glorification, and it does not appear that the apostle made upon this subject a very clear distinction. However, even if the passage where Christ is called "He who knew not sin" (2 Cor. v. 21) relates to the preëxistent Christ, it would at least show that Paul had a belief in the perfect sanctity of Jesus. This, no doubt, is a dogmatic idea—at any rate, it cannot be that the apostle's conception of the historical life of Jesus contradicts it. The exhortations to the imitation of Christ (1 Cor. xi. 1 and Col. i. 10) imply also the idea of this sanctity.

The love of Christ referred to in Rom. viii. 27, being presented as real, must be considered in connection with the glorified Christ. But the gentleness and meekness of Christ, in the name of which Paul exhorted the Corinthians (2, x. 1), refer to His character, since in this passage there is a transparent allusion to a saying of Jesus (Matt. xi. 29). Concerning the middle period of the life of Jesus, the Epistles contain but very little indeed. Nevertheless, as we have seen, Paul knew of the existence of apostles who were associated with the Master's ministry. The cross occupied a predominating place in the preaching as in the theology of Paul (Gal. iii. 1 and 1 Cor. ii. 2).

The death of Jesus was portrayed as an act of obedience towards God and of love towards men (Phil. ii. 8 and Gal. ii. 20). It was brought about by the enmity of the Jews (1 Thess. ii. 15) and through the ignorance of the celestial archons who directed them. Paul is aware that Jesus passed the evening preceding His death with His disciples, and that it was during this last meal that He instituted the Lord's Supper (1 Cor. xi. 23). We shall return to this testimony. Does it also imply that Jesus was betrayed by one of His followers? This cannot be determined with certainty, for the term employed may just as well signify "betrayed" as "delivered over to death." It has sometimes been believed that the execution of Jesus is indicated in the passage in which the apostle assimilates the death of Christ to the sacrifice of the paschal lamb (1 Cor. v. 7). We shall see later that this interpretation is far from being certain.

At almost every page of his Epistles Paul reminds his readers that Jesus died on the cross. He speaks of His violent death (2 Cor. iv. 10), of the shedding of blood (Rom. iii. 25), of the sufferings He endured (2 Cor. i. 5, 7; Rom. viii. 17; Phil. iii. 10), of the exhaustion He passed through before expiring (2 Cor. xiii. 4), of the insults He submitted to (Rom. xv. 3). Finally he specially refers to the burial of Jesus (1 Cor. xv. 4–8), and confirms the tradition concerning the apparitions (1 Cor. xv. 4–8).

When all these indications are grouped together the impression is gained that if Paul does not provide a coherent view of the history of Jesus, he nevertheless possesses one. Furthermore, and more distinctly still, he is a witness of the sayings of Jesus. Resch[42] went much too far in asserting that there were a thousand allusions to the sayings of Jesus[43] in the authentic Epistles. Those which are met with may be divided into three groups: direct quotations, allusions sufficiently precise to authorize the admission that Paul had the saying of Jesus in mind, and finally reminiscences almost unconscious. We shall leave aside this third series of allusions, which cannot be exactly defined, but which are far from being without significance, for they show how the mind of Paul was sustained by the sayings of Jesus. To reassure the Thessalonians, anxious about the fate of believers who died before the second coming, Paul declared to them that at the time of the Savior's return these would be resurrected to join the living, and he gives this teaching "in a word of the Lord" (1 Thess. iv. 15). It is not quite clear what it is in the teaching given which answers to this. The attempts which have been made to rediscover in the text an allusion to a known saying of Jesus, to a passage in the Old Testament, or to an Apocryphal work such as Esdras (iv.), have not succeeded. Some writers[44] think that Paul in this passage speaks by revelation, and that he is writing under the inspiration of the Spirit. This interpretation conflicts with the fact that when Paul communicates any teaching which he holds was revealed to him, he expressly points this out (1 Cor. xv. 51; 2 Cor. xii. 1). The most natural thing is to suppose that Paul is quoting in this passage an agraphon, or in other words a saying of Jesus not incorporated into the Gospel tradition.[45] In the seventh chapter of the first Epistle to the Corinthians Paul gives instructions to married people. "To those who are married," he writes, "my direction is (yet it is not mine, but the Master's) that a woman is not to leave her husband" (verse 10). The saying here referred to is the reply of Jesus to the Pharisees concerning the subject of divorce (Mark x. 11, 12; Matt. xix. 9), preserved in a slightly different form in the Sermon on the Mount (Matt. v. 32). What gives to this citation all its importance is the fact that two verses farther on, considering a particular case (that of a Christian whose wife is not a believer, or on the other hand, that of a Christian woman married to a pagan), Paul writes: "To all others I say, I, not the Master." Similarly, in the course of the chapter, Paul says that, concerning virgins and unmarried women, he "has no command from the Master" (1 Cor. vii. 25; cp. 40). He is content to give his own opinion. If the word of the Master was in Paul a revelation of the Spirit, as M. Couchoud thinks, it would be very surprising that upon a matter so important for the life of the Church, the Spirit produced no oracle. But there is more than this. In the place of the word of the Lord, Paul gives his own opinion, and he attaches great weight to it. It is not the opinion of an ordinary man, but that of one to whom the Master has given the power to be faithful, who can thus boast of being an authorized interpreter of His thought and who possesses the Spirit. Notwithstanding this opinion, Paul takes good care not to claim an authority equal to that of the Master's words. Here is a decisive proof that it was indeed a word coming from Jesus that the apostle meant to cite, and to this word he attributes an absolute authority.

In the same Epistle also Paul cites a saying of Jesus to establish the right of those who preach the gospel to be maintained by the churches. "The Lord has commanded," he writes, "that those who preach the gospel shall live by the gospel." Here is certainly an allusion to the words spoken at the sending forth of the disciples on a mission: "If ye are received in a house, eat and drink what is set before you, for the laborer is worthy of his hire" (Luke x. 7; Matt. x. 10). We now reach the last of the citations of the words of Jesus found in Paul's Epistles, and it is almost the most important and the most discussed among them. In the eleventh chapter of the first Epistle to the Corinthians[46] Paul, in combating the defective manner in which the Lord's Supper was celebrated at Corinth, recalls what took place on the last evening of Jesus.[47] He writes: "I have received from the Lord . . . and I have in turn given to you." Many critics[48] consider that the words "I have received from the Lord" indicate that there was a vision at the origin of the tradition concerning the last supper. They mean "I have received" in the sense "I have it directly from the Lord." Other writers adopt a less radical opinion. Loisy[49] and Bousset [50] think that Paul, by a kind of autosuggestion, reached the point of contemplating in vision the scene that tradition had transmitted to him. Others, like Pfleiderer and Haupt,[52] believe that Paul obtained from a revelation, not the account of the last supper of Jesus, but the knowledge of the sacramental character and significance of the Eucharist.

Nothing in the text of Paul authorizes or justifies such a distinction. Neither can we accept the hypothesis of Lietzmann and Ed. Meyer, who suppose that Paul synthesized in the vision on the Damascus road all that he knew of Jesus. Besides, the initial vision did not determine Paul's knowledge of Jesus; it caused his faith to be born. All intermediate solutions should be put aside. We are in face of a dilemma: Either the entire tradition about the last supper possessed for Paul a visionary origin, or the formula, "I have received from the Lord," means something other than "I know by means of a vision."

If there had been a vision, it would not diminish in the eyes of the apostle the value of the tradition it related. On the contrary, its authority would be the more increased; it would be surprising that the apostle should not expressly relate a detail of a nature to impress his readers.

Paul draws a very close parallel between the two expressions "I have received" and "I have transmitted" (or "passed on"). They are of the same nature, which would not be the case if on one side it was a case of a supernatural communication received by the apostle, and on the other didactic teaching imparted to the Corinthians. And, above all, nothing authorizes us to understand "I have received from the Lord" in the sense "I have it direct from the Lord." The preposition "apo" which the apostle here uses marks the first origin of the tradition, but without excluding an intermediary. What Paul wishes to say is that in the last analysis tradition goes back to the Lord, who pronounced the words which he relates.

When in the Epistle to the Galatians (i. 1) Paul desires to affirm that he holds his apostleship direct from Christ and from God without any human intervention, he uses the two prepositions "apo" and "dia," which proves that he perfectly conceives an apostleship coming from God, but not through human intermediaries. The use in our passage of the single preposition "apo" shows that the apostle only means the first origin of the tradition. What he means to say is that the narrative comes from the Lord by the intermediary of men. This detail did not require to be explicitly announced; for the Corinthians it was clear from the very position of the apostle.

The direct study of the text and its comparison with the form of the tradition fixed in the Gospel of Mark confirms this conclusion. Doubtless the Gospel of Mark was only compiled a couple of decades after the Epistle to the Corinthians, but the date of the compilation of a work like a Gospel must not be identified with that of the traditions it contains.

The two texts read as follows: Mark xiv. 22–25: "While they

were eating, Jesus took some bread, and after saying the blessing, broke it and gave to them, and said: Take it; this is My body. Then He took the cup, and after saying the thanksgiving, gave it to them, and they all drank from it. This is My covenant blood, He said, which is poured out on behalf of many. I tell you that I shall never again drink of the juice of the grape until that day when I shall drink it new in the Kingdom of God."

The first Epistle to the Corinthians, xi. 23–25: "For I myself received from the Lord the account which I have in turn given to you—how the Lord Jesus, on the very night of His betrayal, took some bread, and, after saying the thanksgiving, broke it and said: This is My own body, given on your behalf. Do this in memory of Me. And in the same way with the cup, after supper, saying: This cup is the new covenant made by My blood. Do this whenever you drink it, in memory of Me."[53]

In order to keep to the essential points, we shall note the following peculiarities:

1. Paul gives, after the passing round of the cup as well as after the distribution of bread, an order of repetition. There is none either in Mark or Matthew. Luke (xxii. 19) gives the order only after the distribution of the bread.

2. To the phrase "This is My body," which accompanies the distribution of bread, Paul adds "given for you," which has no equivalent in Mark or Matthew, but only in Luke.

3. Paul has no equivalent to the words which end the repast found in Mark and Matthew—that is to say, no declaration from Jesus that He would drink no more of the juice of the grape before drinking it new in the Kingdom of God. In Luke (xxii. 16) this phrase accompanies the distribution of a first cup. It must, however, be noted that in a fragment which appears no longer to form part of the narrative of the last supper, but which is really the commentary on it, Paul says: "For whenever you eat this bread and drink this cup, you proclaim the Lord's death until He comes" (1 Cor. xi. 26).

This is a reminiscence of the eschatological formula which appears to constitute one of the principal elements of the Lord's Supper.

All these peculiarities have a common character; they tend to assimilate the two elements constituting the rite to each other and to present them as a special institution by Jesus. They progress, therefore, exactly in the same way as the evolution of the rite. This appears to have had a double character, which at first was the transformation into the carrying out of a command of Jesus of that which at the origin had probably only been an instinctive repetition favored by the memory preserved of the last evening passed with Him. On the other hand, the evolution had as its result to form out of the distribution of the cup and the bread two parallel and equivalent symbols, while there is every reason to suppose that at the origin these two actions of Jesus had neither the same object nor the same significance. The distribution of the bread symbolized the gift that Jesus made of Himself to His followers and for His followers; the cup illustrated the meeting place that He gave them in the Kingdom of God. Now the evolution of the texts must have tended continually to conform more closely the narratives to the rite. It is inconceivable, while the believer had the feeling, in celebrating the Eucharist, that he was repeating the actions of Jesus, that additions should have been made to the story which would have differentiated it from the rite. The text, then, of Paul is subordinate compared with the tradition preserved in Mark. Its origin is not to be sought in a supernatural revelation, but in an historical tradition to which Paul is the witness.

Beyond quotations, properly so called, there are in Paul's writings a certain number of allusions to words of Jesus. It will suffice here to indicate the most characteristic:[54]

1 Thess. iv. 4: "Therefore he who disregards this warning, disregards not man, but God, who gives you His Holy Spirit." Compare with Luke x. 16: "He who listens to you is listening to Me, and he who rejects you is rejecting Me; while he who rejects Me is rejecting Him who sent Me as His Messenger."

Gal. iv. 17: "They wish to isolate you." Compare with Matt. xxiii. 13: "But alas for you, teachers of the Law and Pharisees, hypocrites that you are. You turn the key of the Kingdom of Heaven in men's faces. For you do not go in yourselves nor yet allow those who try to go in to do so."

Gal. vi. 2: "Bear one another's burdens, and so carry out the Law of Christ." Compare with Mark ix. 33: "If anyone wishes to be first, he must be last of all and servant of all."

1 Cor. iv. 12, 13: "We meet abuse with blessings, we meet persecution with endurance, we meet slander with gentle appeals." Rom. xii. 14: "Bless your persecutors, bless and never curse." Compare with Matt. v. 11: "Blessed are you when people taunt you, and persecute you and say everything evil about you—untruly, and for My sake." Luke vi. 28: "Show kindness to those who hate you, bless those who curse you, pray for those who insult you."

1 Cor. v. 4: "Having been present in spirit at your meetings when the power of the Lord Jesus was with us." Compare: "For where two or three have come together in My name I am present with them" (Matt. xviii. 20).

1 Cor. xiii. 2: "Even though I have such faith as might move mountains." Compare Matt. xvii. 20: "If your faith were only like a mustard seed, you could say to this mountain, 'Move from this place to that,' and it would be moved." Compare Mark xi. 22, Matt. xxi. 21, and Luke xvii. 6.

1 Cor. xiii. 3: "Even though I give My substance to the poor." Compare Luke xii. 23: "Sell what belongs to you and give in charity." Compare Mark x. 21 and Matt. xix. 21.

2 Cor. x. 1: "I exhort you by the meekness and gentleness of Christ." Compare Matt. xi. 29: "I am meek and lowly in heart."

Rom. xii. 17: "Never return injury for injury." Compare Matt. v. 39: "I say unto you, resist not evil."

Rom. xiv. 14: "I know and am persuaded that nothing is defiling in itself." Compare Matt. xv. 11: "It is not what enters a man's mouth that defiles him."

It is impossible to do anything except speculate on the origin of the acquaintance that the apostle Paul had with the Gospel tradition. The nucleus of what he knew must have dated back to the period preceding his conversion, and have depended upon what was told about Jesus in the first church of Jerusalem. The knowledge which he possessed in his pre-Christian days was enriched and developed afterwards.

The abundance of the allusions to the words of Jesus and the reminiscences found in the Epistles, the fact that Paul appears more often to allude to sayings known to his readers, causes one to think he must have been acquainted with a collection of the sayings of Jesus. The majority of those to which he refers appear to belong to the tradition of the Logia. Hence one is induced to entertain the hypothesis that Paul must have been acquainted with a form of this collection.

The Epistles of Paul afford then precise testimony in support of the existence of the Gospel tradition before him. They presume a Jesus who lived, acted, taught, whose life was a model for believers, and who died on the cross. True it is that in Paul are only found fragmentary and sporadic indications concerning the life and teachings of Jesus, but this is explained on one hand by the fact that we possess no coherent and complete exposition of the apostle's preaching, and on the other hand by the character of his interests. He had no special object in proving what no one in his time called in question—namely, that Jesus had existed. His unique aim was to prove (what the Jews refused to admit) that Jesus was the Christ.

NOTES

1. We consider the letters of Paul as authentic with the exception of that to the Ephesians and the Pastorals (1 and 2 Tim. and Titus). This conception, generally admitted to-day, will be vindicated in Book IV of our *Introduction*. The majority of those who deny the historical character of

Jesus repudiate the testimony of Paul's Epistles. M. Couchoud is the sole exception. The position of Drews is uncertain. Nevertheless, he takes some account of their testimony—not, it is true, without dismissing (as interpolated) certain important texts, such as 1 Cor. xi. 23 *et seq.* (*See Die Christusmythe,* i, p. 121, by Drews.)

2. Among the critics who believe that Paul had seen Jesus we may name Sabatier, Joh. Weiss, Machen. The opposite opinion is held by Renan, Wellhausen, Feine, Prat. Some few writers, like Pfleiderer, consider the question insoluble (*Das Urchristentum*).

3. The time when Paul came into contact with Christianity cannot be very much after the Passion. We consider that Jesus must have died at Easter, in the year 28, and that the conversion of Paul must be placed at the end of 29. Concerning the fixing of these two dates see my works *Essai sur la Chronologie Paulinienne* and *Notes d'histoire evangelique! Le problème Chronologique.* While pursuing an entirely different method from that I have followed, Meyer ends by putting the death of Jesus in 27 or 28 and the conversion of Paul in 28 or 29.

4. Acts xxvi. 14. If this detail is authentic, it is astonishing that it is only met with in one of the three narratives in the Acts. Moreover, we do not believe that these narratives can be taken to be rigorously historical, although sometimes, and especially in recent times, their value has been too much depreciated.

5. There can be no reason to see in the phrase "brother of the Lord" the designation of an ecclesiastical function or title, first because it would be a conjecture resting upon no foundation, and secondly because it would not be possible to differentiate this function from the apostolate, with which, nevertheless, it could not be identified.

6. If, as is done by Catholic exegesis, there were given to the phrase "brothers of Jesus" the meaning of half brothers (sons of a premier marriage of Joseph) or of cousins of Jesus, the force of our argument would not be seriously affected.

7. There is also a reference to the brothers and sisters of Jesus in Mark iii. 31; Matt. xii. 46, xiii. 55; Luke viii. 19; John ii. 12, vii. 3–5; Acts i. 14.

8. Drews, *Die Christusmythe,* i, pp. 125–27.

9. Joh. Weiss, *Jesus von Nazareth.*

10. This follows by comparing 1 Cor. ix. 1 and 1 Cor. xv. 8.

11. The marks referred to in Gal. vi. 17 are in all probability the scars from blows received in the service of Christ.

12. There are three designations of the Jerusalem apostles employed in the Galatians. It appears that Paul alludes to a current designation of the apostles of which it is no longer possible to find the origin.

13. This explains why in 2 Cor. v. 16 Paul seems to deny any value in the fact of having known Jesus.

14. Couchoud, *Le Mystère de Jésus,* p. 131.

15. We shall return in a later chapter to the relations between the prophecy and evangelical history.

16. We put aside two genealogies, which are, besides, not concordant, found in Matt. i. 1–16 and Luke iii. 23–38. Both presume the Davidic origin of Jesus, but they are recent elements of the tradition wanting in Mark.

17. It is the same in the narrative of Matt. ix. 27, which is only a variant of the story of Bartimeus. We do not attach much importance to Matt. xv. 22, where the Canaanitish woman calls Jesus "Lord, Son of David," because a comparison with Mark shows that there is only a literary development involved, nor of Matt. xii. 23, where Jesus, having cured a blind and dumb demoniac, some of the bystanders ask, "Is not this man the Son of David?" because this narrative is an editorial element which offers the starting point supposed by Mark of the accusation of possession brought against Jesus.

18. The text of Zechariah contains no allusion to a Davidic Messiah.

19. It is so because the text goes directly counter to the conception of a Davidic Messiah universally received in the Church since Paul. In the ancient Church only one exception can be found. It is in the Epistle of Barnabas (xii. 10), which is directly dependent on our text, and dominated by the idea of a supernatural birth. It should also be pointed out that the fourth Gospel appears to know of the idea of the Davidic descent, but as an objection to the Messiahship of Jesus. It does not appear that the evangelist (who holds Jesus to be a Galilean) makes a reply to the objection (vii. 42).

20. Zahn (*Das Ev. des Matthaeus*), Wohlenburg (*Das Ev. d. Markus*).

21. This is admitted (with various reservations, varying according to their opinion concerning the question of the Messianic consciousness of Jesus) by Wellhausen, Wrede, Loisy. Klostermann and Joh. Weiss think

the passage only criticizes the Jewish conception of the Messiah. Lagrange thinks that Jesus only wishes to show its inadequacy.

22. Couchoud, *op. cit.,* p. 130.

23. Job xi. 3–12, xiv. i, xv. 14, xxv. 4.

24. Often translated "as a usurpation." This translation does not seem to us permissible, because it assumes His existence in its divine form was equal with God.—Author.

Translator's Note.—Modern English version, based on Westcott and Hort's text, reads: "Though the divine nature was His from the beginning, yet He did not look upon equality with God as above all things to be clung to," etc.

25. Justin, *Dial. c. Tryphon;* Tertullian, *Scorpiace,* viii, *De patientia,* xiv; Origen, *In. Matt.,* xxviii, *Comm. in Matt.,* x. 18, etc.

26. He only attains to this through a supernatural birth (xi. 2–24), which is an evident embellishment, and by which the narrative is related to recent Apocryphal legends.

27. The incoherence betrays itself by an embellishment. In xi. 19 the Well-Beloved, crucified through the action of Satan, descends to the angel of Sheol. In xi. 20 Isaiah sees Him hung on the cross.

28. It does not appear to us that there is any direct contact between Paul and the Ascension of Isaiah. Outside the idea of the descent of a celestial Being, which has a general character, and that of the ignorance of the angels, developed in both in very different ways, there are only two ideas in common, but which are found elsewhere, and these are the idea of celestial garments and that of the superposed spheres, or heavens. But Paul is only carried away to the third and not to the seventh heaven, as Isaiah. In the Ascension the five first heavens belong to the lower world, while Paul has the feeling of having been carried away to a higher world. In Paul the revelation takes place by audition of ineffable words. In the Ascension it is by visions commented upon. Paul cannot repeat what he heard. Isaiah relates his vision to Hezekiah and to other prophets. (Compare 2 Cor. v. 2, xii. 2, and Asc. iv. 16, viii. 14.)

29. Sap. Salomon (Wisdom of Solomon), Enoch xliii. 4 and Enoch (Slavonic) xxiii. 4 and xlix. 2.

30. Enoch, also Esdras. Certain authors hold that in fourth Esdras the conception of the preëxistence of the Messiah may be due to Christian influence. Schürer justly remarks against this idea that post-Christian

Judaism had, in opposition to Christianity, particularly insisted on the humanity of the Messiah, as proved by the declaration of the Jew Tryphon, reported by Justin: "We all expect a Messiah who will be a man born of men" (*Dial.,* xlix. 1).

31. The supporters of the magician Simon also believed that in him was incarnate "the great power of God" (Acts viii. 10).

32. *Translator's Note.*—This passage is taken from the *Twentieth Century New Testament,* translated from original Greek into Modern English (Westcott and Hort's text).

33. Couchoud, *op. cit.,* p. 132.

34. The passage referring to the crucifixion belongs, as we have seen, to a Christian modification (Asc. xi. 19).

35. At any rate, Paul does not say that the archons *were* ignorant of who was Christ. We cannot accept the interpretation of Dibelius, that Paul, like the author of the Ascension of Isaiah, thinks the archons were ignorant of who Christ was.

36. Enoch (lxxxix. 59). There is also a reference in the book of Daniel to an angel of Persia, who fought with Michael, the angel of the people of Israel (see Dan. x. 13–20).

37. They are in any case responsible, since, according to Enoch, they must be judged (xc. 22).

38. Similarly in the Ascension of Isaiah the devil excites the Jews against the Well-Beloved, who crucify Him.

39. See upon this subject Maurice Goguel, *L'ApÙtre Paul et Jésus Christ,* 1904. In this work will be found a bibliography to which the names of Joh. Weiss and P. Olaf Moe must be added.

40. These are only indicated in relation to John the Baptist.

41. In Paul's writings there is no trace of the idea of a supernatural birth (see Lobstein, *Etudes Christologiques,* 1890).

42. Resch, *Der Paulinismus und die Logia Jesu.* Resch has been criticized very severely, but justly, by Wrede and Jülicher.

43. Exactly 925, of which 133 are in Ephesians, 100 in the pastoral Epistles, and 64 in the Pauline discourses in Acts. He only arrived at this result by stating that a parallelism existed between Paul and the Logia, when the two texts compared possessed only one word in common.

44. Lucken, and Couchoud (*Le Mystère de Jésus*).

45. Schmiedel, Dibelius, Feine.

46. Drews (*Die Christusmythe*) rejects this text as an interpolation.

47. Maurice Goguel, *L'Eucharistie des origines à Justin Martyr.*

48. Percy Gardner, *The Origin of the Lord's Supper,* 1893.

49. Loisy, *Les Mystères paiens et le mystère Chrétien,* 1919.

50. Bousset, *D. Schr. d. N.T.,* ii, p. 3.

51. Pfleiderer, *Urchristentum,* i.

52. Haupt, *Ueber die Ursprüngliche Form und Bedeutung der Abendmahlsworte,* 1894.

53. For the question before us we confine ourselves to comparing the texts of Paul and Mark, bringing into the question Matthew only (xxvi. 29) in a subordinate way. The latter, compared with Mark only, offers some unimportant variations. The account in Luke (xxii. 15–20) appears to arise from the combination of two different traditions. For a more detailed study see M. Goguel (*L'Eucharistie,* pp. 105–26).

Translator's Note.—Verses quoted are from text of *Twentieth Century New Testament* in Modern English, based on Westcott and Hort.

54. *Translator's Note.*—The English versions are taken from the *Twentieth Century New Testament,* based on Westcott and Hort's text from original Greek.

CHAPTER VI

THE THEOLOGY
OF THE APOSTLE PAUL

I. THE CHARACTER OF PAULINE THOUGHT

The oldest systematic form of Christian thought which we can discern is that which the Epistles of Paul (whose composition took place approximately between the years 50 and 62) makes known to us. We find therein a theology if not theoretically worked out, at any rate of very coherent character. It is important to examine its character and see whether it may be considered as a development from Jewish and Greek premises, or if it be necessary to its comprehension to bring in an historical factor—the life and death of Jesus.

The fragmentary developments which we possess in the Epistles only deal with the essential points in the system; the picture resulting from their assemblage and combination should nevertheless—with the exception of some unimportant details—give us a fairly accurate sketch of the general aspect that the apostle's teaching must have presented.

If Paul's was a powerful and systematic mind—and the Epistle to the Romans alone suffices to prove it—his teaching was not dominated by philosophic preoccupations. Paul preached a gospel

161

and did not teach a doctrine. He was the bearer of a message of salvation. He desired to pluck men from perdition and death, and assure their access to the Kingdom of God, not to instruct them and reveal to them a history and an explanation of things. Religious affirmations predominate in the Epistles. But these affirmations presuppose a very general conception, which includes not only a history of humanity, but a theory of the world and a doctrine concerning God, celestial beings, and an explanation of the origin of evil, sin and death.

II. GOD AND DEMONS

Although the apostle's thought was rooted in the religious tradition of Israel, his point of view as regards divinity is sufficiently different from the radical and uncompromising monotheism which characterizes certain declarations of the second Isaiah or of Jeremiah:

"Then shall it be for a man to burn, for he will take thereof (wood) and warm himself: yea, he kindleth it and baketh bread; yea, he maketh a god and worshipeth it, he maketh it a graven image and falleth down thereto. He burneth part thereof (tree) in the fire; he eateth flesh; he roasteth roast and is satisfied; yea, he warmeth himself and saith, 'Aha! I am warm. I have seen the fire.' And the residue thereof he maketh a god, even his graven image" (Isa. xliv. 15–17; cp. Jer. x. 3–11).

The point of view of Paul might be better styled "monolatry" than "monotheism." "Although there are," he wrote, "either in heaven or on earth many beings which are called gods. . . . There are indeed many gods and lords, yet is there for us but one God, the Father, from whom all things proceed (and for Him we live) and one Lord, Jesus Christ" (1 Cor. viii. 5, 6). Practically—at least, for him who possesses the gnosis—this formula amounts to that of monotheism, since Paul offers it as a commentary upon the other formula which the Corinthian Gnostics employed: "We are aware that an idol is nothing in the world, and that there is no God but one" (1 Cor. viii. 4). The conclusion drawn by Paul is that he who possesses the gnosis—that is, he who knows the true nature of demons—can enter with impunity into relation with them when consuming food offered to idols. He no longer pays them worship, and he no more seeks their favor than he fears their enmity. But those who have not yet attained this degree of knowledge ought to fly from communion with idols which for them would be pollution.[1] Paul distinctly declares that an idol is nothing—that is to say, it is not a divine being. The worship paid to an idol is not directed to God, but to demons, and has the effect of putting the worshiper into direct relation with them, and thereby exposing himself to divine anger. There exist, therefore, other gods than the Unique Father— these are the demons who, under the guise of idols, are adored by pagans. Idolatry is an insult to God, who alone has the right to be adored. In the very fact that they have claimed worship, the demons have made themselves enemies of God. Although we do not find in the Epistles explicit theories on this point, it is very probable that Paul does not explain the origin of demons by a fundamental and irreducible dualism, but by the theory of Satan, a celestial being who rebelled against God. An allusion to this theory is found in the great Christological passage of the Epistle to the Philippians, where the attitude of the preëxisting Christ is opposed to that of another being who sought to seize for himself full divinity—that is to say, desired to impose himself upon man to be worshiped. Through the rebellion of Satan, who seduced away in his train a faction of celestial beings, there was created in the face of God an army of demons hostile to Him. There are the enemies referred to in 1 Cor. xv. 25, 26. The last to be conquered and destroyed will be Death, who is not to be imagined as an abstract power, but as a personality, Thanatos, probably identical with Satan himself. In the Epistle to the Hebrews, whose thought upon many points is closely related to Paul's, the devil is directly identified with Thanatos in the formula, "he who has the power of death—that is to say, the devil" (Heb. ii.

14). The same identification is not found formally in Paul. It appears, however, to be inferable from fairly precise indications. Paul speaks of a "god of this world" (2 Cor. iv. 4) who is evidently the devil, and on the other hand he asserts the existing world is subjected to the dominion of death owing to sin (Rom. v. 12, vi. 23; 1 Cor. xv. 21). According to 1 Cor. v. 5, the abandonment of the incestuous to the power of Satan will have as its consequence the destruction of the flesh—that is, the death of the guilty one. According to 1 Cor. x. 10, the rebellious Israelites in the desert were delivered over to the exterminator (Satan), who destroyed them.[2] It follows from these passages that Satan and Thanatos are two equivalent terms, or, more precisely, Thanatos is Satan considered as exercising one of his essential functions.

Satan before his rebellion was one of the beings of the army of heaven. The existence of a whole hierarchy of beings inhabiting the heavens—angels, archangels, thrones, dominions, principalities and powers—particularly referred to in the Epistle to the Colossians (i. i6)—has nothing in it which is contrary to the will and design of God. Evil comes uniquely from the action of these beings, who, instead of keeping the subordinate position appertaining to them, dared to rise and oppose themselves to God. Thus is explained the fact that the Pauline theory not only insists upon a disorder introduced into humanity, but also of a disorder within the cosmos, making necessary the redemption not of humanity alone, but of the entire creation (Rom. viii. 19–22)—in other words, the reëstablishing of the sovereignty of God (1 Cor. xv. 24–26).

III. SIN AND EVIL

If this notion of cosmic disorder is fundamental in the thought of Paul, and if the redemption of sinners is with him but a portion of a more general work, in his preaching and his Epistles it is the notion of human redemption which occupies the premier place.

Looked at from the point of view of humanity, evil takes the form of sin. It is a state of things whose essential characteristic is ignorance of God, estrangement and opposition to Him (1 Cor. xv. 34). Sin dishonors God (Rom. ii. 23); it is rebellion against His will and His law (Rom. ii. 8, iii. 5, xi. 30, etc.); it is also a state of weakness (Rom. v. 6, vi. 19). Paul does not only conceive it as an act or series of acts, but as a state characterized by the subordination of humanity to a power hostile to God (Rom. iii. 9, v. 19, vi. 17–20, vii. 20; Gal. iii. 22). It is in the flesh that resides the power of sin, and through which it is exercised (Rom. vi. 12, vii. 5–14, viii. 3).[3] Sin is universal. The whole beginning of the Epistle to the Romans is devoted to establishing this thesis, and particularly that (contrary to an idea cherished by Judaism) the sin of the Jews does not separate them less from God than the sin of the pagans (Rom. ii. 1–3, 18, xi. 32; Gal. iii. 21). The law, indeed, is not a means of escaping from the domination and consequences of sin. Its first task is to reveal it (Rom. iii. 20). In a certain sense it gives sin manifestation by transforming a tendency more or less unconscious into open rebellion (Rom. iv. 15, v. 13, vii. 7–13; Gal. iii. 22). In itself, however, the law is holy, just and good (Rom. vii. 12). It was designed to give life in showing the path to follow to obtain life, or, in other words, access to the Kingdom of God (Rom. vii. 10), but it has been disarmed and rendered impotent by the flesh (Rom. vii. 14, viii. 3). It is the disorder introduced into the world which has prevented the law producing the effects it should have done.

This brings us to the question of capital importance in the interpretation of Paulinism—the origin of sin. Faithful on this point to Jewish dogma, Paul seeks the origin of sin in the disobedience of Adam. His theory is expressed in the parallel between Adam and Jesus Christ, which appears to have been one of the habitual themes of his preaching, and of which we possess two examples, both incomplete, in 1 Cor. xv. 45–47, and in Rom. v. 12–21. The central affirmation is that sin entered the world through the disobedience of Adam (Rom. v. 17–19). This disobedience has introduced a principle which produces consequences even where there are no acts of rebellion similar to that of Adam (v. 21). Paul certainly conceived the disobedience of the first man according to the narrative in Genesis (iii. 1–19), to which he alludes (2 Cor. xi. 3).

But the disobedience of Adam is only an historical explanation of the origin of sin. It shows when, and in what conditions, sin entered the world; it does not explain why it exists. The theory, therefore, only puts the problem further back; it does not solve it. So Paul looks at the problem again and from another point of view, and he indicates—for it is a question of indications only and not of a theory systematically worked out—how the seduction of Satan was exercised and what the relation is between the sin of man and the rebellion of Satan against God. It is in Rom. i. 18–32, where is to be found the sole passage that might be called a philosophy of religion, that these indications are met with. The starting point of the argument is an admission of fact. The wrath of God is manifested from heaven upon the injustice and impiety of mankind (Rom. i. 18). How is it that men are thus so opposed to truth and have refused to worship God? To this question—which is, besides, not expressly formulated—Paul replies by rejecting the idea of a complete ignorance of God on the part of man. God revealed Himself to men, but they fell into idolatry (i. 19–23). The punishment of this attitude is that God abandoned men to their passions, which caused them to fall into all kinds of crime and impurity (i. 24–32). In the beginning there was, therefore, a kind of natural knowledge of God, whose invisible attributes, infinite power and divinity are revealed in creation (i. 19, 20). But man rejected this knowledge of God offered to him (i. 21); he refused to give the worship due to God; his heart became hardened, and has lost itself in vain speculations. Thus came about the adoration of men and animals, rendering to the creature the worship which rightly belonged to the Creator. Idolatry is the root of all sin. The divine wrath which it provoked abandoned man to his evil passions. These without doubt existed before this, but they were to some extent disciplined and kept under control; it was this control which was destroyed. Idolatry does not affect humanity alone. Paul does not conceive it as a perversion of the religious sense which substitutes imaginary beings for its real object. Idolaters adore demons—that is, celestial spirits in rebellion against God. In idolatry we find in alliance two orders of beings in rebellion against God: Satan and his angels, who claim the worship which only belongs by right to God, and mankind, which consents to accord to them the worship which it refuses to God. The second of these facts is a result of the first. In 2 Cor. xi. 3 it is shown that at the beginning of sin there was a seduction by Satan; it is the act whereby the demons obtained the worship of mankind. Human sin is thus in direct relation with the rebellion of Satan. Sin is thus not only a human fact; it is a cosmic fact; it is but one consequence of Satan's rebellion, one special case of the disorder which was thus introduced into the universe. In fact, notwithstanding the extremely valuable indications which are given us in the passage in Rom. viii. 19–22, it is almost exclusively of the consequences for humanity of sin that Paul speaks. Sin involves death. "The wages of sin is death" (Rom. vi. 23). But the mechanism of this consequence, if we may so term it, is presented by Paul under two different aspects. Sometimes we meet with the idea of a kind of logical and necessary relation: sin breeds death. This takes place to some degree of its own nature and without God intervening to exact any sanction. This is what Paul calls "the law of sin and death" (Rom. viii. 2; cp. v. 12).

In consequence of sin man has fallen under the dominion of death, which must reign until at the moment at the end of time, when it will be destroyed by Christ (1 Cor. xv. 24, 25). But beside this, we find almost at every page of the Pauline Epistles the idea that death is the result of a judgment. The concept of judgment and the return of the Lord who will execute it has such precision in Paul's thought that, in a passage like 1 Cor. iv. 3, the word "day"[4] is meant in the sense of judicial authority—of judgment. Paul writes: "We shall all appear before the judgment seat of God"[5]

(Rom. xiv. 10; cp. with 2 Cor. v. 10). With the idea of judgment must be combined that of the divine wrath which at the end of time will fall upon the guilty (1 Thess. i. 10, v. 9; Rom. i. 18, ii. 5, v. 9; Col. iii. 6). There are thus in Paul's thought two conceptions. According to one, God appears as a judge who executes upon sin the penalty it deserves; according to the other, He is a witness, to some degree passive, or rather the penalty He imposes comes, not at the end of time, but at the very moment that sin appears in the world. It consists entirely in the fact that humanity is abandoned to the power of Satan. It is probably because he found these two conceptions in the religious traditions of his nation that Paul allowed them to coexist in his mind, and that he perhaps was unaware of the contradiction existing between them.

IV. THE REDEMPTION

The disorder in the world and the corruption of human nature demands a work of restoration, a redemption. Paul insists greatly on the idea that the initiative of this work belongs to God alone. "But all this is the work of God," he wrote (2 Cor. v. 18). Man here can boast of nothing.[6] It is God who calls men to salvation[7] (1 Thess. ii. 12, v. 9; 1 Cor. i. 9; Rom. viii. 28, ix. 24, xi. 32). Redemption appears at first as an effect of the love of God (Rom. v. 5, viii. 39). It is also an act of the grace of God. This notion of grace, which holds a central position in Pauline thought, is, above all, a practical one. Grace, in the life of Paul, had been an experience before it became an object of his theological meditations. There is noticeable in him a certain lack of homogeneity—at least in expression— redemption being attributed sometimes to love, sometimes to compassion, sometimes to the grace of God. This would be difficult to explain if we were dealing with a logically constructed theory, but, on the contrary, it is very readily explained if experience of redemption had preceded dogmatic reflection. Paul feels that what he is as a Christian and an apostle is the work of the grace of God. "By the grace of God," he writes, "I am what I am." He feels that he had undergone, at the moment of his conversion, a change which his former life had not prepared; that he was thrown outside his routine existence; that he had been coerced. It was this same force which was at work in his apostolic activity (1 Cor. xv. 10; 2 Cor. xii. 9).

Just as the Christian life of Paul in his own eyes is an original creation and not the resultant of earlier factors, so also it is that the notion of grace which explains it has no deep roots in Judaism. Indeed, in the Septuagint the word "grace" means only the ideas of favor, benevolence, benediction, and pardon, and not that of a divine force which creates in man something new. Its origin cannot be looked for in Hellenism either. In Philo's writings grace means the natural gifts which constitute man a reasonable being, but so far away is Philo from Paul's characteristic idea of aid accorded to a sinner, and precisely because he is a sinner, that the assertion is found of the eternal springs of grace being dried up when wickedness began to enter the world (*De opificio Mundi*). In the inscriptions the term "grace" means a gift bestowed by the sovereign authority.

In certain Pauline texts grace appears, without the thought being precisely defined, as the primary source of salvation (2 Cor. viii. 9, xiv. 9; Gal. i. 16). In others it is a divine force which seizes man, calls him, transforms him, justifies him—in other words, makes of him who was condemned a ransomed being, a child of God. It is a power which takes possession of man and permeates his entire life. But its independence of man does not exclude the moral character of its action in producing a renewal and a transformation of the personality (Rom. iii. 24, iv. 4, xi. 5, 6; Gal. i. 15). Sometimes grace is hypostatized; it seems as though it were a personal power—for example, in the parallel between Adam and Jesus Christ (Rom. v. 15–21)—but this is nothing more than a figurative mode of expression.

The essential character of Pauline theology, its originality in comparison with Judaism, is to substitute the notion of grace for that of merit, of justice imputed for that of acts performed. Upon this point Paul is distinctly conscious of separating himself from the religion of his fathers. It is this opposition which explains the energy with which he insists upon the absolutely gratuitous and unearned character of salvation. However, the independence of grace has its limits. From the thesis he affirms with so much fervor, Paul does not draw what would seem to be the logical deduction—namely, that the unique and all-sufficient cause of salvation is to be found in the paternal heart of God. The comparison between Pauline thought and the teaching of the Gospel is here very instructive. In the parable of the prodigal son pardon is not subordinated to the accomplishment of any other condition than the repentance of the sinner—that is to say, it depends upon no relations outside those between the offender and the one offended against. In Paul it is not the same thing. For him salvation would be impossible without the cross. What is the reason of this difference? It is not enough to say that as a Pharisee Paul was too much concerned to safeguard the holiness of God to accept the idea of a free pardon for sin, for besides the holiness of God, Pharisaism insisted also upon His omnipotence. The true reason is elsewhere. Paul was obliged to explain the fact of the death of Christ, which thus appeared as one of the most essential premises of his theology. From the necessity of this explanation arose the Pauline doctrine of redemption.

In Paul's writings the pardon of God is not the effect of a free, spontaneous and immediately efficacious initiative. It is subordinated to the accomplishment of a work of redemption.

For Paul salvation is not only a "processus" within the divine, designed to conciliate love and justice. This order of ideas which is represented in the Pauline doctrine of redemption does not exhaust it. It corresponds to the idea of sin conceived as a violation of the law of God and as rebellion against Him. But the divine pardon granted to man would remain fruitless if it were not accompanied by a victory gained by God over the evil powers, who, owing to sin, exercised their dominion over humanity. God has conceived for the realization of salvation a plan which reveals a wisdom infinitely superior to that of the world. This plan of redemption is the object of the teaching imparted by the apostle to the perfect (1 Cor. ii. 6; Rom. xi. 33). This is the mystery which is revealed unto the elect (Col. i. 25, ii. 2). Redemption has a double object. Man must one day appear before the judgment seat of God, and if he be abandoned to himself he will not escape condemnation.

Redemption has the effect of making him the object of a judgment of acquittal, and thus having part in the divine Kingdom. On the other hand, the sinner must be delivered from the evil powers who have dominion over him. To these two elements correspond two different moments of the work of redemption—justification on one side and redemption properly so called on the other. On one side this distinction corresponds to that which Paul makes elsewhere between the two parts of the redeeming work of Christ, between that accomplished by His death and resurrection and that which will be accomplished at the day of His glorious return at the end of the age. The work of justification is achieved in principle, while that of redemption is only hoped for (2 Thess. ii. 8; 1 Cor. xv. 24). However, if redemption depends upon the victory that Christ is to gain at the end of the age over all His enemies, His triumph is certain, for by His death and resurrection Jesus has conquered and despoiled the powers and dominions—that is, the spiritual beings hostile to God to whom humanity is now enslaved (Col. ii. 15). This it is which gives to the Christian hope of Paul so special a character. The work of justification is described by Paul with much more precision than that of redemption. This is not only because the first develops upon an historical plane, while the second will take place at the end of the age, and will in consequence possess an extrahistorical character. If, in theory, redemption, on Paul's theological system, possesses as much importance as justification, it is not so from the practical point of view. The whole missionary effort of Paul—and Paul was a missionary before all else—is concentrated upon the acceptation of justification by the sinner. This point once gained, everything else followed, for, from the individual point of view, redemption appeared as a consequence of justification, and the spirit which the justified one receives is the assurance of it (Rom. v. 10, viii. 23; Gal. iv. 6).

V. THE CHRIST AND HIS WORK

The fundamental idea upon which the Pauline doctrine of justification rests is that of two worlds, one succeeding the other. The present world, placed under the dominion of evil powers, has for its essential characteristics sin, death and impotence (Gal. i. 4; 1 Cor. i. 20, ii. 6, iii. 18; 2 Cor. iv. 3). It is destined to perish. The world of the future is the Kingdom of Christ and of God. The time which passes between the death of Christ and His return is an intermediate period, in which the two economies (if we may so express it) overlap each other. The old dispensation (or economy) still subsists, since of the powers which reign over it, it is said that they *will* perish (1 Cor. ii. 8, xv. 24); it is never said they *have* perished; their destruction is foretold for the end of time (1 Cor. xv. 26).

The present world is dominated by three facts: Sin, the consequence of Adam's fall, and death introduced by it into the world; the promise given to Abraham, which, amid the darkness of a world condemned, causes hope to shine; and finally the Law of Moses. For each of these points of view the cycle is completed by the manifestation of Christ. Through it sin is vanquished, the faithful are restored to life (1 Cor. xv. 22; Rom. v. 17), the promise made to Abraham is fulfilled (2 Cor. i. 20; Gal. iii. 16), and finally Christ is the end of the law (Rom. x. 4; cp. Gal. iii. 21, iv. 5).

The redeeming work of Christ involves at once God and man. Because of its essentially moral character, it can only be accomplished by a being in close solidarity with humanity, therefore by a man. But as humanity is radically impotent, and the initiative for salvation belongs to God, it can only come through a being who is not himself a sinner but in intimate union with God, therefore by a celestial being. Hence the double character of the Pauline Christ, a human personality and at the same time superhuman, *not* God (the term is not found in Paul), but the "Son of God"—a contradiction that the apostle solves by the idea of the incarnation of the pre-existing Christ. Christ belongs at once to the divine and the human spheres; His personality has a double aspect (Rom. i. 4). But there is nothing in Paul to resemble that which later was to be the orthodox dogma, because his thought does not express itself in theological definitions, and also because he does not picture to himself a combination in the person of Christ of incongruous elements, but rather the succession of diverse phases. The Pauline idea is that of a divine Being, the image of God (2 Cor. iv. 4; Col. i. 15), a celestial man (1 Cor. xv. 48, 49), the first-born of creation (Col. i. 15), who, laying aside His celestial attributes, became man, and who, after His resurrection, received the name of "Lord" (Phil. ii. 5–11).

Everything which concerns preëxistence is outside of experience, as Paul conceives it, and has a double origin. This proceeds from the theological system of Judaism, in which the notion of the Messiah was very developed, but also from the theological reflection. If Jesus, by His death and resurrection, had brought about that which He had, in fact, accomplished according to the experience of Paul, it necessarily follows that His personality must have been unlike that of other men.

The name by which Paul most frequently designates Christ is that of "Son of God." This is but an image, for there is nothing in the apostle's writings which resembles the idea to be met with later, of a Son begotten by God. The Christ remains distinctly subordinate to the Father. He was created by the Father. This follows from the parallel drawn between Adam and Him, but also from the term "image of God," which recalls the narrative of the creation of the first man in the image of God (Gen. i. 27) and also of the term "first-born." The idea of the celestial man or the typical man of 1 Cor. xv. 48 is another form of the notion of preëxistence which is affirmed in a series of explicit texts—for instance, in the declaration of the Epistle to the Romans that God had sent His Son (Rom. viii. 3; cp. Gal. iv. 4; 2 Cor. viii. 9; Phil. ii. 5). It follows also from the part taken by Christ in the creation (1 Cor. viii. 6; Col. i. 15–17).

At the end of time—that is, at the moment chosen by God in the plan conceived by His wisdom (Gal. iv. 4)—Jesus was born in the midst of the Jewish people, a descendant of Abraham and of David (Rom. i. 3). He was in all points obedient unto God (Rom. v. 17–19; Phil. ii. 8) and had in no wise known sin (2 Cor. v. 21). The texts in which a human appearance of Christ is spoken of (Rom. viii. 3; Phil. ii. 7) must not be interpreted against the reality of Jesus, for, as H. J. Holtzmann has very well observed, the Greek word employed is not opposed to the notion of identity, but to that of difference.[8] That which explicitly confirms this interpretation is the fact that Paul attributes to Christ flesh and blood (Rom. i. 3, iii. 25; 1 Cor. x. 16: Col. i. 20), while these are, in his view, elements which characterize human nature, and are foreign to the celestial life (1 Cor. xv. 50). The essence of the work of Christ is His death upon the cross. The cross is for Paul the power and the wisdom of God (1 Cor. i. 18, 23, 24), the sole reason that man can have to be assured of his salvation (Gal. vi. 14), and for this the enemies of the Gospel are called the enemies of the cross of Christ (Phil. iii. 18). If Paul combated with the energy and perseverance known to us the idea of justification by the works of the Law, and particularly by circumcision, it is in order that the offense—that is, the efficacity of the cross—may not be diminished (Gal. v. 11, vi. 12; 1 Cor. i. 17). It is upon this idea that the apostle insists with the greatest emphasis (Gal. i. 14; 1 Cor. xv. 3; Rom. iv. 25, v. 10). Several concepts are introduced to explain it—for instance, that of Christ as the paschal lamb (1 Cor. v. 7), that of Christ as propitiation (that is, a means of salvation conceived as a levitical sacrifice) (Rom. iii. 25), and also that of the sacrifice by ransom (Rom. vi. 17; Gal. iii. 13). But the governing thought which explains the process of justification is that of the condemnation of sin in the flesh of Christ (Gal. iii. 13; 2 Cor. v. 21; Rom. viii. 3). Jesus, while being perfectly holy, was treated by God as though He were sin personified and condemned. This is not the idea of expiatory sacrifice incidentally indicated in Rom. iii. 25, for the victim of this sacrifice had to be of perfect purity, while the death of Jesus on the cross was that of one condemned, loaded with sin. Neither is it the equivalent of ransom, for the punishment of sin in the flesh of Jesus was a legal sanction and not a satisfaction accorded either to God or devil. Neither can it be said, as does M. Loisy, who assimilates the death of Christ to the sacrifice of the ram dedicated to Azazel, that Christ took upon Himself the sins of men. These sins, in fact, are not destroyed by His death. They subsist after it, with all their consequences, and are only destroyed by the virtual death of the believer realized by mystical union with Christ. We have in Paul an original conception in which juridical notions play a much greater part than in the Jewish conception of sacrifice.[9]

The death of Christ without His resurrection would be without efficacy. The resurrection is not only for Paul a reparation accorded to Christ, a recompense for His sacrifice; still less is it a consequence of His divine nature. If Christ died without subsequent resurrection, His sacrifice was in vain (1 Cor. xv. 14–17). He was raised again for our justification (Rom. iv. 25). When Paul uses the verb "to rise again" in the active voice it is always God who is the subject of the sentence. Christ did not return to life by Himself.[10] It is God who raised Him (1 Thess. i. 10; Gal. i. 1; 1 Cor. vi. 14, xv. 15; 2 Cor. iv. 14; Rom. iv. 25). Through His resurrection Christ was restored to the rank and to the possession of the attributes which He had in His preëxistence, and He is even placed at a higher rank than that which He occupied (Phil. ii. 11), and seats Himself at the right hand of God (Rom. viii. 34; Col. iii. 1). He enters into the possession of the divine glory. In His glorious existence Christ was essentially spirit (1 Cor. xv. 45), and even *the* Spirit[11] (2 Cor. iii. 17; Rom. viii. 9, 10). The phrase "Christ, power of God" (1 Cor. i. 24) makes of Him almost a "mode" of the divine activity.

The death and resurrection of Christ also modify His position relatively to demoniacal beings. Henceforward, indeed, they have no power over those who belong to Christ (Rom. viii. 37). He has gained the victory and reëstablished order in the cosmos (Col. i. 18–20). He has taken the first place and brought into subjection all other powers. Nevertheless, according to 1 Cor. xv. 24, 25, the victory of Christ can only take place at the end of time. The reconciling of these two things, in appearance contradictory, seems attained by the idea that in the text of the Epistles to the Philippians, Romans and the Colossians they are considered as principles and in the absolute, while in the first Epistle to the Corinthians they are considered in their chronological development. In the Epistle to the Romans it is a question of a certain victory, but one which does not exclude a struggle. The Satanic powers are not destroyed; they can still wage the last battle with Christ, but they will be unable to triumph. In the Epistle to the Philippians (ii. 9–11) Christ receives a name before which every knee shall bow, but this does not imply that they will not attempt to rebel. On the other hand, in the first Epistle to the Corinthians, if there is a battle, the issue is fixed in advance. The victory of Christ is certain. According to Col. i. 20 Christ gains the victory by the blood upon the cross. This may be compared with 1 Cor. ii. 8, where the statement is made that if the archons of this world had known the wisdom of God—that is, understood His plans—they would not have crucified the glorious Lord. Why is this? Because they would not have devoted their efforts to the realization of a work which must have for them as consequence their overthrow and spoliation. The cross is thus the means by which the princes of this world are to be annihilated and despoiled. It is impossible to interpret with precision the thought of Paul on this point, for it proceeds only by allusions which are concerned either with the teaching he had himself given, or with the current ideas of his time—for example, those developed in the Ascension of Isaiah, and which, to appeal directly to the intelligence of his readers, it sufficed to evoke.

The full and complete victory of Christ over the spirits would only be gained at the end of the age. After His resurrection Christ is seated at the right hand of God (Rom. viii. 34; Col. iii. 1). He will reign until all enemies have been put under His foot, and the last enemy of all—death. Then He will surrender the Kingdom to His Father, and this will be the end (1 Cor. xv. 24, 26).

How is this Pauline Christology formed? It is often said that the apostle was the creator of Christology. This formula is only exact if the word "creation" be understood, not in the sense *ex nihilo,* but in the sense of a synthesis formed from preëxisting elements. The Pauline thought appears as an original solution of a problem which arose out of the circumstances themselves, for the Christological problem existed from the very moment that one single man continued to believe in Jesus in spite of the ignominy of His death. But the solutions or the outlines of them were swept aside by the powerful synthesis of Paul, which dominated all later Christian thought. Certain elements of the Christology of Paul have a speculative origin. These are specially the notions of saintliness—in so far as it is not the observation of a fact but the affirmation of a principle— and of preëxistence. The notion, too, of the Messiahship has a theoretical and absolute character. The drama proceeds according to a necessary plan, while if we adopt the idea in the parable of the vineyard, according to the thought of Jesus, we are led to the conception that the arrival of the Messiah was a last attempt at redemption, which would not have taken place if the wickedness of mankind had not rendered fruitless the mission of the prophets. The doctrine of the necessity of the death of Christ marks, indeed, an essential point of difference between the thought of Paul and that of Jesus. For Jesus death is the supreme proof of love for His fellow men, which He will give them if it be necessary. It is like His entire ministry, but not separated from it; it is an appeal addressed to sinners; it is not—what it is according to Paul's thought—the very cause of the pardon of God. Reflection and speculation are dominant in Paul. As for the preponderance accorded to the cross—one might almost say the eclipsing of Christ's ministry in face of the unique and extraordinary radiance of His cross—it can only be explained by the angle under which Paul entered into contact with the Gospel.

There is in Paul an element whose origin is in the Jewish Messianic doctrine.[12] Brückner has shown that after eliminating what is specifically Christian in the Pauline Christology there is found a system of coherent ideas which finds its place in the most natural manner in the development of the Jewish Messianic doctrine. This Christology existed in Paul's mind before his conversion. Certain Hellenic elements are also to be recognized—those treating of the relations of Christ with the spirits—but they may have been incorporated with Jewish ideas before Paul. Nothing, however, would be more erroneous than to consider the Pauline Christology as only a simple development of Jewish or Judeo-Hellenic premises. That which gives him his originality is the synthesis built up of these elements and the historical episode of the life and death of Jesus.

It is not possible to reduce to a common element the historical and dogmatic constituents of the Pauline Christology, as M. Couchoud would do. This is proved by the fact that we do not find in Paul a homogeneous conception of the cause of Christ's death, as should be the case if the entire history of Jesus, and of His death in particular, had been the postulates of a dogmatic system. According to 1 Cor. ii. 8 Christ died crucified owing to the acts of the archons or rebellious angels against God. According to Rom. vii. 3 He died (although He was not in person a sinner, but through solidarity with humanity accepted by Him) because God treated Him as though He were sin itself, and inflicted the chastisement which sinners deserve. These two conceptions are not dialectically irreconcilable. One might imagine the archons as agents used by God to punish sin. Doubtless the two conceptions are far from having the same compass or being on the same plane. The first is only indicated in a quite incidental manner, in a dissertation which treats, not of the death of Christ, but of the wisdom of God. The second is in direct relation with the doctrine of justification, which is at the heart of the apostle's thought. The coexistence of these two explanations proves, however, that we are not dealing with a ready-made conception, nor with a system developed from myth or doctrine, but from the interpretation by this doctrine of an historical fact.

VI. THE JUSTIFICATION AND REDEMPTION OF THE SINNER

The same conclusion follows, with better evidence still, from the study of the Pauline theory of the justification and redemption of the sinner. The death of Christ, as we have seen, abolishes the consequences of sin, and contains in germ the defeat of the demons to whom humanity is subject and whose action produces sin and death. But, however efficacious it be, this death does not abolish the actual consequences of sin. The theoretical destruction of its power does not save mankind from continuing to bear as a fact the consequences of sins committed, and if the demon-powers are in principle condemned, mankind still undergoes the effects of its subjection to them in the past. Moreover, their power continues to be exercised up to the time when their defeat will be fully consummated.

The work accomplished by Christ in dying on the cross does not at once justify sinners *ipso facto* by one act, to some extent magical; it merely makes justification possible—that is to say, the acquittal of man before God's tribunal. Justification opens to the believer access to the Heavenly Kingdom and gives him assurance of his future redemption.

Salvation can only be attained for the individual by a moral act. This plainly follows from the term of reconciliation employed by Paul. This term implies the change of the relation between persons. "We beseech you in the name of Christ," writes Paul, exercising thus what he calls the ministry of reconciliation, "be ye reconciled with God" (2 Cor. v. 20). To the act of God giving His Son there must correspond an act of man. God calls the sinner; the latter must respond. Justification is the act of imputing to the sinner the justice attained by Christ, who, considered as sinner, has put Himself through His death right with the Law, and who lives henceforth a life freed by the power of God from the dominion of sin and death. The starting point of justification is faith. This term and words derived from it are often found in Paul.[13] Faith is the specific phenomenon of the religious Christian life. The type of believer is Abraham. In what did his faith consist? In this, that God, having promised that he should be the father of a large posterity, he had confidence in this promise at the time when his age and that of his wife rendered its realization improbable (Rom. iv. 17–21). Faith is therefore not founded upon the evidence of a truth, but upon the confidence inspired by God and His omnipotence. According to 1 Cor. ii. 4, 5 faith has its origin in the power of God, and not in human reasoning. Faith is faith in God (1 Thess. i. 8), but there is also faith in Christ (Gal. ii. 16; Rom. iii. 22), because it is through Christ that God keeps His promise. To believe in Christ is to believe in the promises of God; it is therefore also to believe in God. Faith has for its origin the preaching of the Gospel by the apostles and the missionaries whom God has appointed for this object (Rom. x. 14); it includes an intellectual element, the idea of God who by His power raised up Jesus from the dead. Paul mentions it between the gift of wisdom and that of knowledge (1 Cor. xii. 8, 9). But faith is not only knowledge and confidence; it is also (and this is the most original element in the Pauline conception) mystical union. The believer united to Christ is made a participator in everything touching Him, and particularly in His death and resurrection. According to 1 Thess. v. 10 Jesus died in order that believers, whether sleeping or waking, may be with Him. This supposes the establishing of an indissoluble bond between the believer and the Savior. In 1 Cor. i. 9 "communion" with the Son of God, the Lord, appears as an ideal held up to the faithful. He who is united with the Lord becomes a spirit with Him[14] (1 Cor. vi. 17). In Gal. ii. 19, 20 Paul declares himself to be crucified with Christ: "It is not I that live; it is Christ that liveth in me," and this suppression of the individual life has for its consequence the suppression of all accidental differences of race, sex and social situation (Gal. iii. 27, etc.). According to Rom. viii. 29 the object of predestination is that believers may be made like unto the image of the Son of God, so that Christ may be the first-born among many brethren (Rom. vi. 3–5, xiv. 9; 2 Cor. iv. 10, 11, xi. 2).

The explanation of this union is furnished by the idea of the death of Christ in solidarity with humanity. "As one died for all, therefore all died; and He died for all, so that the living should no longer live for themselves, but for Him who died and rose for them" (2 Cor. v. 14, 15). The mystical union has for its effect the rupture of the bond uniting the man to the world. He asks again: "Can it be that you do not know that all of us who were baptized into union with Christ Jesus in our earthly baptism shared His death? Consequently, through sharing His death in our baptism, we were buried with Him that just as Christ was raised from the dead by a manifestion of the Father's power, so we also may live a new life. If we have become united with Him by the act symbolic of His death, surely we shall also become united with Him by the act symbolic of His resurrection. We recognize the truth that our old self was crucified with Christ, in order that the body, the stronghold of sin, might be rendered powerless, so that we should no longer be slaves to sin. For the man who has so died has been pronounced righteous and released from sin. And we believe that as we have shared Christ's death we shall also share His life. We know that Christ, having once risen from the dead, will not die again. Death has power over Him no longer. . . . So let it be with you; regard yourselves as dead to sin, but as living for God, through union with Christ Jesus" (Rom. vi. 2–11).[15] There is here no image, but a precise formula which is to be taken literally. Christ is free in regard to sin because in dying He paid His debt. Sin, death and the law have no more dominion over Him. The same thing is also true of the believer mystically united with Christ. He also is free with regard to sin, death and the law.

In the last passage cited, what is said about baptism might be

interpreted symbolically. But other passages show that this explanation does not suffice, and that to Paul, baptism is more than a symbol.
It effectively brings about the union of the believer with Christ, "For
we were all baptized to form one body, whether Jews or Greeks,
slaves or freemen" (1 Cor. xii. 12). Faith and baptism are thus presented in Gal. iii. 27 as the two means through which is realized the
union of the believer with the Lord, "For all of you who were baptized into union with Christ clothed yourselves with Christ."[16]

That which is true of baptism is also true of the Eucharist. This,
for Paul, is an act instituted by Jesus in commemoration of His sacrifice, and as a means of entering into relation with Him in His
death. In this act, with which the entire Church is associated, the
faithful are invited to sit down at the Lord's table and receive His
cup. The bread and the wine distributed to them are the flesh and
blood of Christ. They put those who consume them in direct relation with Christ through His death. The fruit the believer obtains by
his participation in the repast is the consciousness of being by its
means intimately united to the dying Christ (1 Cor. x. 16, 17).

Baptism and communion, then, occupy in the Pauline system
exactly the same place as faith. Like it, they are the means through
which mystical union is attained. What relation exists between
these two things? Have we here two notions which, if not contradictory, are at any rate different as to their origin and not reducible
to each other—the idea of mystic union through faith which represents Paul's thought, while the theory of the sacraments is only an
interpretation of the rite practised in the Church? This solution
seems to us to encounter several difficulties. If the sacraments were
in the background of Paul's thought it would be comprehensible
that he should have spoken of them in 1 Cor. xi, where there was an
abuse to be attacked, but not that on a quite practical question (the
consumption of meat sacrificed to idols) he should have relied upon
the meaning of the communion as a decisive argument. Neither
would the texts relating to baptism be comprehensible. On the other
hand, seeing that in so systematic a mind as the apostle's the simple

juxtaposition of two different conceptions is very improbable, one is forced to suppose that the mystical union attained by faith and that attained through the sacraments are only two aspects of the same fact. The link uniting them is not the idea that the sacrament is only a symbol of the faith alone efficacious. The apostle, in fact, attributes a real, though harmful, action to the communion when observed without reverence (1 Cor. xi. 27–30). The sacrament acts of itself *ex opre operato* and without the intervention of faith, but faith—that is, the conscious desire to become one with Christ—is necessary to direct its action. To understand this it is necessary to get rid of the modern ideas opposing symbol and reality to each other, and to remember that for the mind of antiquity the symbol partook of the reality of that which it represents; for instance, a name was not a simple designation, but the very substance of the thing named.

The mystical union accomplished for every believer that which had been accomplished for Christ by His death and His resurrection. This is implied in the fundamental affirmation of Paulinism, "the believer is justified by faith." Certain texts seem to favor an interpretation imputing to Paul the idea of effective justification—that is, a transformation of the believer. In Rom. viii. 4, for instance, it is stated that God "condemned sin in the earthly nature (of Christ) so that the requirements of the Law might be satisfied in us who live now in obedience, not to our earthly nature, but to the Spirit." But it is a question here not of justification, but of sanctification, which while intimately related to, is still different from it. Similarly the exhortation to sin no more which is addressed in Gal. ii. 17 to those who have been justified by faith in Christ would have no meaning if justification were identical with sanctification. Justification is forensic; it is the act of God the judge, who proclaims "just" (that is, acquitted) the sinner who appears as the accused before Him. It is an anticipation of the Last Judgment.

The mystical union in linking the fate of the believer to that of Christ breaks the fetter which keeps man the slave of sin and death.

In like manner as Christ, who lived in the flesh during His earthly ministry, has become spirit, the believer also is no longer flesh, but spirit (Rom. vi. 12). But if in *theory* the believer has broken with sin and the carnal life, in *practice* this rupture is not consummated. It suffices to show this to recall the important place filled in the Pauline Epistles by exhortations to sanctification (for instance, Gal. v. 1–6, 10). In fact, sanctification is never completely realized, and it is this which explains the somewhat special character which the Pauline morality assumes.[17] The fundamental idea upon which it rests is that of the abolition of the Law[18] (Gal. iii. 24, iv. 4, 5, v. 18; Rom. vi. 14, vii. 1–6). "I am dead unto Law," wrote Paul (Gal. ii. 19). The believer is then a free man (Gal. v. 1; Rom. vi. 18, 22; 1 Cor. ix. 1–19, etc.). His activity should, in principle, be spontaneous. Since he belongs to God, he ought to live according to God; since he is a spirit, he ought naturally to produce what Paul calls the fruits of the spirit (Gal. v. 16; Rom. viii. 12).

Things are not, however, so simple in reality, and obligation, abolished in principle, is restored in fact. That which seems as though it should be shown as a consequence is formulated as a postulate.[19] Man should strive to realize the fruits of the spirit, which are in harmony with his new nature. He ought to struggle and labor to escape indeed the very law which in theory no longer exists for him (Gal. v. 13; Rom. vi. 15, viii. 7, 8).

The morality of Paul answers to the dualism of the fact of flesh and spirit which subsists in the believer until redemption is achieved; it possesses, therefore, only a temporary value, and will be abolished when believers shall fully live the life of the spirit.[20] There lies here a difference between theory and practice which must be explained. Paul has expressed in touching words which remain classic the sense of this imperfection of sanctification: "For I am so far from habitually doing what I want to do that I find myself doing the very thing I hate. . . . But when I do what I want not to do, I am admitting that the Law is right. This being so, the action is no longer my own, but that of sin which is within me. I

know there is nothing good in me—I mean in my earthly nature.
. . . Miserable man that I am! who will deliver me from the body
that is bringing me to this death?" (Rom. vii. 15–24).[21] Doubtless
the apostle gives a cry of triumph to follow this lament—"Thanks
be unto God through Jesus Christ our Lord"—but the motive of this
cry is the hope of being delivered in the future. The liberation of
those who are in Christ is therefore only a *potential* liberation.

This dualism which exists in man after justification is explained
by the fact that the believer, although dead to the flesh, continues to
live *in* the flesh. Neither his body nor the world in which he lives
has been transformed. He has only received the promise of the
Spirit as surety of that which will be fully realized later (2 Cor. i.
22, v. 5; Rom. viii. 23). Glory, the celestial attribute reserved for the
elect, is only promised him (Rom. v. 2, viii.18). Salvation is not
fully accomplished. "By our hope we were saved." Again he writes:
"Our salvation is nearer now than when we first believed" (Rom.
xiii. 11). In the same Epistle further he writes: "If while we were
yet sinners Christ died for us, how much more now that we are justified by His blood shall we be saved by His life?" The Epistle to
the Philippians similarly affirms that salvation is not yet attained (i.
6). It is at the second coming of the Lord that it shall be fully realized (Rom. viii. 18–25).

VII. THE GENESIS OF THE
PAULINE THEOLOGY

How are we to explain this seeming contradiction in Paul's conception of the position of the justified man, which is not in fact
what in theory it ought to be? For the faithful it is only at the end
of time that will be consummated the thing which in principle follows from the new situation in which he finds himself through mystical union with Christ. This is one of the most difficult and delicate
problems which the interpretation of Paulinism presents. It is by no

hazard that it is so; it is the consequence, we would say without hesitation it is the penalty of the association in Paul's thought of two incongruous elements. There is, indeed, something more than the complex situation in which man struggles between two antagonistic forces which alternately attract and repel him. The contradiction is much deeper; it lies at the very root of Pauline thought. In the way Paul conceives it, the situation of man between justification and redemption is of a provisional and temporary character. Paul expects the return of Christ at a very early date to complete the work begun.[22] Justification and redemption, although separate, remain organically linked one to the other. They are two acts of the same drama. So inter-related and complementary are they that their separation can only be conceived by a complete dislocation of the Jewish doctrine of the Messianic redemption. There is no equivalent for this dislocation in the whole Jewish Apocalypse. We do not think that it is possible to give any other explanation than the following: The conception of redemption, in Paul, is anterior to his Christian faith. As a Rabbi, he already expected the arrival of a Savior who would rescue men from the dominion of sin and death to bring them into the Kingdom of the Spirit, whose advent would be marked by the triumph of the Messiah over the enemies of God.

This faith was his at the time when Jesus in his eyes was only a justly condemned blasphemer. Then happened the mysterious event upon the Damascus road which gave him the conviction that Jesus was living and in glory. From this he concluded that what His disciples had said about Him was true: that Jesus had been the holy Son of God, sent upon earth to accomplish His work. Hence was established an unexpected synthesis between the doctrine of redemption (already in his mind) and the story of the Nazarene Jesus, crucified by Pontius Pilate, but raised again from the dead since He showed Himself to His friends and to Paul himself, and henceforward was living in the spirit life.

The synthesis of these two elements (the story of Jesus and the doctrine of redemption) Paul was unable to effect completely at once. There were in the mission of the Savior-Messiah certain elements which did not permit of their relation to Jesus of Nazareth. These were all those which (to put it in one word) related to a triumphant Messiah, restorer of the sovereignty of God. Paul resolved the difficulty by dividing the mission of the Messiah into two parts and in reserving for the glorious return of Christ (which he considered very near) everything it was impossible to discover as accomplished in the life, death and resurrection of Jesus. The Pauline doctrine thus proceeds from a dislocation of the work of redemption. It therefore has no single source; it is not born out of the elaboration or the transformation of a myth, but proceeds from the interpretation of an historical fact by a doctrine already preëxisting it: the fact constituted by the life and the death of Jesus and by belief in His resurrection. The theology of Paul assumes therefore a double starting point for its development. One is a doctrine of redemption whose origins must be sought in Judaism;[23] the other is an historical episode, the life of Jesus. It is not possible, as M. Couchoud has attempted, to attribute to it a more homogeneous character, and by reducing one of these elements to the other to maintain that the history of Jesus was deduced from a drama of redemption. Indeed, it would not be possible to find in the history of Jewish thought— more or less syncretic—an analogy to the process that must be admitted in Paul; for to presume the existence of certain forms of Judaism of the Diaspora sensibly differing from that of Palestine and which would not have been without a strong influence on rising Christianity would not be to state a true parallel.

We know of nothing, in fact, in the Judaism of the Diaspora which offers any real analogies with the Pauline speculations on this point, and it would be unquestionably making use of an inadmissible historical method to attempt the explanation of a given fact by something which is only a conjecture. But it is not entirely the absence of any parallel which forbids us to see in Paulinism an exclusive product of speculation; it is also the existence of incoherences and internal contradictions which we have pointed out. If the Christian doctrine had come forth in its entirety from the brain of Paul, as Minerva did from that of Jupiter, it would present a homogeneous character. The manifest traces of the sutures we have discovered plainly prove its double origin and justify us in affirming that the Pauline system of theology assumes and certifies the historical tradition about Jesus.

NOTES

1. Concerning communion with demons, see Maurice Goguel, *L'Eucharistie,* p. 167.

2. "Through the jealousy of the devil, death entered the world" (Wisdom of Solomon). "The devil was a murderer from the first" (John viii. 44). "Satan, the Evil One, and the Angel of Death are identical" (Rabbi Simon ben Lakisch).

3. We may leave aside the question, difficult enough to answer, as to whether the flesh is the cause or only the seat of the sin, and if it is so by its very nature or as a result of a fall.

4. Day of Lord's return.

5. There is a certain amount of incoherence in Paul's thought on this. The Judge is sometimes God and sometimes Christ (2 Cor. v. 10). The first is related to the ancient Hebrew tradition of Yahweh (judge); the second is more Messianic. Dialectically, the contradiction is resolved by the idea of God judging through Jesus Christ (Rom. ii. 16). In a subordinate position is found in Paul the idea of judgment of the world by the saints (see 1 Cor. vi. 2).

6. In his struggle with Judeo-Christianity he insists much upon the idea that the Law is impotent to effect salvation. See, for example, Rom. ii. 13, iii. 20; Gal. ii. 16.

7. We may leave aside the question whether He destines all to salvation, or a part of mankind only, and whether the fact that all are not saved is explicable by divine decree or by human freedom.

8. It may appear, given the notion of the flesh, that there is a contradiction between the humanity of Christ and the fact that He is without sin. The solution of this is given by the parallelism drawn between Adam and

Jesus Christ. Just as Adam, before the fall, was at the same time man and without sin, so it is possible to conceive that God had realized for Christ what Adam had been at the creation. It is to be noted that Jewish thought does not rigorously affirm the universality of sin. A Jewish Apocryphal book, fourth Esdras, says that nearly all men are sinners and that very few are not. This offers some striking affinities with Paul's thought (vii. 139).

9. The question whether Paul taught a doctrine of expiation has been much discussed. There are many texts which seem to hint at it; those on which it is said that Christ died "for us" or "for our sins," but it is not certain that "for us" means "in our place" and not "in our interest," and that "for our sins" may have the sense of "accepting responsibility for our sins," and not "because of our sins." It is rather the idea of solidarity which seems to adapt itself to Paul's thought (2 Cor. v. 15).

10. As in the case of the Johannine conception, "I have power to lay down my life and power to take it again" (John x. 18).

11. Believers mystically in union with him ceased to be flesh to become spirit (Gal. v. 24; Rom. vi. 1).

12. Concerning the Jewish Messianic doctrine see Schürer (*Gesch.*), Bousset (*Die Religion des Judentums*), Baldensperger (*Die Messianis-chapokalyptischen,* etc.), Brückner (*Die Entstehung der Paulischen Christologie*).

13. About 280 times in the authentic Epistles.

14. In this passage the idea of the union of believers with the Christ serves as the starting-point of the argument, which proves that we are concerned with one of the fundamental ideas of the apostle with which the faithful must have been very familiar.

15. *Translator's Note.*—English version from *Twentieth Century New Testament,* based upon Westcott and Hort's text.

16. This is confirmed by the practice of baptism for the dead to which Paul alludes in 1 Cor. xv. 29, without pronouncing any censure or making any reservation. (*Author's note.*)

17. Upon the Pauline morality see Wernle, *Der Christ und die Sünde bei Paulus;* also R. Bultmann, *Das Problem der Ethik bei Paulus.*

18. By this is meant the abolition of the ritual part of the Law, not of its moral part. But the inadequacy of the terminology which does not allow the apostle to distinguish exactly between the two things prevents his reaching an exact statement, as is seen by the passage 1 Cor. ix. 20,

where Paul declares that he is not under the Law, although he cannot be without a law, since he is under the law of Christ.

19. A curious fact must be pointed out that in the exposition of the Epistle to the Romans where the *modus operandi* of redemption is analyzed the argument ends by an exhortation, "Being justified by law, let us have peace with God." Logical consistency seems so plainly to require a declaration that many manuscripts have substituted *"we have"* for *"let us have."*

20. Concerning the Pauline morality should be noted among the motives proposed by the apostle the place occupied by the idea of the imitation of Jesus (1 Thess. i. 6; 1 Cor. xi. 1; 1 Col. iii. 13).

21. *Translator's Note.—Twuentieth Century New Testament,* Westcott and Hort's text.

22. In 1 Thess. iv. 15 and 1 Cor. xv. 51 Paul conceives that the return of Christ will take place during his life. He had announced this to the Thessalonians in such a way that the latter had begun to suppose that the faithful who died before the Savior's return would be excluded from salvation (1 Thess. iv. 13).

23. In a Judaism which, no doubt had not been entirely uninfluenced by foreign ideas, principally Greek and Persian.

CHAPTER VII

THE NON-PAULINE EPISTLES OF THE NEW TESTAMENT

I. THEIR CHARACTER

The interpretation of the testimony which the non-Pauline Epistles give concerning Christ calls for the same observations already made concerning those of Pauline origin. These documents are the Epistle to the Ephesians, attributed to Paul, but in which one is obliged to perceive a secondary imitation of the Epistle to the Colossians; the pastoral Epistles (1 and 2 Tim. and Titus), in which there appear to have been inserted fragments of authentic Pauline letters; the first Epistle of Peter, at the basis of which are found the essential ideas of Paul; the Epistle to the Hebrews, written by a man very familiar with the Alexandrine philosophy and exegesis; the second Epistle of Peter and that of Jude, closely related to each other, and apparently of fairly recent period; and lastly, the Epistle of James, who makes use of the traditional Jewish and Greek ethic, and shows very striking analogies with the literature of the Wisdom of the Old Testament.[1] With the exception of the Epistle of James, all these works belong to the literary species which Paul created by his correspondence, and all betray the influence of his theology.

None of these letters pretends to be a complete exposition of Christian faith. They are written to believers, and only expound the ideas and the beliefs which they assume to be those of their readers.[2] Several among them, so far as their date can be fixed with any preciseness, were written at the time when the Gospel literature began to be spread abroad. All these Epistles should be considered as the commentary upon certain points of Christian doctrine and tradition; it is illegitimate to employ in what concerns them the argument *ex silentio*—that is, to suppose their authors were ignorant of certain ideas because they do not give them expression.

Very frequently in the Deutero-Pauline literature the idea of the imitation of Jesus is met with. The idea could only have been a moral force for men who were acquainted with the human history of Jesus. The author of the Epistle to the Hebrews, after having proposed to his readers the imitation of the heroes of the faith spoken of in the Old Testament and Jewish tradition (xi. 1–40), concludes by exhorting them to fix their eyes upon Jesus, who "endured the cross and despised the shame" (Heb. xii. 1, 2). The way in which this exhortation is connected with the examples given in the eleventh chapter is only comprehensible if this also is referred to an historical model. The author also exhorts the faithful to suffer insult as Jesus Himself had done (xiii. 13). The writer of the first Epistle of Peter declares to his readers who are called upon to suffer persecution that they ought to find consolation in the thought that Christ also suffered in the flesh (iv. 1), and has left to them an example that they may follow in His footsteps. Thus he makes his thought precise: "Reviled, He reviled not again; He suffered, but He did not threaten; He entrusted His cause to Him whose judgments are just"[3] (ii. 21–23).

The author of the Epistle to the Ephesians, exhorting the faithful to live in love for one another proposes that they should follow the example of Christ, "who loved us and gave Himself for us" (v. 2).

II. THE PASTORAL EPISTLES

It is true that in the pastoral Epistles the name of Jesus is never found, but always "Jesus Christ," with or without the epithet of the Lord, which is a designation of the celestial Christ, not of Jesus in His earthly ministry. It is also true that there is no direct mention of His death in certain passages where an allusion would seem natural[4] (1 Tim. i. 14; 2 Tim. i. 9, etc.; Titus iii. 4–7). The writer specially speaks of the manifestation of the glory of God in Jesus Christ (1 Tim. i. 15; 2 Tim. i. 9, etc.; Titus iii. 4, etc.); and if he insists upon the human character of this manifestation, he does so without citing any concrete detail, no doubt because these details were in the minds of his readers. Concerning this manifestation, he employs the word *epifaneia* (2 Tim. i. 10; Titus iii. 4), which appears to put it in the same category with the manifestation of Christ at His return[5] (1 Tim. vi. 14; 2 Tim. iv. 1, 8; Titus ii. 13), but it must not be forgotten that the identity of the Christ expected at the end of the age with the Jesus who had already appeared in history had for the Christian faith much importance.

In the first Epistle to Timothy there is a definite allusion to a testimony given by Jesus in the presence of Pontius Pilate. The writer urges Timothy to fight the good fight of faith, to seize hold upon eternal life to which he had been called, and of which he had made confession in the presence of several witnesses. "I urge you as in the sight of God, the source of all life, and of Christ Jesus, who before Pontius Pilate made the great profession of faith—I urge you to keep His commandments without stain or reproach until the appearing of our Lord Jesus Christ" (1 Tim. vi. 12–14). The mention of the Roman Procurator in the same conditions, found in Ignatius and Justin, has given rise to the suggestion that the phrase in the first Epistle to Timothy might be a first sketch of the article in the creed "He suffered under Pontius Pilate."[6] M. Kattenbusch thinks that the testimony of Timothy which is referred to is that given by him at the time of his baptism. Concerning Jesus Christ, the phrase "give testimony" may have a double meaning, and relate both to the declarations of Jesus and to His sufferings. In the article of the creed the mention of Pilate is only a chronological indication. It is too brief to have been introduced in an apologetic interest to confirm the reality of the crucifixion.[7]

M. Kattenbusch believes that the phrase in the creed arises from the transfer of a formula of exorcism, "In the name of Jesus Christ, crucified by Pontius Pilate."[8] This theory gives rise to various objections. The parallelism which exists between the confession of Timothy and that of Jesus Christ compels us to give the term the same meaning in the two cases, and negatives the introduction (even in a subordinate manner) into the confession of Jesus Christ of the notion of suffering and death, which would not apply for Timothy. The idea of the suffering of Christ is so all-important in Christian thought that it could not have been merely suggested. This idea once excluded, there is no longer any connection (according to M. Kattenbusch's view) between the passage of the first Epistle to Timothy and the article of the creed. Nevertheless, it is difficult to admit that the coincidence between the two phrases is quite fortuitous.

The explanation offered by M. Kattenbusch of the article of the creed is no more satisfactory. If the mention of Pontius Pilate possessed a chronological interest, an indication of this kind would have been more in place in reference to the birth of Jesus. The insertion into the creed of a formula of exorcism which does not seem to have had wide currency does not appear to be more natural either.

An interpretation of the passage in the first Epistle to Timothy, infinitely more satisfactory than those hitherto proposed, has been offered by M. Baldensperger, who seems to us to have definitely explained the meaning and scope of the text simultaneously with its relations to the article of the creed.[9] We shall sum up in its main features his illuminating study, of which all the conclusions (it seems to us) must be accepted. The phrase concerning the testimony of Jesus could not have had for its object to fix the time in which He lived. Neither Timothy nor the other readers of the Epistle required enlightenment on this point. Besides, the writer has no care for history or chronology. His eyes are fixed on the future and not on the past. Neither does he dream of affirming the reality of the facts of evangelical history, or, as the mythologists have it, of making history out of a myth. The mere mention of Pontius Pilate would, besides, be quite inadequate to do that. One of the preoccupations dominating his thought was the contest against heresies. Those which he attacks have a practical character and a reference to the life of the Christians. What is known by us about the author's thought permits us to affirm that if he had found himself confronted by a negation respecting the reality of the life of Jesus, he would not have confined himself to a combat on a side issue by the phrase, "He rendered testimony before Pontius Pilate"—a phrase which, besides, was a simple allusion to an episode known to his readers and in no wise in doubt among them. The mere mention of the fact permits the argument to be drawn from it. It was a question of testimony and not of suffering; there is therefore no reason to suppose an anti-Docetist polemic as is the case in other texts where Pilate is mentioned.[10] The starting point of the argument is not the testimony of Jesus, but that of Timothy. It is only incidentally, and as an encouragement for Timothy to persevere in his attitude, that the testimony of Jesus is recalled. M. Baldensperger does not think that it is Timothy's baptismal confession of faith which is referred to, but a testimony which Timothy had given of his faith before the magistrates who had interrogated him on the subject. "One is justified in saying," writes M. Baldensperger, "that Timothy, like Christ, had been summoned before the Roman magistrates and that he had publicly confessed his faith. In this way the text of 1 Timothy is replaced in the historical environment to which it belongs by origin. It is a period of persecutions. The duty of the leaders of the Church was clearly marked out; they were obliged to insist that the disciples of Jesus should publicly confess their faith without lending themselves to more or less formal denials to save themselves from persecution."[11] And M. Baldensperger points out very appositely that a whole series of maxims found in the New Testament recalls this duty of public confession. "Whosoever shall confess Me before men," said Jesus, "I will confess him before My Father who is in heaven. Whosoever shall deny Me before men, the same will I deny before My Father who is in heaven" (Matt. x. 32, 33). Doubtless all these declarations did not have their first origin at the period of the persecutions, but the way in which they stand out in relief reveals clearly an undeniable solicitude and shows anxiety to outline clearly to Christians their duty, as is also done in his exhortation of the First Epistle of Peter: "Sanctify the Lord in your hearts, being always ready to give an account before whomsoever may question you of the faith which is in you"[12] (1 Pet. iii. 15). Under these circumstances, given the importance which the idea of the Christ as a model possessed in Christian thought, it was natural that the episode of the interrogation of Jesus by Pilate should come to be insisted upon. In this was seen a living example of the attitude incumbent upon the faithful when interrogated by the judicial authorities. But why did the writer of the Epistle propose to Timothy the example of Jesus when He had already given testimony?

The answer is—the history of the persecutions proves it—that generally one single interrogation of the Christians was not considered sufficient. In 2 Tim. iv. 16 there is a reference to a first appearance before the magistrates, which implies necessarily that there will be a second, and Pliny expressly states that he was in the habit of interrogating accused persons two or three times. This is the reason that Timothy was exhorted to persevere in his attitude. In the critical circumstances through which Christianity was passing, exhortation to fidelity in the confession of faith was always a present need. It was therefore originally the idea of the "Christ as model" for the confessors of the faith which gave birth to a symbolical formula destined to enter later into the Apostles' Creed. There remains to explain the transformation by which the phrase "He suffered under Pontius Pilate" was substituted for "He gave testimony before Pontius Pilate." M. Baldensperger supposes an error of interpretation of the word *marteria,* taken in the sense of martyrdom and not of confession. This explanation is perhaps not sufficient. It is difficult to accept in respect of a phrase which must have long had for Christians a great practical value. Perhaps it might be possible to think of another explanation. The various phrases of the creed which refer to Christ are so arranged as to constitute a summary of His history, and it might be asked if it was not through an assimilation with what is stated concerning the crucifixion and death that the general idea of martyrdom (which besides also included the notion of testimony) has been substituted for the narrower one.

Whatever the explanation may be, the scope of the passage 1 Tim. vi. 13 stands out clearly through the exegesis of M. Baldensperger. It is no question of the evolution of history from a myth, as M. Couchoud thinks, nor of an effort to crystallize by a chronological detail a history which might seem inconsistent, but the utilization, with an immediately practical aim in view, of a detail in the tradition known to every one, teaching a lesson upon which it was necessary to insist.

This conclusion illuminates this fact: that for the writer of the pastorals the Christian faith rested upon real history. This affirmation is found in such a form that it proves the writer had no sentiment of making an innovation.

III. THE EPISTLE TO THE HEBREWS

Although the writer of the Epistle to the Hebrews makes current use of the name of Jesus, and not only of Jesus Christ or the Lord, the historical person of Jesus does not in his thought possess very special importance. He who is designated by the name of Jesus is the glorified Lord who preëxisted and who is now in heaven. Thus it has sometimes been thought that the Christ of the Epistle to the

Hebrews was a purely mythical personage,[13] and, indeed, as Windisch[14] has observed, this Jesus was a celestial Being, and not a man who had made a profound impression upon those who had known Him. His history is presented in abstract terms which almost all apply to the traditional type of the Messiah, borrowed from the Old Testament, and especially from the Psalms. What is said about His death is in some aspects lacking in everything of historical character. The Jesus of the Epistle to the Hebrews is a High Priest who offers His own blood in sacrifice (ix. 11); He is not the condemned of the Sanhedrin, executed by the Romans.[15] But these features, which have considerable importance, are not the only ones to point out. If Christ preëxisted, and if He is now in celestial glory, the link which unites these two periods of His history is His incarnation. Herein, as Von Soden has well observed, is a conception closely related to that of the Epistle to the Philippians. The idea of the human life of Jesus in the thought of our author does not play a purely minor part; it explains the redemption accomplished by Jesus—a redemption at the center of the author's thought.

He emphasizes certain features which clearly show that a history of Jesus, and in particular of His death, was familiar to him, and forms the foundation of his theology. He indicates that the manifestation of Christ took place at a recent date, in a period which he considers the last in the world's history (i. 2). The message had been brought to him by those who had first heard the preaching of Jesus (ii. 3). He describes the sufferings and temptations of Jesus in words which would be with difficulty explicable as theoretical views, and he maintains that they should be a model and a consolation to men who also have to support suffering and persecution. "Because He Himself has suffered, being tempted, He is able to succor those who are tempted" (ii. 18). "Although He was the Son of God, He learned obedience from His sufferings; and being made perfect, He became to all those who believe in Him the author of eternal salvation" (v. 8, 9). The lot of Christ is exactly the same as that of all men, who must die once, after which is the judgment (ix. 27, 28). The whole constitutes a summary of Christ's sufferings; there is no intention by the author to rewrite a history that in any case his readers know, but there is a certain care to depict in it a drama of redemption and the desire to attach a practical lesson to it.

One single detail concerning the Passion is related in the Epistle to the Hebrews. This is that Jesus died *outside* the city (xiii. 12). This detail is not found in any of the Gospel narratives, but seems to be implied by John (xix. 20). This is, besides, extremely probable, and seems to be presumed in all the accounts. Because the writer of the Epistle to the Hebrews brings this detail into relief owing to the allegorical significance which he accords it, there is no legitimate reason to suppose that he postulates it for ulterior convenience. In a speculative construction this detail would not be thus isolated; it would form part of a general picture interpreted as an allegory. In the conditions in which it is found, it is only to be explained by supposing that it is borrowed from a narrative of the death of Jesus, from which it is detached because of its allegorical interest.

IV. THE FIRST EPISTLE OF PETER, EPISTLE OF JUDE, THE SECOND EPISTLE OF PETER AND THE EPISTLE OF JAMES

The first Epistle of Peter, if we except the concept of the Christ as the model of the faithful, does not contain any allusion to the facts of the life and death of Jesus. The Gospel history is presented as the realization of a prophetic program. The holiness of Jesus is based upon Isaiah (liii. 9) and in 1 Pet. ii. 22, when referring to His sufferings, the writer quotes the same prophet (liii. 4–6). The first Epistle of Peter shows how the theological interpretation of the Gospel history, already vaguely outlined in the preceding generation, tended to become substituted for the history itself. The Epistle of Jude is too brief to authorize any conclusions whatever, for it is rash, seeing the vagueness of the expressions employed, to suppose as does Weinel, that verse 4 is a polemic against Docetism. Admitting the date of its composition as probably fairly late, we might pass over the second Epistle of Peter[16] written at a time when the Epistles of Paul already formed a collection of recognized authority (iii. 15, 16)—that is to say, when Christianity and its doctrines were settled in their essential features. The author alludes to the account of the transfiguration as related in the Synoptic Gospels (i. 16–18). He very distinctly places himself on the ground of the Gospel tradition. This does not prevent his considering the person and work of Jesus from a uniquely dogmatic point of view. Here is a manifest proof—and it does not apply to the second Epistle of Peter alone—that a theological conception of the Christ in no wise excludes the historic tradition. This is an idea which must not be lost sight of when one begins an examination of the Epistle of James. This has a peculiar physiognomy which is not to be found in any other book of the New Testament. No allusion is found to the history of Jesus, even when the line of thought would seem necessarily to require it, as in Chapter v. 10.

Beyond the opening salutation (i. 1) the name of Jesus Christ is only found once (ii. 1), and it is introduced[17] in a way that might suggest an interpolation. Hence the hypothesis which considers the Epistle to be a Jewish work in which the name of Jesus Christ has been introduced in two different places.[18] This hypothesis does not appear admissible owing to the numerous reminiscences of Gospel phrases found in the Epistle and because they are the Pauline formulas concerning justification by faith (somewhat inaccurately transmitted, it is true) which the writer has in mind in the second chapter (ii. 14–26). The Epistle introduces us to an original type of Christianity conceived as a rule of life and a source of moral inspiration. The Gospel is the perfect law of liberty (i. 25) or the royal law (ii. 8). These are practical instructions given by the writer. He does not place them in any relation with a drama of redemption, historical or mythical. It is evident that from such a work no conclusion as to the character of the evangelical tradition can be drawn, the latter being ignored, or, to be more precise, they are left aside.

V. CONCLUSION

In their entirety the non-Pauline Epistles of the New Testament show us, then, the continuation of the development which we have already recognized in the Pauline Epistles. The Gospel history serves as the base of the development of a doctrine of redemption, and the further we advance the more does the doctrine grow in importance and tend to substitute itself for the history of which originally it was the interpretation.[19]

NOTES

1. The three Epistles of John, which cannot be considered separately from the fourth Gospel, are not mentioned here.

2. This is illustrated by a significant fact. In the Johannine Epistles, which, as all are aware, are closely related to the fourth Gospel, there is no allusion to the facts about the life of Jesus.

3. Immediately after the author speaks of the death of Christ on the cross (1 Peter ii. 24). It is evident that there is an allusion here not to an Apocalyptic drama, but to the crucifixion.

4. But account must be taken of the effect upon the mind of his readers of the form of words used by the writer.

5. Von Soden, *Das Interesse des apostolischen Zeitalters an der Evangelischen Geschichte* (Freiburg im Br., 1892).

6. Von Soden, *op. cit.;* Kattenbusch, *Das apostolische Symbol.*

7. If such were its character, the function of Pilate should be stated.

8. This formula is attested by Justin, by Irenæus and by Palladius.

9. Baldensperger, *Il a rendu témoignage sous Ponce Pilate* (*Revue d'hist.,* Paris, 1922).

10. For instance, Ignatius, *ad Magn.,* xi; *ad Smyrn.,* i. 2; *ad. Tral.,* ix, 1.

11. Baldensperger, *op. cit.,* p. 20, etc.

12. Concerning the importance of testimony at the period of persecutions see Apoc. ii. 13. The fact that the Christians of Pergamos did not deny their faith at the time of the martyrdom of Antipas has caused the

presence of Nicolaites among them to be considered as having little importance, while the struggle against heresy was one of the dominating occupations of the author of the letters to the seven churches.

13. Drews, *Die Christusmythe;* Smith, *Ecce Deus;* Couchoud, *Le Mystère de Jésus.*

14. Windisch, *Der Hebrärbrief.*

15. Von Soden, *op. cit.,* p. 120.

16. It is unnecessary to say that our observations would only have more force if the authenticity of the Epistle be admitted, as is done by Catholic exegesis and certain Protestant critics—for instance, Spitte (*Der Zweite Brief des Petrus*) and Zahn (*Einleitung in das Neue Testament*).

17. "Jesus Christ, our glorified Lord."

18. Massebieau, *L'Epitre de Jacques est elle l'Œuvre d'un Chrétien?;* Spitte, *Der Brief des Jakobus,* etc. It is interesting to note that Spitte and Massebieau developed their theories independently of each other.

19. The same development continues in the writings of the Apostolic Fathers (Clement, Ignatius, Polycarp, Barnabas), but it shows less and less originality. It is unnecessary to examine this in detail, for these documents were written at a time when doctrine and tradition were fixed in their essential elements.

CHAPTER VIII

THE CHRIST
OF THE APOCALYPSE

I. CHARACTER OF THE APOCALYPSE
("REVELATIONS")

The Johannine Apocalypse, as we have it, dates from the last decade of the first century—that is, from a period when a Gospel literature existed—at least in its essential elements—and the author of the Apocalypse appears to know it. There is no direct reference to the contents of this literature in his book, but the nature of the work sufficiently explains it. On the other hand, one lights upon reminiscences which are clear enough to prove that the author knew the Gospel tradition. "Unless you are on the watch," says the Angel of the Church of Sardis, "I shall come like a thief, and you will not know at what hour I am coming." This is almost a quotation from Matt. xxiv. 43, 44 and Luke xii. 39, 40: "If the master of the house had known at what watch of the night" (Luke, "at what hour") "the thief would come, he would have watched." "Be ye ready, for the Son of man will come at an hour when ye think not." "He who overcometh," is read in the conclusion of the same letter, "will I confess before My Father and before His angels." This reminds us of Matt. x. 32, Luke xii. 8: "Whosoever shall confess Me before men, the same will I confess before My Father who is in Heaven" (Luke has it, "before the angels of God"). The phrase in the Apocalypse (xiii. 10), "Whoever shall kill with the sword, the same shall be killed with the sword," recalls Matt. xxvi. 52, "All they who take up the sword shall perish by the sword." Finally, the illustration of the Water of Life in xxi. 6 and xxii. 17 is too similar to what is found in John iv. 10, etc., vii. 37, to permit the supposition of a chance coincidence.

The Apocalypse must not be taken alone. In order that it may be correctly interpreted, all the ideas and all the knowledge which it presumes must be taken into account.

The Christ of the Apocalypse, notwithstanding the name Jesus by which He is most frequently designated, is a celestial Being. He is the Lord in the heavens, whose return is awaited (i. 5–13 and iii. 11), and the testimony[1] rendered to the Christ, who occupies so great a place in the book, is a testimony rendered to the Lord in the heavens, as may be inferred from Chapter ii. 13. Could it be otherwise in a book whose entire outlook is towards the future? Nevertheless, this celestial Being has had a human history. The writer makes no direct mention of this, but he presumes it in saying, for instance, that He died (i. 5, v. 9) or that He had been crucified at Jerusalem (xi. 8), and it is precisely this which explains his celestial dignity. It is the lamb who was slain who alone is worthy to break the seals of the book (v. 6).

Among the most characteristic details of the figure of Christ is that which states that He died and returned to life. The frequent mention of the blood of the lamb and its purifying action presumes a doctrine of redemption, which, like those of Paul and the Deutero-Pauline Epistles, is a theological interpretation of the drama of Calvary. There is not to be found in the Apocalypse any detail which recalls the Gospel accounts of the Passion, but to appreciate this fact at its true significance allowance must be made for the allegorical character inherent in the Apocalyptic writings. The mere mention of the death of the lamb evokes for the readers of the book the souvenir of the Passion with sufficient clearness.

There are, on the other hand, in the Apocalypse certain pictures which have a distinctly mythical character. The Messiah there appears completely stripped of all human features. He is a Being entirely ideal. How ought these images to be interpreted? To reply to this question certain principles which are essential to the interpretation of the Apocalypse must be remembered.[2] The Johannine Apocalypse belongs to a group of books whose composition in the bulk is distributed over the two centuries which preceded and the two centuries which followed in the Christian era. This species of literature possesses its rules, its habits, its methods, which are found almost identical in all the writings belonging to it—Jewish as well as Christian. There is an Apocalyptic tradition which explains the affinity observed between the various works. There are always the same images and symbols to be found, the same activities at work. But this is not all. The writers of this Apocalyptic literature must not be considered as visionaries—notwithstanding the important part played by inspiration in the Christian productions—but as "rabbis," not ignorant of the works of their predecessors. On the contrary, they carefully studied them, discovered their prophecies, corrected, modernized, and adapted them to new surroundings. Often they introduced in the works they composed descriptions more or less elaborate, borrowed from an older Apocalypse. The author of the canonical book has not departed from this procedure. Thus are to be explained the incoherences, the doublets, the repetitions so frequently found in his work, and of which it will suffice to give as an instance the juxtaposition of the scene at the breaking of the seven seals (v. 1–8) and that of the seven trumpet blasts (viii. 2–11), to which may be also added that of the seven bowls (xv. 1–16). Hence a double duty is incumbent upon the interpreter of the Apocalypse. The writer is far from being a mere compiler; he does not restrict himself to sewing together and framing the fragments of previous works. If he has made use of already existing material, in adding thereto portions that literary analysis cannot fail to identify, it is in order to express his own ideas and personal sentiments, and to press them into the service of the object he aimed at. Above all it is necessary to disentangle his personal thought and the signification of the picture he drew. Bousset, who has done more than any one to influence the study of the Apocalypse by the analysis of its sources, has strongly and judiciously insisted upon this point. He wrote that "the main task is to understand the Apocalypse as a personal and original work possessing its literary unity." It would be a grave error to attribute directly to the author of the Apocalypse all the ideas and sentiments found in the documents he used without taking into account the corrections in detail he made, and, above all, the indications which follow from the main plan of his work and of the part played in its development by fragments borrowed from earlier documents.

Certain of these fragments express ideas and sentiments they were not in their origin destined to convey, and among those which the writer has adopted to express an idea which dominated his mind are to be found others which are not his at all, and which have only penetrated into the book in its actual form owing to their solidarity with others belonging to the primitive document.[3]

II. THE VISION OF THE WOMAN AND THE DRAGON

This rule of interpretation should particularly be applied to Chapter xii,[4] in which M. Stahl and M. Couchoud, independently of each other, have thought they found the concept of a Christ purely ideal.

The vision of Chapter xii forms a whole complete in itself, and which possesses no organic relation either with what precedes or with what follows it. It is permissible therefore to consider it in itself.

The seer says that a great portent[5] shows itself in the heavens:

A woman appears, clothed with the sun; she has the moon under her feet, and upon her head is a crown of twelve stars; she is with child, and upon the point of giving birth to it. Another portent also appears in the heavens. It is a great fiery dragon with seven heads with seven crowns. His tail swept away and hurled down to the earth the third of the stars of heaven. The dragon stood before the woman about to give birth to the child and prepared to devour her child as soon as it was born. The woman gave birth to a son destined to rule the nations with a rod of iron. The child is carried away to the presence of God—before His throne. The woman flees away into the wilderness, where for a period of 1,260 days she is nourished and tended.[6] Then ensues a battle in the heavens. Michael and his angels fight against the dragon and gain the victory—they drive their enemies from the heavens. They are not to be found again. The great dragon, the old serpent, he who is called the devil and Satan, he who deceives the inhabitants of the earth, is hurled to the earth, and his angels share his fate. In heaven a voice is heard celebrating the victory. Now is the day of salvation and power and dominion of our God, and the rule of His Christ, for the accuser of our Brethren had been hurled down, he who ceased not, night and day, to accuse them before our God. Their victory was through the blood of the lamb and by the word of their testimony. In their love of life they shrank not from death. Therefore rejoice, ye heavens, and ye who inhabit them! Woe unto the earth and the sea, for the devil has descended unto you in fury, knowing that his days are counted. When the dragon saw he was conquered he pursued the woman who had given birth to the male child. But to the woman were given the wings of the great eagle, so that she might fly to the wilderness, where she is nourished for one year, for two years, and for half a year.[7] Then the dragon poured water from his mouth like a river so that she might be drowned. But the Earth came to her help and opened its mouth and drank up the river which the dragon had poured from his mouth. Then the dragon went away to make war upon the rest of her children—they who observe the commandments of God and are faithful to the testimony of Jesus—and he took his stand upon the seashore.[8]

This passage is not a free creation, but the adaptation of a more recent Apocalyptic fragment. The interest which is centered at the beginning on the Messiah's birth turns in the divine canticle and its conclusion upon the destiny of believers. In the verses 7–9 the victory over the dragon is gained by Michael and his angels. According to verse 11, on the contrary, it is by the martyrs, who through the blood of the lamb and by the faithfulness of their testimony have overthrown their accuser. There is another incoherence not less significant between the picture given in verses 1–9 and that outlined in verses 13–18. The two flights of the woman into the desert, the refuge which in both passages is represented as prepared for her, the duration of this retreat, all manifestly form a doublet. But while in the first passage the woman is the mother of the Messiah, and may, therefore, be identified as the people of Israel,[9] in the second passage she is the mother of believers—that is, the Church.[10]

The image of the battle against the dragon is not one and the same throughout the chapter either. In the first passage the Messiah plays no part; He is only the king destined to reign with power when order is restored in the world. It may perhaps be imagined that He will be called upon to play a part in the last phase of the struggle, but up to the supreme moment He is held in reserve in heaven and in shelter before the throne of God, the victory being gained by Michael and his angels. In the celestial hymn, on the contrary, it is through the blood of the lamb—that is thanks to the Messiah's work—that the martyrs gain the victory.

It may be added that no organic relation is perceptible between the statement (in the first portion of Chap. xii) of Satan being hurled to earth, and the mention of the same thing in Chapters xix, xx—chapters which, in their essentials at least, there is good reason to attribute to the writer of the Johannine Apocalypse.

As for the character of the fragment utilized at the beginning of Chapter xii, it does not seem possible to hesitate in recognizing it. The quite secondary part played in it by the Messiah indicates that it must be Jewish and not Christian.[11] In whatever way the primitive origin of Christianity may be conceived, how can it be supposed that at the end of the first century a Christian could have imagined Christ as rapt up to the heavens immediately after His birth, while completely suppressing His historical ministry and the redemption drama?[12]

While borrowing this Jewish fragment, the Christian author has made additions to it which entirely change its character. The defeat of the dragon, for the sake of which he collected this fragment, must in the original have been final; in *his* work it is no more than a stage of the great struggle and the guarantee of future victory. The writer makes use of it to express one of the ideas to which he was most addicted, which in his readers' eyes had the greatest practical value and reality—the idea that the very rage of the devil against the Christians, as manifested in the persecutions, was the consequence of his first defeat, and that this rage would continue to be powerless provided only that the Christians remained faithful and were able to bear their sufferings without yielding to weakness.

We are unable, then, to discern in the idea of the newly born Messiah, immediately caught up to the heavens and transported before the throne of God, the primitive form of Christian Christology; it is an element borrowed, and which does not express the thought of the author of the Apocalypse. If at the beginning of the chapter there is indeed the idea of a purely mythical Messiah, it is a Jewish and not a Christian idea. Chapter xii, therefore, cannot be legitimately invoked by the supporters of the nonhistorical character of Jesus, and the considerations above offered to support the thesis that the Apocalypse assumes the Gospel tradition maintain their force.

NOTES

1. The word is found no less than nine times, without counting the noun "witness" (five times) and the verb "witness" (four times).

2. Consult on this subject the introduction to the various commentaries, particularly those of Bousset, Charles, and Loisy.

3. The failure to recognize these principles vitiates radically the studies of MM. Stahl and Couchoud; Stahl, *Le Document 70;* Couchoud, *Le Mystère de Jésus.*

4. Upon this chapter see Wellhausen (*Analyse der Offenbarung Johannis*) Stahl, Couchoud.

5. Wellhausen and Stahl think that the first scene takes place in reality on the earth, and there is only in the heaven a sign which announces it. It would be difficult, according to them, to conceive an accouchement in the very heavens, and besides, the child, as soon as he is born, is caught up into the heavens, and finally it is said that the woman fled into the desert, which is opposed not to the heavens, but to another place in the earth. None of these three arguments can be admitted. One cannot insist that an Apocalyptic scene should be probable. The theory of superposed heavens allows us to conceive readily that the child born in one of the lower heavens, or rather (seeing that stars are mentioned) in the firmament, is immediately after carried away to a higher heaven. He is, in fact, placed before the throne of God. This is not the place of his birth. Finally, the fact that the return of the woman on the earth is not expressly mentioned is nothing more than a piece of negligence in the form of the account.

6. These 1,260 days represent 42 months—that is, 3½ years, the half of a week of years, the unit of time for Apocalyptic calculations since Daniel. Wellhausen and Stahl consider these 3½ years to be the duration of the Jewish war, but as M. Alfaric remarks, with reason, the 3½ years only fit this period very imperfectly. And besides, the figure of 3½ years is traditional in the Apocalypse. In his work of 1907 Wellhausen has not reproduced the interpretation which he gave in 1899.

7. That is to say, 3½ years, "for a time, and times, and half a time."

8. This last part of the sentence serves to connect with the picture which follows.

9. It is extremely probable, as M. Loisy has shown, that the woman was originally an astral personage and that this is a portion of an astrological myth. But for the writer the entire interest of the picture is centered in the fight with the dragon.

10. Wellhausen (*Analyse*), followed by Stahl, considers the woman

to be Zion and the first child to be the Jewish Messiah. The other children would therefore be Jews who had fled from Jerusalem because they did not rely upon arms, like the Zealots, but only on God, to reëstablish the Theocracy. Under these conditions it is strange that no mention is made of the first group of the children of Zion. It would thus be necessary to suppose much mutilation of the source of the passage, not only at the end but in the middle, which would seem improbable. It is for this reason that we prefer to consider the verses 13–17, which follow a portion due to Christian inspiration (verses 10–12), as a glossing over the theme (developed in the Jewish fragment found at the beginning of the chapter) by the Christian editor.

11. Wellhausen (*Analyse*), while admitting that this idea of the Messiah rapt up to the heavens immediately after his birth is not attested in Judaism, maintains that it is possible to see in it a compromise between two Messianic conceptions—the Messiah coming from the people of Israel and the Messiah of Daniel coming from heaven. This idea is found in the rabbinical tradition. (Cp. Israel Levi, *Le ravissement du Messie enfant*.)

12. Wellhausen, *Analyse*, p. 20.

CHAPTER IX

THE THEORY OF THE PROPHETIC ORIGIN OF THE GOSPEL TRADITION

I. THE FUNCTION OF THE PROPHETIC ARGUMENT IN PRIMITIVE CHRISTIANITY

The preceding chapters have led us to the conclusion that the theology found in the Epistles of the New Testament and in the Apocalypse necessarily presume the existence of the Gospel tradition. It is with this tradition that we have now to deal. But before beginning the direct study of it, we shall find it convenient to examine a theory which, if well founded, would offer in favor of the thesis of the mythologists an argument of great weight: this is the theory which holds that the Gospel narratives—or at least the most important among them—are developed from themes supplied by the Old Testament.

Already had Schelling, in a course of lectures upon the philosophy of art given at the beginning of the last century, observed that the history of Jesus was completely enveloped in fables whose creation and development had been suggested by prophecies in the Old Testament.[1] After him Strauss sought to find in the Old Testament one of the sources of the Gospel myths. After this critics occupied with the history of the Gospel tradition recognized the profound influence exercised upon it by the Old Testament.

Returning to their observations, M. Salomon Reinach has stated in very harsh terms the problem which this contact poses. The solution which he gives of it is distinctly unfavorable to the historical character of the events related in the Gospels. His observations are confined to one particular point, the history of the crucifixion of Jesus. Indeed, here is the knot of the problem, for according as one admits or denies the reality of the cross, the historical character of the person of Jesus will be substantiated or will fall to the ground. We may, therefore, confine our observations to this point of capital importance: Is the account of the crucifixion of Jesus the relation of a real fact, or is it derived from the supposed fulfillment of certain prophecies previously read in the Old Testament?

In M. Reinach's opinion,[2] and M. Couchoud entirely shares his point of view,[3] the problem presented is a very simple one. We are in face of a dilemma. Given agreement between a prophecy and a narrative, and two explanations only are possible: Either the prophecy is, in fact, what it is taken to be by orthodox traditional theology—that is, it rests upon a supernatural and anticipated knowledge of events—or the narrative has been suggested, and, so to speak, engendered, by the prophecy, and ought to be considered as totally without value. To admit the first hypothesis would be to accept a dogmatic *a priori* and consequently to place oneself outside the conditions of historical research.

Are we, therefore, forced to accept the second alternative, and to conclude that all the portions of Gospel history in which the recognition of the fulfillment of prophecies is possible are of a purely mythical character, even including those in which the Gospel tradition itself has recognized them? First of all must be noted the conditions in which the prophetic argument first appeared and developed in early Christianity.[4] Before everything else there existed an apologetic method of which the Christian missionaries made use. The history of Jesus bewildered the Jews, so contrary was it to the way in which they conceived the Messiah. The cross of Jesus had been to Paul the object which prevented his belief in what the Christians said about Him. That which was true of Paul was certainly also true of all those who had received a similar education. The Jew Tryphon is prepared to yield to Justin's argument claiming to prove by scriptural demonstration that the Messiah is called upon to suffer,[5] but he absolutely refuses to admit that the Christ had perished by the infamous punishment of the cross. In his eyes, as in those formerly of Paul, the phrase of Deuteronomy remains an invincible obstacle: "Cursed be he who is hung on a tree" (xxi. 23).

Says Tryphon: "Your pretended Christ was without honor and without glory, to such a degree that He was under the most extreme malediction of the Law—He was crucified!" (*Dialogues,* xxxii. 3). Again he writes: "We are aware, accepting the argument of Justin, that the Christ must suffer . . . but that He had to be crucified, that He had to die a death of such a degree of shame and dishonor—a death cursed by the Law—prove this to us, for we are totally unable to conceive it" (xc. 1, lxxxix. 2, xciii. 4).

Tryphon was no exception. He represented a point of view which had already evolved towards the idea of a suffering Messiah.[6] Before his time the passage in Isaiah (Chap. liii) had not yet been connected with the Messiah.[7] It is impossible to say precisely if Christian ideas did not influence Judaism on this point. At all events, what is found in the pre-Christian period concerning the efficacy of suffering is at the most merely the germ of later development.[8] The idea of the redeeming utility of suffering concerning the martyrs of the time of Antiochus Epiphanius is found in the second book of the Maccabees, especially in the celebrated episode of the death of the mother and of her seven sons: "As for me, said the last of them, like my brothers, I give my body and my life for the laws of my fathers, praying to God to show mercy quickly to my people. May the anger of the Most High, justly incited by our race, be ended at my and my brother's death" (2 Macc. vii. 37, 38). The same idea is found in the fourth book of the Maccabees, which dates from the first century of our era. At the point of expiring, the martyr Eleazar addresses this prayer to God: "Have compassion upon my people; for their sake be satisfied with my punishment! Make of my blood a means of purification, and accept my life for their ransom" (4 Macc. vi. 29).

Notwithstanding the interest and importance of the indications to be gleaned in these and some other texts, it is only possible to recognize in them materials which have been utilized later in the elaboration of a doctrine of the Messianic sufferings. But this doctrine did not exist in the Judaism of the first century, and it is this fact which made the task of the Christian apologists and missionaries a difficult one.

The problem presented to Justin was presented from the first days of the life of the Church. A considerable effort must have been made to discover in the Scriptures a demonstration of the necessity of the Messianic sufferings. To find this must have required a quite special acquaintance with the prophecies. The apostle Paul explains that if the Jews did not find in the Scriptures the same thing as the Christians, it was because, while reading Moses, they had a veil over their intelligence (2 Cor. iii. 15, 16). When the disciples met with Jesus on the road to Emmaus, it was necessary for Him to "open up to them the Scriptures" (Luke xxiv. 32). While commencing with Moses, He expounded to them everything in the prophetic writings concerning Himself, as well as the necessity for the Christ to suffer to enter into His glory (xxiv. 26, 27). The concept of the sufferings and the death of the Messiah, which the Christians had so great a *need* to discover in the Old Testament, was therefore, by their own admission, only contained there in such an obscure manner that a special capacity was required to find it. This renders the hypothesis that the Scriptures suggested the idea of the crucifixion of the Messiah one of very small a priori probability.

II. THE RELATIONS OF PROPHECY AND THE GOSPEL HISTORY

The problem of the relations between prophecy and the Gospel history is not so simple as the dilemma formulated by M. Salomon Reinach would suppose. It is convenient, we think, to distinguish between several cases.

1. Creations Due to Prophetic Exegesis

There is first of all among these a series which support M. Reinach's theory. These are the episodes or details which for the main part are only found in the youngest Gospel narratives. If the influence of prophecy does not suffice to explain them completely, it certainly appears to have taken some part in their genesis. It will suffice to mention here some examples:

The most ancient tradition seem to have considered Jesus the son of Joseph.[9] The idea of the supernatural birth, as it is found developed in Matthew (i. 18), arises partly from the application to Mary and her Son of the passage in the prophet Isaiah (vii. 14), thus phrased in the Septuagint version: "A virgin shall conceive and bear a son"—a prophecy whose realization is emphasized by Matthew[10] (i. 22, etc.) in the narrative of the birth of Jesus.

Similarly, primitive tradition represented Jesus as a Galilean, born at Nazareth; but as a prophecy of Micah (v. 1) had announced that the Messiah would be born in Judea, it was found necessary to put history in harmony with it. Matthew and Luke have done this in two different ways, which, besides, are not to be reconciled with each other. Matthew[11] states that after His birth the parents of Jesus went to reside at Nazareth to flee from the wrath of Herod and his heirs (ii. 19–23). Luke affirms that the parents of Jesus resided at Nazareth, but that Jesus was born at Bethlehem, where His parents had come upon the occasion of the census taken by Quirinius (ii. 1–39).

In the gospel of the infancy it is also possible to instance the flight into Egypt as having a prophetic origin (Matt. ii. 13–15), fulfilling the words of Hosea, which in the original text related to the people of Israel and not to the Messiah: "Out of Egypt have I called My Son." There is also to be noted in this connection the massacre of the innocents (Matt. ii. 16–18), in which the evangelist saw the fulfillment of the words of Jeremiah (xxxi. 15).

2. Modifications Due to Prophetic Exegesis

Sometimes prophetic exegesis has only caused the modification or the addition of one detail. Thus Matthew (xxi. 14–16) records that after He had driven the dealers out of the Temple, Jesus was the object of an ovation on the part of the children. This detail was certainly suggested by the words of the Psalm (viii. 3): "Out of the mouths of babes and sucklings Thou hast called forth praise." Certain details of the history of the Passion must have the same origin. Mark (xiv. 11) and Luke (xxii. 5) relate that the chief priests promised Judas a sum of money if he would deliver Jesus to them. Matthew (xxvi. 15) specifies that the sum was thirty pieces of silver, and he later (xxvii. 3–10) relates that Judas, seeing how events had happened, returns to the chief priests and the elders to say, "I have sinned in delivering up the blood of the innocent," and he then flings the thirty pieces on the floor of the Temple and goes out to hang himself. The priests decide that this money, being the price of blood, cannot be paid into the treasury, so they employ it in the purchase of a plot of ground belonging to a potter, to be a burial ground for foreigners. Matthew himself reveals the origin of this story by saying: "Thus was fulfilled the prophecy of Jeremiah: they took the thirty pieces of silver—the price of Him who was valued by the people of Israel—and gave them for the potter's field as the Lord had commanded me."[12]

Mark relates how, at the moment when Jesus is to be crucified, He is offered aromatic vinegar to drink. The women of Jerusalem were in the habit of giving to condemned persons a stupefying drink to attenuate their sufferings.[13] Matthew (xxvii. 34), remembering doubtless a passage in the Psalms, "they made me to eat gall" (lxix. 22), has substituted "gall" for the aromatic drink, and has thus changed the significance of the detail.

In Luke (xxiii. 6–16) the episode of the appearance of Jesus before Herod—an episode whose historical character cannot possibly be admitted[14]—probably owes its origin not only to the memory of the hostility which Herod had shown to Jesus in Galilee (Luke xiii. 31–33), but also to the words of the psalmist: "The kings of the earth and the great ones have assembled together against the Lord and against His Anointed" (Psa. ii. 2), the great ones being represented by the Jewish authorities and Pilate. Herod has been added to them to fulfill more completely the prophecy. Two of the phrases on the cross which do not belong to the most ancient tradition (since Luke is the only one to record them) have their origin in prophecy. It is said of the Servant of the Eternal, "He interceded for the guilty" (Isa. liii. 12). Luke attributes to the crucified Jesus this prayer: "Father, forgive them, for they know not what they do"[15] (xxiii. 24); and at the moment where Mark (xv. 37) and Matthew (xxvii. 50) relate that Jesus expired in giving a loud cry, Luke puts into His mouth the sentence, inspired direct from the Psalms (xxxi. 6): "Father, into Thy hands I commend My spirit" (xxiii. 46).

In John's Gospel the episode of the spear-thrust (xix. 31–37) fulfills that which the Law prescribed regarding the paschal lamb, whose bones must not be broken (Exod. xii. 10–46; Num. ix. 12; cp. Psa. xxxiv. 21). The evangelist remarks: "This was done in order that the Scripture should be fulfilled: A bone of His shall not be broken" (xix. 36, 37). This influence of prophecy may have also reacted upon certain narratives of the common tradition. The forty days' fast in the desert (Mark i. 13; Matt. iv. 2; Luke iv. 2) suggest, notwithstanding the different circumstances, the forty days which Moses passed before the Lord (Exod. xxiv. 18 and xxxiv. 28), or the forty years during which the Israelites ate manna in the desert

(Exod. xvi. 35).[16] The idea of the Spirit descending upon Jesus at the moment of baptism (Mark i. 10; Matt. iii. 16; Luke iii. 22; cp. John i. 32, 33) might have as its origin the passage in Isaiah. "The Spirit of God shall rest upon Him" (xi. 2). It is not impossible that the crucifixion of the two robbers (Mark xv. 27) may have been suggested by Isaiah (liii. 12), "He was numbered among the transgressors."[17] With the cases which we have been citing may be compared those where some distortion or adaptation of certain narratives has taken place under the influence of a prophecy.

In the account of the entry into Jerusalem the four evangelists represent the ovation made to Jesus in the form of the messianic acclamation in Psa. cxviii. 25, 26.

The announcement of the treachery of Judas seems to have been made during a repast, because a passage in Psa. xli. 10[18] has been taken literally: "He who has eaten My bread has raised his heel against Me." Mark states that Jesus during the meal declared: "One of you will betray Me—he who dips his hand with Me into the dish." Matthew relates this, presenting the episode in the form "he who dips his hand with Me into the dish" as an act actually performed at that very moment, introducing in this way into the account the designation of the traitor. Luke also refers to a gesture; his account, however, does not involve the personal designation of the traitor. John has combined the two traditions, placing side by side a public announcement of the treachery (xiii. 18–22) with a designation of the traitor Judas in words spoken aside (verses 23–26). After this Judas, into whom Satan had entered, rises from the table according to the request which Jesus had made to him to do quickly that which he had to do (verses 27–30). The Synoptic Gospels, which all agree in presuming that Judas was present at the beginning of the evening, do not state that he left Jesus and His companions. Nevertheless, at the Mount of Olives he is at the head of those who come to arrest Jesus. His departure is too important for tradition to allow it to pass without a word.[19] In its *primitive* form the tradition could not have presumed the presence of Judas,

and it is perhaps the fact of his absence at this time which gave substance to the suspicions that Jesus must have had, and which
revealed to Him the knowledge that the circle of His enemies was
closing up around Him, and that He would no longer be able to
escape them. It is because the expression borrowed from the
psalmist had been taken literally that the presence of Judas at the
last repast has been presumed.

The account of the insults which the passers-by threw at Jesus
when crucified (see Mark, Matthew and Luke) betrays by the use
of certain words[20] the influence of Psa. xxii. 8; and Matthew has
emphasized this by introducing the words which recall verse 9 of
the same psalm: "He trusted in God; let God deliver Him now if He
will have Him" (xxvii. 43). Nevertheless the entire scene cannot
have its sole origin in the psalm.

The episode of the vinegar given to Jesus at the moment He was
about to expire is important to consider. Mark recounts that after
Jesus had cried out, "Eloi! Eloi! Lama sabachtanei?" certain among
those present said, "He is calling upon Elias"; another, soaking a
sponge with vinegar and offering it to Him, said: "Let be; let us see
if Elias will deliver Him." This scene is enigmatical in that it attributes contradictory sentiments to those standing by—the derision
implied in the sneer about Elias and the pity which inspired the gesture of the one who offered the sponge. Vinegar was the usual bev-
erage of the soldiers, and Jesus was only offered some in order to
procure Him some slight relief. The intervention of the second soldier tends to hinder the compassionate gesture of the first. Matthew
(xxvii. 47–49) has here slightly modified the account of Mark, and
in so doing he has transformed the significance of the scene. It is one
of those who had uttered the sarcasm who offers the vinegar to
Jesus. His action thus becomes a gesture of derision, and that is
probably because Matthew had been influenced by the passage in
Psa. lxix. 22: "To assuage my thirst, they make me drink vinegar."[21]

In John's Gospel (xix. 28, 29) the episode is transformed under
the influence of the prophecy. At the moment He was about to

expire, Jesus said, in order that the Scripture might be fulfilled, "I thirst"[22]; it is then that He is offered a sponge soaked in vinegar.

Let us point out another detail. Both Mark and Matthew state that during the crucifixion the women stood looking on some distance away. To the women Luke adds the friends of Jesus, possibly to avoid the appearance of the disciples being disinterested in the fate of their Master, but doubtless also under the influence of two passages in the Psalms: "My friends and my acquaintances forsake me . . . my kindred remain apart" (xxxviii. 12) and "Thou hast removed my friends far from me"[23] (lxxx. 9).

The examples just cited bring into prominence the fact that prophecy suggested, or at least influenced, certain Gospel narratives. We must now consider another series of facts in which the influence of prophecy does not seem to us in any way to exclude historical veracity.

III. INFLUENCE OF PROPHECY ON THE FACTS

In certain instances the influence of the Old Testament has been exercised, not on the narratives, but on the facts themselves, by inspiring certain actions, sentiments, or sayings of Jesus. His thought and His pity were nourished by the Old Testament, particularly by the prophecies and the Psalms. He was constantly inspired by them, and devoted Himself to fulfilling the program which He there found traced out. In the oldest account of the baptism of Jesus—that in the Gospel of Mark—there is a reference to a vision of Jesus when He acquires the belief of being the Son of God.[24] It is Jesus who sees the clouds opening and who hears the celestial words. It is not astonishing that the experience then realized by Him was expressed in a phrase inspired by various passages of the Old Testament, particularly by the verse of Psa. ii. 7: "Thou art My Son; this day have I begotten Thee."[25]

In several episodes, as in the preaching of Jesus at Nazareth (Luke iv. 16–30) and the reply to the messengers of John the Baptist (Matt. xi. 2–6 and Luke vii. 18–23), the ministry of Jesus is expressly portrayed as the accomplishment of the Messianic program in Isaiah (xxxv. 5, lviii. 6, lxi. 1, 2). If it be granted that Jesus was persuaded He was called by God to carry on His work and to be His Messiah (with which important point we shall deal later), then these episodes explain themselves, and there is no necessity at all to attribute a purely literary origin to them. The narrative of the entry of Jesus into Jerusalem is the staging of the prophecy of Zechariah: "Be joyful, O daughter of Zion! Shout for joy, O daughter of Jerusalem! Behold thy King cometh unto thee, just and victorious. He is humble and rideth upon an ass—upon an ass and the foal of an ass" (Zech. ix. 9).

Doubtless Matthew has exaggerated (xxi. 8) in speaking of a great multitude who acclaimed Jesus. Mark has the Greek word which may signify "some," and it is probable that it was solely from the little band who accompanied Jesus that the ovation came.

The incident must have passed almost unobserved, and this it is which explains the absence of any allusion to it either in the contests of Jesus with the Scribes and Pharisees or in the account of His trial. Jesus was inspired by the idea of the humble and gentle Messiah which He found in Zechariah, and so He organized His entry into the Holy City to make of it the fulfillment of the prophet's words.

The purification of the Temple, as recounted in Mark, rests upon the contrast of two prophetic texts—that of Isa. lvi. 7, which portrays the Temple as a house of prayer for all nations, and that of Jer. vii. 11, which accused the Jews of having made of it a den of thieves. To grant that Jesus was more impressed by these two texts, and forced to act by the words in the Psalm (lxix. 10), "The zeal for Thine house hath eaten me up," which the fourth Gospel (ii. 17) quotes in reference, is more natural than to suppose that these texts have only been remarked and illustrated by tradition.[26] The reply of Jesus to the adjuration of the high priest, "Ye shall see the Son of man seated at the right hand of power and coming upon the clouds of heaven" (Mark xiv. 62; cp. Matt. xxvi. 64 and Luke xxii. 69), is inspired directly from Daniel (vii. 13). This reply is no creation of tradition, but an authentic declaration of Jesus, for the idea of resurrection upon the third, or after three days (current in primitive Christianity), is not found in it. What is found is the idea of the return upon the clouds of heaven—an idea doubtless often met with in the most ancient Church, but which was never separated from faith in the resurrection.

Finally we shall cite a last example characteristic of the influence of the Old Testament on Jesus Himself. At the moment He was about to expire upon the cross He gave expression to the despair filling His soul by the sentence borrowed from Psa. xxii. "My God! My God! why hast Thou forsaken Me?" and the words were spoken in Aramean (Mark xv. 34 and Matt. xxvi. 40). Although it is not possible to know—given the absence of friends or disciples of Jesus from the foot of the cross—how the memory of these words could have been preserved, we are unable to see in them a creation of Christian tradition. Indeed, they express an idea (that of Jesus abandoned by God) which is quite opposed to the way the ancient Church conceived the relations between Jesus and God. Tradition may have preserved such a phrase, but it is impossible to imagine that it invented it. John has not repeated it, and Luke himself has replaced this exclamation of despair by a declaration of perfect and filial abandonment to the divine hand: "Father, into Thy hands I commend My spirit" (xxiii. 46).

IV. FULFILLMENT OF PROPHECIES DISCOVERED AFTER THE EVENT

There is still a third series of facts to examine. These are the facts in which the correspondence of the Gospel record with the Old Testament has only been noticed "a posteriori" during a secondary stage of the Gospel tradition. Its discovery took place during the course of the search for proofs drawn from the Old Testament, which the necessities of apologetic defense at an early date imposed upon the preachers of the Gospel. In these cases also the concordance of history with prophecy is not a proof of their nonhistorical character. The agreement, besides, most frequently only extends to general features, and possesses nothing very characteristic.

Matthew is particularly given to recognizing the fulfillment of prophecies in the Gospel history. In the cures made by Jesus at Capernaum (viii. 16, 17) he finds the accomplishment of the words of Isaiah (liii. 4): "He took upon Himself our infirmities and bore the burden of our diseases." (In the way Matthew cites this passage of Isaiah there is no trace of expiatory or substitutionary suffering.) The cures of the demoniacs also fulfill Isaiah (xlii. 1–4). The theory of parables[27] is based upon Isa. vi. 9, 10 and upon Psa. lxxviii. 2—texts which are not cited by Mark in this connection.

Sometimes it is at a period prior to the composition of Mark's Gospel that the interpretation of history by prophecy is made. This is the case, for instance, in the application of the prophecy of Isaiah (xl. 3) to John the Baptist (see Mark i. 3; Matt. iii. 3; Luke iii. 4; John i. 23), or that of Malachi (iii. 1) (see Mark i. 2; Matt. xi. 10; Luke vii. 27).

It is naturally to the history of the Passion (the first part of the Gospel history which may have been compiled, and that which manifestly had the greatest importance for Christians) that it was specially sought to apply prophetic interpretation.

It frequently happens that a text from the prophets or the Psalms describes a situation of a fairly general character—for instance, that of the righteous man surrounded by enemies who puts his trust in God and is cruelly maltreated. We should not be able, however, to conclude from the comparisons made by the primitive Church between these facts and the sufferings of Jesus that the idea itself of these sufferings was found in the Psalms or the prophets. The passage is familiar in which Plato paints the lot of the persecuted upright man, maltreated and finally nailed to the cross (Plato, *Republic*). No one, however, would dream of deriving the history of the Passion from the text of the *Republic*. The Christians who read the Old Testament with the conviction that the history of Jesus was foreshadowed there did not fail to note that what was said of the persecuted righteous man applied admirably to Jesus. Their attention had been particularly drawn to Psa. xxii., of which Jesus upon the cross had cited a verse. They did not fail to emphasize in the records which they gave of the Passion the similitudes—in their eyes providential—which they discovered therein.

A very simple criterion enables us to recognize these harmonies established a posteriori and to distinguish them from those which are explicable as history evolved from a prophecy. In the latter the concordance is perfect, starting from the oldest accounts, and it is generally emphasized by a quotation. On the other hand, when the harmony between the prophecy and the story has only been recognized after the fact, as a rule it is only by degrees that it has gained precision. It is possible to follow the progress of the assimilation by comparing the various forms of the tradition with each other. One example will illustrate our point. Mark (xv. 24) states that after Jesus had been crucified the soldiers who had carried out the sentence shared His garments among them, drawing lots for them.[28] In ancient times the clothing of the victims belonged to the executioners[29]; there is, therefore, in the detail given nothing out of the ordinary, and the first narrators who related it merely desired to illustrate their story by a concrete detail. Later on it was observed that in Psa. xxii. the righteous man persecuted had said: "They parted my garments among them and drew lots for my vesture"; and thus had a detail of the story of the Passion been prophesied by the psalmist. Matthew, who, as we have recalled, attached so much importance to the realization of the prophecies in the Gospel story, had not yet remarked this concordance, since he makes no reference to the psalm.[30] The fourth evangelist has not only noticed and emphasized the words of the psalmist, but what is more, referring the two parallel expressions of the psalm to two different actions, he has made a distinction between the drawing of lots for the robe[31] and the sharing of the garments, justifying the procedure by the fact that the robe of Jesus was without any seam[32] (John xix. 23–24). Complete harmony with the prophecy only exists here at the end of the development of the record. It would have been entirely different if the episode had been inspired from the words in the psalm. The problem of the relation between prophecy and the Gospel history thus appears, when we attempt to get close to the subject, vastly more complex than the dilemma formulated by M. Reinach would assume.

V. THE CRUCIFIXION

Let us now leave aside the problem of the general relation between history and prophecy in order to examine the essential thesis stated by M. Reinach[33] and endorsed by M. Couchoud.[34] Their thesis is that in Psa. xxii the idea of the crucifixion is found, and particularly in verse 17, as given in the Septuagint version: "A crowd of dogs encircled me; a band of malefactors surrounded me. They pierced my hands and my feet."[35]

If this passage of the psalmist were really the source of the belief in the crucifixion of the Messiah, it is surprising that it has not been cited in connection with the event before the time of Justin Martyr.[36] But this is not all, nor is it even the essential point. If we look at the totality of the tradition we find that the Psa. xxii was first applied to Jesus in an Aramean context, since Mark (xv. 34) and Matthew (xxvii. 46) relate that it was in Aramean that Jesus when on the cross cried aloud: "Eloi! Eloi! Lama Sabachthanei"—that is, "My God! My God! why hast thou forsaken Me?"[37] Now, in the Hebraic text of the psalm no allusion to the crucifixion is to be discovered. The Palestinian tradition know of no interpretation which referred to it, since Aquila, Symmachus and Jerome have translated by "they have bound" the words which the Septuagint has rendered by "they have pierced." It was, therefore, only at a secondary stage of the evolution of the tradition that it was possible to discover in this psalm a passage relating to the punishment of the cross.

Would it have been discovered if it had not been known in advance that it must have been there—that is, if the very idea of the crucifixion had not been anterior to the interpretation of the psalm? MM. Reinach and Couchoud have no doubt of it. The reading of the psalm does not appear to confirm their opinion. In its entirety Psa. xxii is the cry of anguish from a man surrounded by enemies and threatened from every quarter. His situation seems desperate, but notwithstanding he still hopes and places his confidence in God. He recalls the deliverance formerly accorded by Jehovah: "Thou dost inhabit the sanctuary. Thou art the glory of Israel. In thee did our fathers trust. They had confidence and Thou didst deliver them. They cried unto Thee and were saved. They put their trust in Thee and were not deceived" (verses 4–6). In the verses which follow (7–9) the wretched man describes his misery, and then gives his reasons to hope: "Yea, it is Thou who hast brought me forth from the womb of my mother. . . . Go not far from me, for I am in tribulation. Come nigh unto me, for there is none to help me."[39] (See verses 10–12.)

After the verses 13–19, which describe the situation of the afflicted one, there comes an invocation to Jehovah: "But Thou, Jehovah, be not far from me! Thou art my strength; hasten to help me! Deliver my life from the sword. My only Good,[40] (deliver me) from the dog.[41] Save me from the jaw of the lion." (See verses 20–22.)

The psalm ends in the praise of Jehovah, who has delivered the one who called upon Him: "I will proclaim Thy name unto my brethren, and will praise Thee in the midst of the congregation. Ye who fear Jehovah praise Him. . . . Let all the race of Israel tremble before Him. For He has not spurned nor rejected the prayer of the afflicted; neither has He turned away His face from him" (verses 23–25).

If the desire had been to interpret in one narrative the subject matter of the psalm, one would have spoken of an afflicted man threatened by his enemies, but whom God marvelously protects from their assaults. Without doubt it may be understood that the deliverance means the resurrection, and this is what Messianic exegesis has done. But would this interpretation be given unless the reading of this psalm was begun with the conviction that in it was related the story of the death and resurrection of Jesus? Besides, do the words "they have pierced my hands and my feet" constitute a very distinct allusion to the crucifixion? When the cross is referred to, there are brought into prominence the two notions of hanging and exposure on the cross. The fixing of hands and feet by means of nails did not itself cause death—it was only an accessory to the punishment. Furthermore, it is by no means certain that the hands of the victim were always fixed by nails; as for the feet, it is more doubtful still. The archæologist, Victor Schultze, writes: "As regards the means employed (the cross properly so called), stake or gibbet, and for the method of attaching the victim thereto, the executioners seem to have had the greatest liberty allowed. Ropes alone were used, or ropes and nails. In these latter cases sometimes the hands only, and sometimes hands and feet, were fixed by nails."[42] Dom Leclercq, whom no one will suspect of treating tradition with lack of respect, writes: "The condemned approached the gibbet, to which he was bound, his hands on the crosspiece and his feet placed upon a small board." As for nails, the learned Benedictine does not even mention them.[43] In fact, the most ancient Gospel tradition makes no mention of nails. There is a reference to them for the first time in the Johannine account of the Resurrected One,[44] Thomas having said: "Unless I see in His hands[45] the marks of the nails, and unless I put my hand into His side, I will not believe." Jesus invites him to put his finger into His hands and his hand into His (Jesus') side (John xx. 25–27). The wounds in the hands appear then, at the same phase of the tradition as the wound in the side— in other words, as one of the latest elements of the Johannine narrative.[46] There is also a reference to nails in the hands found in the

Gospel of Peter (xxi) but no mention of nails in the feet is found before Justin Martyr (*Apol.,* i. 35).[47]

If the history of the Passion had as its principal source a passage where it is a question of pierced hands and feet, it would be very strange, it must be admitted, that no mention of nails in the hands is found before the fourth evangelist[48] nor of nails in the feet before Justin Martyr.[49]

From these considerations it cannot be admitted that the story of the crucifixion has been drawn from verse 17 of Psa. xxii. It is only after the event that this text was related to the story of the cross. As for the fifty-third chapter of Isaiah, which has so greatly influenced Christian thought and piety, it cannot either be considered as one of the sources of the idea of the death of the Messiah and of the accounts dealing with it. Let us first of all remember what has already been pointed out, that it was only after the beginning of the Christian era, and under conditions which do not permit us to exclude a priori the possibility of the influence of Christian ideas, that this chapter was interpreted as relating to the Messiah. In several passages of the New Testament it inspired the interpretation given of the death of Christ, either by supplying the terms employed as in 1 Pet. ii. 22–25, or in Acts viii. 32, etc., where the instructions given by Philip to the Ethiopian queen's eunuch take the form of a commentary upon Isa. liii. 7, 8, or, again, where this text has inspired in a more general way the formulas employed in John i. 29–36, Rom. iv. 25, and 1 Cor. xv. 3. In all these passages, of which several are of a fairly recent date, it is not a question of the fact of the death of Christ, but of its significance. In Paul's own writings Isa. liii. 1 is only expressly cited in Rom. x. 16, not in reference to the death of Christ, but to the opposition against Christian preaching.[50] Elsewhere it has been remarked (by Schweitzer) that the ideas of Paul cannot be explained as due to the influence of the fifty-third chapter of Isaiah, because this passage develops the idea of the value of the sufferings of the servant of Jehovah, while Paul attributes a redeeming character not to the sufferings, but to the death of Christ.

With regard to the influence of this chapter of Isaiah upon the narratives of the Passion, we have seen that it is very limited. It inspired the declaration of Jesus before His arrest: "This that is written must yet be accomplished in Me. And He was reckoned among the transgressors" (Luke xxii. 37), and also in Luke the intercession of Jesus for His executioners (xxiii. 34; cp. with Isa. liii. 12).

VI. CHRIST THE PASCHAL LAMB

M. Couchoud thinks, indeed, that the idea of the paschal lamb exercised a profound influence on the genesis of the tradition concerning the death of Jesus. The identification of Jesus with the paschal lamb is, in fact, current in ancient Christianity. It is very old, since it is already found in the first Epistle to the Corinthians. The apostle addresses the faithful, exhorting them to be pure, and in referring to those guilty of incest he points out the danger to which the Church will expose herself by allowing the leaven of wickedness, liable to corrupt the whole, to subsist within her. It is therefore necessary, he says, to purge out thoroughly the old leaven,[51] and to celebrate the feast[52] in purity and in truth. "For Christ our passover is sacrificed for us" (1 Cor. v. 7).

Let us first observe that if the assimilation of the death of Christ to the sacrifice of the lamb was already current—and how could it have been otherwise if it was the primary nucleus of tradition?—it would not be easy to understand the precision of the explanation that the lamb was Christ. The Corinthians would have well known, without Paul being obliged to tell them expressly who this paschal lamb was of whom he wished to speak. The whole passage is figurative; it contains nothing to show that Paul conceived the death of Christ under the category of the paschal lamb or of any other Levitical sacrifice other than as a simple illustration.[53] It is merely an elucidation, for it is not as a sacrifice, but as a juridical condemnation, that Paul interprets the death of Christ in his doctrine of redemption.

The assimilation of Christ to the paschal lamb is also found, but in conditions which indicate the influence of yet other ideas, in the Johannine formula "the lamb of God, which taketh away the sins of the world" (John i. 29–36).

But it is in the tradition concerning the Lord's Supper that the idea of a Christian passover is specially developed. The comparison was very natural, and suggested by the date itself of the death of Jesus. There is reason (as an increasing number of critics admit) to fix this, as indicated by the fourth Gospel, at the fourteenth day of Nisan[54]—that is, upon the very day when the paschal lamb was offered in sacrifice. The conditions in which the idea of Christ the paschal lamb was developed are characteristic, and clearly show that we are in presence of an assimilation made "a posteriori." In the Synoptic Gospels the idea is developed by attributing to the last repast of Jesus the paschal character which it does not seem to have had in the primitive tradition[55]; in the fourth Gospel[56] the development of the idea is indicated in a portion belonging to the most recent stratum, where it is stated that the legs of Jesus were not broken, as in the case of the thieves, thus fulfilling the prescriptions of the Law concerning the paschal lamb.[57]

NOTES

1. Schelling, *Sämmliche Werke*, 1856, Stuttgart.
2. Salomon Reinach, *Orpheus; Le Verset 17 du Psaume xxii; Bossuet et l'argument des propheties*, etc.
3. Couchoud, *Le Mystère de Jésus*, p. 49, etc.
4. See concerning this subject the interesting studies of Weidel, also of Feigel; also compare with Nicolardot, *Les Procédés de redaction des trois premiers evangelistes*.
5. (*Dialogues* lxxvi. 6 and lxxxix. 2). Justin does not confine himself to invoking the Scriptures to fix the meaning of the death of Jesus.

He makes use of them, also the very fact of the death (see *Apol.,* i. 35), where he invokes the testimony of Psa. xxii.

6. Schürer writes that it is "impossible to deny that in the second century of our era certain Jewish circles were familiar with the idea of a Messiah suffering to expiate the sins of men."

7. Referring to the idea of the Messiah's sufferings in the period following, see Dalman. See also Volz, *Jüdische Eschatologie von Daniel bis Akiba.* It should be noted, however, that even at the period where the idea of the suffering Messiah is commonly met with in Judaism, interpretations are given to Isaiah (Chap. liii) which do not relate to the Messiah. Origen, for example, cites, in his work *Contra Celsum,* the opinion of a Jew who referred the prophecy to the Jewish people, obliged to suffer, and be dispersed in the world so that many proselytes might be won over.

8. We do not attach much importance to the idea found in a passage of the fourth book of Esdras, where it is stated that the Messiah must die after reigning 400 years. There is no question there of expiation.

9. This idea is presumed, in their primitive form, by the genealogies given by Matthew and Luke. Compare the Syraic version of Sinai of Matt. i. 1–16: "Joseph, to whom the Virgin Mary was betrothed, will beget a son." This reading is supported by certain manuscripts of the old Latin version. Neither John nor Paul make the slightest reference to a supernatural birth. (See M. Goguel, *Introd. au N.T.,* I, p. 469.)

10. The Hebrew text has a word which signifies "young woman" and not "virgin." It has no relation whatever to the Messiah. The prophecy of Isaiah relates to the deliverance of Jerusalem, besieged by the king of Syria. A sign is given to Achaz—a young woman will became enceinte, and (it is announced to the king) before the child is born and "knows how to reject evil and choose the good" (that is to say, in a very short time) "the country whose two kings thou fearest shall be abandoned."

11. By the way, he finds in the arrival of Jesus at Nazareth the fulfillment of a prophecy (ii. 23).

12. This passage is not found in Jeremiah. It is borrowed from Zechariah (xi. 12) with the addition of some details taken from Jeremiah (xviii. 2, xxxii. 6).

13. This custom, attested by the Talmud (Wünsche), may originate in a passage in Proverbs: "Give strong liquors to him who perishes and wine to him who has bitterness of soul. Let him drink and forget his poverty

and let him no more remember his pain" (Wünsche, *Neue Beiträge zur Erlänterung der Evangelien,* etc.).

14. Indeed, one cannot imagine how the Procurator, so jealous of his authority, could have recognized, even as an exceptional thing, any right of jurisdiction to Herod at Jerusalem.

15. There is, furthermore, reason to doubt the primitive character of this sentence in Luke. The verse 34 of Chapter xxiii is lacking, in fact, in certain good texts (Sinaiticus, Vaticanus, Codex Cantabrigiensis, and others), and no reason can be seen to explain its suppression.

16. The accounts of the temptation in Matthew and Luke abound with citations from the Old Testament. It is not, however, certain that they are creations of prophetic exegesis. They must evidently be taken for symbolical narratives, which leads one to consider what the influence of the Old Testament could have been upon Jesus Himself.

17. Luke (xxii. 37) certainly quotes this passage, but not directly concerning the crucifixion of the two thieves. The account we mention has been considered from antiquity as proved, that in certain manuscripts of Mark there is to be read: "Thus was fulfilled the word of the Scripture: He was numbered among the transgressors"—a version which it is impossible to consider as primitive (Mark xv. 28).

18. R. Bultmann seems to us to go too far in explaining the formation of the accounts concerning Judas to the influence of this psalm. The tradition, which plainly tends to glorify the apostles, would not have imagined the betrayal by one of them of Jesus (*Geschichte der evangelischen Tradition*).

19. John is so much aware of this importance that he expressly mentions the departure of Judas, and takes the trouble to explain why this departure did not surprise the other disciples (xiii. 27–30).

20. See Mark xv. 29; Matt. xxvii. 39; Luke xxiii. 35.

21. In the Gospel of Peter (xvi) it is evidently with the object of magnifying the sufferings of Jesus that He is made to drink vinegar mixed with gall.

22. The evangelist seems to think of this passage in Psa. xxii. 16: "My strength is dried up like clay and my tongue cleaves to the palate."

23. Perhaps it is convenient to mention, to complete these remarks, certain rather superficial resemblances which the evangelists do not appear to have noticed—for example, the false witnesses at the trial of Jesus (Psa. xxvii. 12, xxxv. 11, cix. 2). This is a detail which naturally had

its place in the narrative of the sufferings of an innocent person. We may also mention the silence of Jesus before His judges (cp. Isa. liii. 7; Psa. xxxviii. 14, 15). Besides, the silence of Jesus is not complete. Even the Gospel of Peter, which expressly lays emphasis on it, relates one remark of Jesus spoken on the cross (xix).

24. In Matthew and Luke the vision becomes an objective revelation for the people. Its evolution in John is still more advanced when the scene of the baptism is replaced by a sign given to John the Baptist, who states who it is whose coming he had announced without recognition.

25. In passing may be noted the influence of 2 Sam. vii. 14, and for the explanation of the term "well beloved" that of Isa. xlv. 4. What is said concerning the baptism may be repeated in regard to the phrase which accompanies the Transfiguration (Mark ix. 7, etc.), where the partial influence of Deut. xviii. 15 and Isa. xlv. 4 may be observed. It should, however, be noted that the history of the Transfiguration, as we possess it, appears to be the end of a fairly complex evolution.

26. It cannot be objected against the historical veracity of the incident of the purification of the Temple that the intervention of Jesus had no direct serious consequences for Him, while, nevertheless, it was a provocation offered to the Jewish authorities. The latter, indeed, could not reprove Jesus for what was a proof of zeal for the Temple. Indirectly, however, the censure of the authorities implied in the action of Jesus must have had its influence upon the measures taken against Him later.

27. The idea that the parable was a method in use by Jesus to disguise His thought from noninitiates must be regarded as a creation by tradition or by Mark (iv. 11, 12). This theory owes its origin to the idea that if Jesus was not understood it is because He did not desire to be understood. In reality the parable was a method of exposition adapted to the popular audiences to whom Jesus appealed.

28. Matthew (xxvii. 35) and Luke (xxiii. 34) say the same thing.

29. Fulda, *Das Kreuz und die Kreuzigung.*

30. One is unable, indeed, to consider as authentic the received text which adds at the end of Matthew's account, "In order that it might be fulfilled as spoken by the prophet, they parted my garments among them and drew lots for my robe." This reading is only attested by certain Western manuscripts based upon certain forms of the Latin, Syrian and Armenian versions. It is an addition which comes from John xix. 24.

31. Just as Matthew (xxi. 7), interpreting Zechariah literally, represents Jesus as riding upon an ass and on its foal as the same time (Zech. ix. 9).

32. Similar to the robe of the high priests (Josephus, *Antiquities,* iii). The seamless robe of the high priest may have its origin in the interpretation of Leviticus. It is possible the fourth evangelist may hint here at speculations analogous to those made by Philo concerning the sacerdotal robe which is assimilated to the Logos (*De profugiis,* 20).

33. Salomon Reinach, *Le Verse 17 du Psaume xxii.*

34. Couchoud, *Le Mystère de Jésus.* M. Couchoud does not seem to know M. Reinach's works, since he does not quote them.

35. The Hebrew text, very probably corrupted, runs: "A band of scoundrels prowls around me, as a lion to seize my hands and my feet." The *Bible du Centenaire* gives up the translation of the last line and has the following note: "The text runs: 'like a lion my hand and my feet,' which yields no acceptable meaning. The ancient versions run: 'they have pierced (Greek), or they have bound (Hebraic Psalmbook of Jerome), or they have insulted (second version, Aquila, Midrasch) my hands and my feet.' These read therefore 'kâ'rou,' instead of 'kâ'ari' (like a lion). This verb in any case cannot mean 'they have *pierced,*' as the current version has it."

36. Justin Martyr (1 *Apol.,* 35) is the first author who has applied Psa. xxii. 17 to the story of the Passion. In the New Testament are to be found several citations or reminiscences of this psalm; none relates either directly or indirectly to the story of the Passion. We have already pointed out the influence exerted by the psalm on certain details of the story of the crucifixion.

37. It is not possible to explain this fact as an effort of the narrator to give his account an archaic color, since the use of the Aramaic language is confirmed by the fact that the soldiers believed Jesus had invoked Elijah.

38. See Loisy, *Revue d'histoire et de littérature religieuses,* 1913.

39. That is to say, "Thou has adopted me from my birth." He who received the new-born child on his knees (whether natural or adopted father) recognized the child as his own by that fact (see Gen. 1. 23; cp. Gen. xlviii. 12 and Job iii. 12).

40. Poetical expression signifying the life, the soul (see Psa. xxxv. 17).

41. Literally, "against the hand of the dog." (This note and the two preceding it are borrowed from the *Bible du Centenaire*.)

42. Von Schultze, article "Kreuz, Kreuzigung," *Real Encyclop. Protestantische Théologie*.

43. Dom Leclercq, article "Croix," *Dict. d'Archéologie Chrétienne*, Paris, 1914. In the article "Clous," of the same dictionary, Dom Leclercq makes no reference to nails of the cross either.

44. In Luke xxiv. 39 the Resurrected One says to the disciples, frightened of His apparition, thinking they are in presence of a ghost: "See My hands and My feet. It is I—feel Me and see. A spirit has not flesh and blood as ye see I have." It is not a question of the recognition of Jesus as the crucified, but to notice that it is a real being before them.

45. This text does not speak of the feet.

46. Maurice Goguel, *Introd. au N.T.*, ii, p. 336.

47. Ficker believes he finds in a passage of the *Acta Petri cum Simone*, (in a reference to a young man, nude and bound) an allusion to the crucifixion without nails. W. Bauer remarks that the ropes do not necessarily exclude nails, and thus the importance (already dubious enough) of the passage in the *Acta Petri cum Simone* is still further diminished.

48. Not in reference to the crucifixion, but in an account of the resurrection. It is known that these have been most influenced by apologetics.

49. In the account of Jesus' burial, Mark and Luke say that the body is taken down from the cross. Matthew and John say it is taken from the cross. The Gospel of Peter alone says that the nails are removed (xxi).

50. The same text is also cited in John xii. 38, in a passage which is not put into the mouth of Jesus, but which contains the reflections of the evangelist about the failure of the ministry of Jesus.

51. As was done in Jewish homes on the 14th day of Nisan, the day of the preparation of the Passover.

52. There is no reference here to a private feast, of which there is no trace in primitive Christianity, but of the Christian life, in its entirety, inaugurated by the death of Christ. It therefore seems to us very conjectural to suppose, with Johannes Weiss and others, that this image had been suggested to Paul by the fact that he was writing about the time of the Passover Feast.

53. In Rom. iii. 24 it is, on the contrary, to the sacrifice of the feast of expiation that Paul compares the death of Christ. This duality would be

difficult to understand if the crucifixion had been deduced from the Jewish doctrine of sacrifice. It is, on the other hand, quite natural if the assimilation had been made "a posteriori."

54. Maurice Goguel, *Les Sources du recit Johannique de la Passion,* 1910.

55. *Id., L'Eucharistie.*

56. *Id., Introd. au N.T.,* ii.

57. We do not speak here of Psa. xxiv, of which Paul cites a verse in a passage (1 Cor. x. 26) where there is no question at all of the Gospel history. M. Couchoud believes that primitive Christianity had found in this psalm "the lament of the Son of God, fallen into the hands of cruel archons." What we have said above concerning the passage of 1 Cor. ii. 8 proves that this text has not the significance which M. Couchoud attaches to it.

CHAPTER X

THE GOSPEL TRADITION

I. COMPOSITION OF THE GOSPELS

The Gospel tradition is presented in the form of four narratives,[1] whose parentage is certain and whose three first members are even parallel for a considerable part of their content. Before it is possible to come to any conclusion concerning this tradition there is a question of literary history to be solved—that of the relations which these narratives have to each other.[2] It is necessary to examine the group of the first three Gospels, known as the Synoptics, and the fourth separately.[3]

The most ancient of the Synoptics is the Gospel of Mark. It must have been composed—perhaps at Rome—at a date a little later than A.D. 70. Its author seems to have been of Palestine origin, perhaps the John Mark of whom the book of Acts speaks (Acts xii. 25). It is a work of some complexity, whose author has utilized traditions of different sources, doubtless inserting them into the framework created by him.

Among these sources the two best are a collection of narratives going back to the apostle Peter, which were the echo of his missionary preaching, and a selection of discourses, the Logia, whose first origin seems very ancient, but of which Mark has borrowed relatively little, doubtless because he knew it was in the hands of readers for whom his work was designed.

Some ten years or so after its composition the Gospel of Mark seems to have undergone some revision which has not perceptibly modified its general aspect.

The Logia with which Mark was acquainted, and which he used with discretion, should in our opinion be considered rather as a collection than as a literary work well put together and arranged according to a rational plan. This collection became richer as it grew, and by that very fact more varied in character, because, as would be natural, each person inserted in it sayings and discourses attributed to Jesus of which he knew, but which had been neglected or ignored by the first editors. It is still possible to distinguish with sufficient precision three stages of the collection. The first, which no doubt is not the primitive form but only the most ancient within our reach is made up of elements of the collection which Matthew and Luke have borrowed and which appear in their versions in the same order. It is one form of this primitive stage that Mark seems to have known and made use of. The two other stages are those which Matthew on one side and Luke on the other had at their disposal. To each must be attributed not only those portions which Matthew and Luke possess in common, and are wanting in Mark, but also other portions which are only found in one of them, but belong to the same type as the portion common to both,[4] or which are in close relationship with them.[5] Some are found in the first and in the third Gospels in forms which differ too much from each other to permit of their belonging to the same source.[6]

The Gospels of Matthew and of Luke are, to put it simply, two attempts, parallel but independent of each other, to concentrate the Gospel tradition. Their authors (who appear to have worked, Luke somewhere between the years 75 and 85; and Matthew between 80 and 90) desired to write in one single work the two principal documents existing in their time upon the Gospel history: the narrative of Mark and the Logia. Furthermore, both gleaned from various subsidiary sources. Luke's aim, moreover, was to give a coherent account, complete and well arranged. His work thus shows an attempt to include narratives which originally were works of edification into the literary domain proper. Notwithstanding this, the Gospel of Luke is of the same type as those of Mark and Matthew.

The fourth Gospel must have been composed between the years 90 and 110. Although it is, like the Synoptic Gospels, an apologetic and missionary and not an historical work, it possesses certain features which are peculiar to it. It assumes that its readers not only are familiar with the Gospel tradition, but also that they have certain narratives in their hands (most probably our Synoptic Gospels) to which it frequently alludes, either by explicitly correcting them on some points or in supposing as known to its readers certain facts to which it makes no allusion itself, but which are recorded therein. The fourth evangelist did not claim to substitute his work for that of his predecessors; to a fairly large extent it would not be clearly intelligible without them; he only desired, on the basis they offered him, to develop a certain number of meditations upon themes of the Gospel history which he has inserted (a fact betraying the influence of the type created by the Synoptics) between a narrative about the opening of the ministry of Jesus and one concerning the Passion.

The objective of the fourth evangelist—essentially theological and religious—being admitted, a very delicate problem is encountered concerning the methods used by him. Some critics, like Jean Reville[7] and M. Loisy,[8] consider that all the deviations from the three first Gospels which are found in the fourth are explicable in terms of allegory and symbolism; others, like Godet,[9] and Zahn,[10] and in a less absolute manner the Father Calmes,[11] think that John, in order to correct the narratives of his predecessors, was guided by direct and personal experience. To a certain extent, however, the conservative critics agree that the souvenirs of the old apostle were somewhat vague, and that he did not distinguish with clearness between the Jesus he had followed in Galilee and Judea and the ideal Christ who lived in his heart. None of these theories seems to us to take complete account of all the somewhat complex factors of the problem. We believe that although he may not have attached great importance to historical necessities, the fourth evangelist was acquainted with data and written and oral traditions which it is impossible to reconstruct with precision, nor even to describe or date with certainty, but several of which show themselves to be excellent in comparison with the Synoptic tradition. Without having any intention to utilize historically the sources at his disposal, John had borrowed data from them; sometimes even it has happened that he has inserted some fragments in his own narrative. We should, for instance, be inclined to recognize some of these sources as evidence for the narratives which portray Jesus baptizing by the side of John (iii. 22), or coming to Jerusalem for the Feast of Tabernacles (vii. 1, etc.), or as being arrested by the cohort led by the tribune (xviii. 3–12). These data are only preserved in the fourth Gospel in a sporadic manner, and this fact is characteristic—we would be prepared even to say symbolical. It shows that the Gospel literature was not primarily interested in the history of the ministry of Jesus. It only preserved the memory because of its religious value.

II. THE GOSPEL IDEA

Luke, at the beginning of his book, tells Theophilus, to whom he dedicates it, that he had undertaken to write it to convince his friend of the certainty of the things in which he had been instructed (Luke i. 4). John also says in his conclusion that Jesus wrought many miracles besides those which he has recorded, and he continues in these words: "These have been written in order that you may believe that Jesus is the Christ, the Son of God, and, believing, may have life in His name" (xx. 31). A gospel, therefore, is before everything else, not a book of history, but a book of edification and religious teaching. History is the method of instruction; it is not an object in itself.

This is also shown by the examination of the word "gospel" itself. In the Greek Bible, if the word *euanggelia*[12] is only found in the material sense of good news,[13] the verb of the same root, *euaggelizein*, is sometimes met with—and particularly in the second book of Isaiah—having a sense which announces and prepares the way for the Christian idea of the gospel.[14] The Old Testament thus contains (at least implicitly) the idea of a gospel as the proclamation of a divine deliverance. That which invests this fact with its full significance is that the evangelists expressly portray the ministry of Jesus as the fulfillment of these prophecies.[15]

Upon Christian ground, it is with the apostle Paul that, so far as we know, there appears for the first time the word "gospel," sometimes without limitation as "the gospel," sometimes specialized as the "gospel of God," "my gospel," or the "gospel of Christ." The "gospel" in its unlimited sense is the doctrine preached by Paul, the mystery of the redemption of sinful humanity ransomed by the death and resurrection of Jesus Christ (1 Cor. xv. 1), in this sense the gospel is the power of God (Rom. i. 16). From this fundamental signification is derived another, that of the preaching of redemption (Phil. i. 7 and ii. 22). The gospel of God is the gospel which comes from God, which the apostle has been charged by Him to preach (Rom. i. 1, xv. 16, etc.). As for the phrase "gospel of Christ," this is not to be understood in the sense of the teaching given by Jesus, but in that of the teaching of which Christ is the essence[16] (1 Cor. ix. 12, etc.). The gospel, therefore, to Paul meant the preaching whose subject or content was Christ the Redeemer. This is not a history, although the historical element may have its place and be at its base. It is the same conception also found in all the other books of the New Testament outside the Gospels. The books relating the history of Jesus are called Gospels because they were composed, not in an historical or biographical, but in a missionary interest. They are books of exposition of apostolic doctrine, preaching the Christian faith. "Gospel of Jesus Christ" in Mark i. 1 does not mean a gospel preached by Jesus Christ, but a doctrine whose essence and content is Jesus Christ. The author of the Gospel is only the interpreter of the doctrine of salvation. This it is which explains the objectivity with which works of this kind are called categorically "the Gospel," and the modesty with which their presumed authors are referred to is shown by the simple phrase "according to." It was only at a relatively late period that the word "gospel" was interpreted in the sense which subsequently prevailed—that is, a book which narrated the history of Jesus.

Jesus does not appear to have used the word "gospel" Himself.[17] It is only put into His mouth by Matthew and Mark,[18] each upon two occasions (Mark xiii. 10; Matt. xxiv. 14; Mark xiv. 9; Matt. xxvi. 13). In each passage the "gospel" means not the teaching of Jesus, but the future preaching of the apostles. In each it is more than doubtful whether the word "gospel" comes from Jesus Himself. In the first case, the editors have used the word which meant in the time they wrote "Christian teaching." As for the second, there are good reasons for thinking that the portion in which it is found (the episode of the ointment at Bethany) did not form part of the most primitive deposit of the Gospel tradition, and in the solemn affirmation that the act of the woman would be narrated wherever the Gospel would be preached, there certainly seems to be a reminiscence of the period when this portion did not yet form part of the Gospel.[19]

With the Apostolic Fathers and the Apologists is seen the rise of the idea of the gospel as narrative or document alongside the idea of the gospel as a doctrine. That which we have seen concerning the meaning of the word "gospel" in the first Christian generations shows that it was not in an historical interest that the traditions concerning the life and teachings of Jesus were collected, preserved, and committed to writing. The thought of the early Christians was entirely turned toward the future and not to the past. They expected the early return of Christ, whose task was to complete the work of redemption already begun, and all interest in organization was completely foreign to their minds. In so far as they had need of an authority, they found it in the Old Testament and in the persuasion that they had been inspired and guided by the Spirit. Still, it was impossible that those who had lived in the companionship of Jesus should not carefully preserve the memory of what He had been, of what He had said and done. For them these things were a source of inspiration and an example.

When upon the morrow of the Passion a Christian theology began to form, the meditations of the disciples of Jesus were centered around an historic fact, the death of the Lord. This death contradicted the impression produced by His life and teaching, since it represented Him as if abandoned and even cursed by God. The necessity of solving this contradiction was for Christian thought the most powerful of stimulants.

Jesus, for those who had lived with Him, had been the incarnation of the highest moral authority. They had formed the habit of looking to Him, of expecting His counsel, of being inspired by His example. He, having disappeared, the moral authority of His personality did not disappear; it became transformed and attached itself to the memory of His acts and His words.

A triple interest, therefore, assured the preservation of memoirs of the Gospel history—a sentimental interest first of all. Those who had been in contact with Jesus could not let His memory fade away in their minds and hearts; in the next place there was a moral interest, the words and actions of Jesus being considered as offering or inspiring the solution of the moral and practical problems which they found facing them; finally there was a theological interest, for it was impossible to ignore what they considered the human episode of the grand drama of redemption.

At the beginning, at least, no special value was attached to the tradition preserving a coherent history of the life of Jesus. From the speculative point of view, the sole thing of importance was the simple fact of His death; from the moral point of view, the important things were the words, the acts, the attitudes in which the soul of Jesus was manifested. Thus from the beginning the Church had need of traditions concerning His life, but fragmentary memoirs were amply sufficient for her needs.

It is to this situation that the Epistles of Paul, for instance, correspond, which, as we have seen, presume the knowledge of many details of the Gospel history and the memory of many of the Master's words, but not a coherent, organic and systematic tradition about His life. Without doubt it was in a less definite form that the first evangelists found the substance of their narratives.

III. THE ABSENCE OF CHRONOLOGICAL CONSIDERATIONS

Two facts are thus understood which strike one at once when the Gospel tradition and the conditions in which it is presented are studied. The first is that we have neither in the canonical tradition nor in that which is extracanonical any precise indication concerning the times in which the facts of Gospel history took place; the second is that the plan upon which this history is arranged in the Synoptics [20] is artificial. It was arbitrarily created by the first evangelist to group together memoirs which tradition furnished him as isolated units.

It will be convenient to examine these two considerations in succession. As regards the appearance of Jesus in history, Paul merely says that God had sent Him in the fullness of time (Gal. iv. 4). This is a dogmatic concept which needs to be kept in mind as meaning that it was in the last period of the history of the world (that world to which Paul had the sentiment of belonging) that the Gospel history is to be assigned. This at once shows that the absence of all chronological details in Paul's writings must not be interpreted as a proof that in his thought the drama of redemption was devoid of all contact with historical reality. The close relationship which he establishes between the death of Christ and His return, which he believed to be imminent, also proves that it could only have been at a quite recent period that the Gospel drama had taken place.

It should be added that Paul had no reason to repeat in his Epistles what he doubtless on frequent occasions had expounded in his oral teachings concerning the death of Jesus.

In the Gospels of Mark, Matthew and John the date of the death of Jesus is (indirectly, at any rate) indicated by the mention of Pilate, although the narrators did not mention him to give any chronological indication, but because of the part he had played in the history of Jesus.[21] The first writer in whose work there appears a real chronological sense is Luke, who indicates by a series of synchronisms (iii. 1, 2) the period at which the ministry of John the Baptist began. The value of the data which he gives is a question of small importance. The interesting thing is that he had considered it necessary to give them.[22]

The chronology of the life of Jesus presents in later tradition a singular vacillation. Certain authors—for instance, M. Salomon Reinach—have drawn from this an argument against the historical character of the tradition. Let us see how matters stand.

Irenæus (*Hær.*, ii. 22–25) declares, basing his statement on the fourth Gospel and on the presbyters who had known John—that is to say upon the work of Papias[23]—as admitted by all critics, that Jesus died not at the age of thirty, but at the age of fifty,[24] and it is certainly Irenæus who is the authority for writers attesting the same belief.[25] Irenæus is familiar with the canon of the four Gospels, and attributes to it an absolute value, leaving no place for the Apocryphal Gospels.[26] It is, therefore, highly improbable that he was inspired by a tradition differing from theirs. His ideas originate in a particular interpretation of the Gospel data. Corssen has observed that in the very passage of which we are speaking Irenæus declares that after His baptism Jesus came three times to Jerusalem for the Passover. In this statement he is in flagrant contradiction with himself. Two indications have been found in Irenæus which put us upon the track of the explanation sought for. In the first place, in the same passage where he gives his opinion as to the age of Jesus at death, Irenæus says that He must have sanctified by His death all the periods of human life (*Hær., xxii*). This is a dogmatic observation which scarcely fits in with the authority of the Gospel traditions which he recognizes. In the second place, Irenæus (ii. 22–25) relies on the authority of the fourth Gospel and the tradition of the presbyters who had known John—that is, upon Papias. It is possible to trace the exegetical process by which the idea of Jesus dying at the age of fifty years has been extracted from the fourth Gospel. In John viii. 57 the Jews say to Jesus, "Thou art not yet fifty years old." There is evidently here no indication as to the real age of Jesus at the time, but Irenæus, and no doubt the presbyters before him, being desirous of representing Jesus as sanctifying the age at which it was supposed that a man attained the plenitude of his powers, have understood this passage to suggest that Jesus was nearly fifty years old.[27] One other text of the Gospel may have suggested or confirmed this interpretation. In the episode of the purification of the Temple the Jews asked Jesus to justify by a miracle the authority which He had claimed in expelling the traders. He replied: "Destroy this temple, and I will rebuild it in three days" (ii. 19), which remark, observes the evangelist, did not refer to the Temple of Jerusalem, but to the body of Jesus (ii. 21). The Jews retorted: "Forty-six years was this Temple in building, and Thou wilt rebuild it in three days!" (ii. 20). It only required to apply the same symbolism to this reply of the Jews as to the declaration of Jesus to arrive at the same idea that Jesus was forty-six years old at the time of the incident of the purification of the Temple.

There is, therefore, in the work of Irenæus no tradition on behalf of which it is possible to criticize that of the Gospels. There are only speculations inspired by allegorical principles and dogmatic considerations. The opinion of Irenæus and of those who followed him cannot be interpreted as the proof of the existence of doubts and hesitations concerning the current tradition. And it is deducing from very inconsistent premises conclusions singularly unwarranted to suppose, with M. Salomon Reinach, that a tradition which represented Jesus as dying in the reign of Claudius—that is, after A.D. 41—could not originally have mentioned Pontius Pilate, who was disgraced in A.D. 36, for this presumes that the most ancient narrative of the Passion must have contained no mention of the name of the Roman Procurator. The point it is necessary to remember about traditions like those of Irenæus is that during a long period the indifference was maintained which the first generation had shown to everything concerning Jesus which only possessed biographical interest.

IV. THE PLAN OF THE GOSPELS

The same conclusion follows also from the fact that during the generation after the death of Jesus interest was centered only in isolated souvenirs, without any conscious attempt to form them into a coherent group, in harmony with the real development of facts. It is this which is shown by the character of the setting of the Synoptic Gospels.

The Gospel of Mark is composed of an introduction and of four portions of which the first may be subdivided into eight sections.

The introduction consists of three brief accounts of John the Baptist, the baptism, and the temptation of Jesus (i. 1–13). The first part (i. 14 to viii. 26) gives a picture of the Galilean ministry of Jesus and of His preaching of the Gospel to the multitudes. The return to Galilee, the calling of the first disciples, the journey to Capernaum, the itinerant preaching and the healing of the lepers, make up a first section which portrays the activity of Jesus as welcomed by the crowd (i. 14–45). Then comes a series of conflicts which take place between Jesus and the Pharisees, ending in a cabal between these and the Herodians who wish to destroy Him (Chap. iii). It is the second section which immediately after the opening success portrays the difficulties, ever increasing, until the final drama. The third section is a kind of interlude, Jesus not allowing Himself to be discouraged by the opposition He encounters, but continuing His ministry of healing while He prepares the future by the institution of the apostolate (iii. 7–19). With the fourth section (iii. 20–35) the conflict becomes more acute. Even the kinsmen of Jesus accuse Him of being out of His senses, and the Pharisees declare that He is possessed by Beelzebub. The fifth section gives a specimen of the teaching of Jesus, consisting of three parables, accompanied by explanations and theoretical reflections. In this section the evangelist explains the failure of Jesus already announced in preceding sections. Being unwilling to admit that this was not intentional, he develops the theory of the hardening of men's hearts consciously provoked, Jesus using parables designed to conceal His real thought from those who were not initiates (iv. 1–34).

A sixth section (iv. 35 to vi. 6) shows Jesus quitting the Galilean territory to begin His action on pagan soil at Gerasa. He is not, to speak exactly, ill received, but the time for acting upon the non-Jews has not yet come. The episode of Gerasa must be looked on as prefigurative of the Christian mission. Having returned again to Galilee, Jesus heals the daughter of Jairus and the woman with the issue of blood, then returns to Nazareth, where He is repulsed by His compatriots.

Just as after the conflicts narrated in the second section Jesus had prepared for the future by the institution of the apostolate, so after His rejection at Nazareth He sends forth the apostles on a mission. To this episode there is attached in a somewhat artificial way the narrative about the perplexity of Herod and retrospectively that of the death of John the Baptist (seventh section, vi. 6–30). The narratives which follow up to the close of the first part of the Gospel (eighth section, vi. 31 to viii. 26) show a very characteristic arrangement. The same episode (the multiplication, or rather the distribution, of loaves) is related twice under two forms sufficiently like one another to prevent any hesitation in recognizing in them two variants of the same theme, and it appears that the events which follow the second multiplication of loaves (the crossing of the lake, the discussion with the Jews, and the healing) correspond fairly closely with those accompanying the first. This doublet shows the importance which this part of the narrative had for tradition.

The distribution of loaves has been considered to be the anticipation of the Lord's Supper, as a supreme attempt made by Jesus to win over the people who had not been gained to His cause either by appeals or by healing.[28] The failure is manifested by the Jewish opposition, which raises after the first distribution the discussion concerning the pure and the impure, and after the second demands from Jesus a sign from heaven. Henceforward the fate of the public ministry of Jesus was sealed—failure was complete and irremediable. Jesus to some extent resigns Himself to the inevitable, and renounces all public teaching designed to win the people's support.

In the second part of the Gospel (viii. 27 to x. 52) it is solely to His disciples that Jesus addresses Himself.[29]

At the same time His teaching is about to assume a new character. It is no longer the Gospel of the Kingdom but that of the Messiah. Jesus reveals to His disciples the fate which awaits Him in Judea, and announces His resurrection to them, but they do not understand His teaching. After each of three prophecies of sufferings—which form, so to speak, the framework of this part of the Gospel (viii. 31, 32, ix. 30–32 and x. 32–34)—is placed a narrative in which the disciples' lack of intelligence is startlingly manifested. A peculiar importance as regards the arrangement of the Gospel of Mark belongs to the first passage of this second part, where the author narrates the confession of Peter near Cæsarea Philippi (viii. 27–30). Starting from this passage, the notion of the Messiahship dominates the narrative and forms the central subject of the teaching given to the apostles.

The third part of the Gospel begins with the entry of Jesus into Jerusalem, and ends at the time when the Jews are preparing to form a plot against Him (xi. 1–13, 37). This portion contains an account of the discussions between Jesus and the Jews and the teaching given to the disciples. The narratives are arranged in well-marked progression. After Jesus, by His solemn entry into Jerusalem (xi. 1–11) and by the purification of the Temple, has, so to speak, taken up His position, there is placed a series of discussions which accentuate the conflict and make it a definite thing. This is shown by the invectives against the Pharisees, which are the last words of Jesus pronounced in public (xii. 38–40). After this the evangelist narrates the teachings given by Jesus to His disciples touching final things (xiii. 1–37). This is a kind of testament which He bequeaths them. One single episode of this portion of the Gospel presents a character different from the others: it is that of the widow's mite (xii. 41–44), which the evangelist has placed here because the act, taking place in the Temple, could not be well put elsewhere.

The narratives of the Passion, which form the last portion of the Gospel (xiv. 1–16), are so intimately inter-related that it is unnecessary to show that they form one complete group. They are linked with each other in a necessary way, beginning with the plot of the Jews up to the arrival of the women at the sepulcher, which they find empty.[30]

The plan upon which the Gospel of Mark is arranged has a triple character: it is psychological, since it rests upon the idea of the development of the Jewish opposition and the disciples' lack of intelligence; it is logical and chronological, since it shows in the events the reaction after the welcome given to Jesus; it is geographical, since it divides the history of Jesus into three great periods: Galilean ministry, itinerant ministry, and Jerusalem ministry.

It is on the plan adopted by Mark that the narratives of Matthew and Luke also rest, and nothing perhaps shows better than this fact the dependence of the first and third evangelists upon the second. Both, however, have been obliged to modify to a certain extent the arrangement adopted by Mark so as to enable them to introduce into their narratives the elements they wished to add to those given by him.

In the immense majority of cases the portions borrowed by Matthew from Mark are found in his work in the same order. As in Mark, the account is divided into two portions by the episode of Cæsarea Philippi. But in the first portion Matthew has not reproduced the somewhat elaborate composition which we find in Mark. This is not because he has represented the order of events differently, but the ordering of Mark's work was much too compact to permit the insertion of elements which Matthew desired to add.

The Gospel of Matthew opens by an introduction (i. 1 to iv. 11) which, in addition to what is given in the Gospel of Mark, contains the gospel of the infancy, but in a somewhat detailed way as regards John the Baptist and the temptation.

The account of the Galilean ministry (iv. 2 to xvi. 12) is divided into four sections. The first (iv. 2 to ix. 34) is formed, after a short preamble, by two pictures: the preaching by words (v. 1 to vii. 29) and the preaching by deeds (viii. 1 to ix. 34), which illustrate the two terms, "preaching and healing," employed in iv. 23 to characterize the activity of Jesus. The Sermon on the Mount (v. 1 to vii. 29) has been inserted as a specimen of the teaching of Jesus at the place in Mark's Gospel where for the first time the teaching had been referred to[31] (Mark i. 21, 22). The picture of the activity of Jesus consists of a series of portions borrowed either from Mark or from other sources; it is arranged in such a way as to illustrate the reply of Jesus to the question of the Baptist: "The blind see, the lame walk, the lepers are cleansed, the deaf hear, the dead are raised" (xi. 5). This picture is drawn with a certain objectivity in the sense that the evangelist does not relate the impression which the acts of Jesus produced.

It is in the second section (ix. 35 to x. 42) that the welcome given to Jesus is shown in relief. In the first place, by anticipation on the order followed by Mark, we have the sending forth of the disciples on a mission, and reproduced according to the Logia and not according to Mark, the discourse which accompanies their departure. It is specially the idea of the difficulties that the missionaries will encounter and the hostility which will assail them which is developed (ix. 35 to x. 42); then comes, after a note about the itinerant preaching (xi. 1), the question of the messengers sent by John the Baptist to Jesus, followed by the testimony of Jesus to John, the phrase about the Kingdom of God suffering violence, and the parable of the children (xi. 2–19). These portions show the forerunner himself losing faith. The words concerning John the Baptist are immediately followed by the malediction pronounced upon the unbelieving Galilean towns, and, whether it be that the evangelist did not wish (xi. 20–24) to terminate this portion by a note exclusively negative, or whether he merely copied the arrangement of his source, there comes next the doxology upon the revelation made unto infants (xi. 25–27) and the call to the weary and heavy laden (xi. 28–30). In Chapter xii Matthew takes up again the thread of the narrative of Mark with the two accounts about the disputes concerning the Sabbath (xii. 1–14) and a general notice about the healings accomplished by Jesus and of the crowds who came to Him (xii. 15–21). Still following Mark, he relates next the accusation of possession by evil spirits and the reply of Jesus (xii. 22–50), but in a more developed form. Then comes the chapter of parables (xiii. 1–52), which, although in a manner less obvious than in Mark, has also the character of a theoretical reflection upon the failure of Jesus.[32] The rejection of Jesus at Nazareth brings us to the end of this section (xiii. 53–58). For the third section (perplexity of Herod and death of John the Baptist, xiv. 1–13) and for the fourth (the group of the multiplication of loaves, xiv. 13 to xvi. 12) the narrative of Matthew is exactly parallel to that of Mark.[33]

In the second part of the Gospel, extending from Peter's confession to the healing of the blind men at Jericho (xvi. 13 to xx. 34), Matthew follows very closely the narrative of Mark. In no detail has he any different order. He confines himself to omitting two short passages (Mark ix. 38–41 and 49, 50) and to adding some others.[34]

The relationship of Matthew's narrative with that of Mark in the third part, which deals with the Jerusalem ministry, is the same as in the second. One single passage has not been introduced, namely that of the widow's mite (Mark xii. 41–44). On the other hand, Matthew has added some portions. In the account of the Passion and the resurrection, which constitutes the fourth and last part of the Gospel (xxvi. 1 to xxviii. 7), there is neither omission nor transposition to be noted, but only the addition of certain elements of clearly secondary importance.

Finally, Matthew continues his narrative beyond the point at which (for us) Mark stops; he finishes his work by the narrative of the apparition in Galilee and of the mission given by Jesus to His disciples (xxviii. 8–20). It is thus only in the first part of his narrative that Matthew diverges sensibly from the arrangement adopted by Mark. This he does for two reasons—to incorporate in his narrative the substance of the Logia and to group in compact groups the similar elements furnished by either of the two sources at his disposal.

The introduction of new matter has not led in Luke's Gospel, as in that of Matthew, to a transformation or retouching of the primitive plan. The new matter is, generally speaking, intercalated in the structure of the second Gospel. Luke opens his work with a dedication to Theophilus, in which he explains the object he has in view (i. 1–4). Then comes the introduction (i. 5 to iv. 13), consisting of two elements, a gospel of the infancy differing from that of Matthew (i. 5 to ii. 52) and the narratives concerning John the Baptist, the baptism and temptation of Jesus, this last narrative being preceded by a genealogy (iii. 1 to iv. 13). The first part of the Gospel of Luke contains the account of the Galilean ministry of Jesus (iv. 14 to ix. 17), arranged somewhat differently from the account in the second Gospel. After a short reference to the itinerant preaching (iv. 14, 15), there comes the scene of the preaching of Jesus at Nazareth (iv. 16–30), which anticipates a story that Mark gives a little later. Luke has here made a displacement, for the episode at Nazareth supposes continuous and organized activity of Jesus at Capernaum (iv. 23), as will be recorded in iv. 31. The displacement gives to the opening of the ministry of Jesus a dramatic character, and illustrates two dominating ideas, the first being that the Gospel was the accomplishment of prophecy; the second that it was not welcomed.

After the scene of Nazareth, Luke gives the narratives about Jesus at Capernaum (iv. 31–41), the flight of Jesus to a desert place (iv. 42–43), the itinerant preaching in Galilee (iv. 44)—told more briefly than in Mark, certain elements of his account being taken from elsewhere—and the healing of the lepers (v. 12–16).

These incidents follow in the same order as in Mark, but before the last of the series Luke inserts the episode of the miraculous draft of fishes (v. 1–11), which replaces the more simple narrative of the vocation of the disciples found in Mark. The picture of the early activity of Jesus is followed, as in Mark, by a second section, wherein a series of conflicts already announces the failure of the preaching of Jesus (v. 17 to vi. 11). The third section (apostleship and healing, vi. 12–19) again reproduces the arrangement of Mark. In what follows there is found, on the contrary, nothing which corresponds to the fourth section of Mark (accusation of madness and possession).[35] On the other hand, Luke inserts here two sections which are peculiar to him; the fourth consists of a discourse on the plain (vi. 20–49), which is the equivalent, although in a less well-developed form, of the Sermon on the Mount given by Matthew. The fifth section consists of a series of passages lacking in Mark, and of which a portion only is found, again in Matthew (Luke vii. 1 to viii. 3). These portions are fairly dissimilar, and it is difficult to see why they were inserted at this place. It may be supposed that Luke, who seems to make it a point to interrupt as rarely as possible the thread of Mark's narrative, has made use of what he had left out to place at the end of the discourses of Jesus a series of fresh narratives.

The sixth section of Luke (viii. 4–18) corresponds to the section of parables in Mark, but with certain simplifications. In the seventh

(viii. 19–56) and eighth sections (ix. 1–9) Luke only diverges from Mark upon secondary points. The ninth and last section of the first part shows, when compared with Mark's narrative, considerable simplification. It only contains the narrative of the return of the disciples and the first multiplication of loaves (ix. 10–17). In the second part of the Gospel, which opens with the Messianic confession of Peter, Luke begins by following very closely Mark's narration as far as the episode of the miracles worked in the name of Jesus[36] (ix. 18–50). Then from ix. 50 as far as xviii. 14 he abandons the narrative of Mark in order to record a whole series of episodes peculiar to himself, and which constitute a third part of his Gospel. Jesus appears in this to be constantly on the road; and although the geographical development is not distinctly marked, He appears to be going towards Jerusalem. Analysis shows that this account (which is frequently called, by the way by no means too correctly, the narrative of the journey or ministry in Perea) is not homogeneous.[37] Whether the subject under consideration be the questioners of Jesus, the circumstances supposed attending each episode, or the transitions between them, one becomes convinced that the successive narrations forming this part of the Gospel have no real unity, but that they have been borrowed from various sources and grouped together artificially. It appears as though Luke had interrupted the narrative of Mark at a point chosen in an arbitrary manner in order to insert a series of passages which he did not wish to lose, but which he did not know where to place. In xviii. 15 he resumes the thread of Mark's narrative exactly at the point where he had left it, and the fourth part of his narrative (xviii. 15 to xix. 27) corresponds almost exactly with Mark to the end of the second part of the latter.[38] The account of the Jerusalem ministry, which forms the fifth part of the Gospel (xx. 28 to xxi. 38) is also fairly similar to that of Mark. Luke omits the curse upon the fig tree, and gives no division into days, stating only at the end of his narrative that Jesus taught during the daytime in the Temple and at night he retired to the Mount of Olives.[39]

The sixth part, consisting of the account of the Passion and resurrection (xxii. 1 to xxiv. 53), is in its general arrangement sufficiently close to the corresponding part of Mark's narration, but from many points of view it presents a rather special physiognomy owing to the disposition or the form of certain of the more important narratives of which it consists. There is here presented a problem peculiar to the point of view of the sources which Luke has followed in his narrative of the Passion. The account of the resurrection consists, after the discovery of the empty tomb, of the apparitions to the two disciples upon the road to Emmaus and to the apostles assembled at Jerusalem. This last account is followed by that of the Ascension (xxiv. 1–53). It should be noted that Luke knows only of Judaic apparitions. It follows from the preceding analysis that the plan of Luke's work has no independent value of its own. It is a mere enlargement of that of Mark.

The fact that neither Matthew nor Luke have attempted to arrange their narrative of the life of Jesus otherwise than Mark had done, and that they confined themselves to retouching the arrangement adopted by their predecessor, where it was necessary to permit the introduction of new matter, is in itself significant. It proves that Matthew and Luke, who had at their disposal sources of information which Mark had not, found nothing therein which supplied them with information concerning the arrangement and the order of the facts. This premier observation is already unfavorable to the hypothesis according to which the development of Mark's narrative corresponded to the real course of events.

The problem, however, can only be solved by direct examination of Mark's plan. We shall confine ourselves here to some remarks which do not pretend to exhaust the problem of the life of Jesus, but which should at least serve to explain the character of Mark's plan. The first remark will bear on the notion of the Messianic secret. The episode of Cæsarea Philippi (viii. 27–30), in which Peter recognizes Jesus as the Christ, and the story of the Transfiguration (ix. 2–8), which serves as celestial confirmation for him, form the pivot around which is articulated the entire construction of the Gospel. From this time onward the disciples being prepared to receive this quasi esoteric teaching, Jesus attempts to make them understand the necessity of the sufferings and death of the Messiah. Does this construction of Mark answer to the real development of the facts? There is reason to doubt it. There are found in the first part of the Gospel passages which clearly present Jesus, not, doubtless, as the Messiah in the traditional sense, but at least as One sent from God, as the Son of man—that is, some one charged by God to accomplish the work of redemption. We shall not, to establish this, refer to the account of the baptism (i. 9–11), where there is an express Messianic declaration, since it seems that originally it was related as a vision of Jesus and not a revelation accorded to the people or to the disciples.[40]

But it must be asked if episodes such as the calling of the disciples (i. 16–20), the institution of the apostleship (iii. 13–19) and the sending forth of the disciples on mission (vi. 6–13) do not assume that the narrator had the idea that He who acted with such authority must, to be thus obeyed, have revealed who He was to those whom He chose and sent forth? Certain narratives, such as the healing of the paralytic (ii. 1–12), with the declaration that the Son of man has the power on earth to forgive sins (ii. 10), would have no sense if Jesus had presented Himself only as a doctor or even as a prophet. The healings of the demoniacs, and the discussion about Beelzebub connected with them, are in this connection particularly characteristic. The expulsions of demons are not, in the evangelist's eyes (and they were not for Jesus) simple acts of power and mercy—they were acts essentially Messianic. They assume, in fact, a victory gained over Satan, the prince of demons—in other words, the realization in power of the very work which was expected from the Messiah, or at least an anticipation of this victory. This is shown by the reply of Jesus when the Pharisees accuse him of casting out demons by the power of Beelzebub, the prince of demons (Mark iii. 22). Jesus replies first by reducing the argument to an absurdity. If Satan makes war upon himself, he will not be able to stand; his kingdom will come to an end (iii. 23–26). Then He gives the explanation of these expulsions, and this He does in the parable of the strong man: "No one can enter into a strong man's house and spoil his goods except he will first bind the strong man" (iii. 27). The strong man here is Satan, the prince of demons. Jesus is unable to "spoil his goods"—that is, snatch from him those whom he holds dominion over—if He has not first of all conquered him. This victory gained over demons is essentially a Messianic act, and the assertion of Jesus has for the evangelist the quality of a Messianic declaration. This is shown by the text of Luke, which adds this declaration: "But if I, with the finger of God, cast out devils, no doubt the Kingdom of God is come upon you" (Luke xi. 20). One other fact proves that the Messianic proclamation of Mark viii. 27 could not possess the importance (if the data of Mark are adhered to) which the evangelist himself attributes to it, and marks the appearance in the Gospel tradition of a new idea, and this is the recognition of Jesus as the Son of God by the demoniacs.[41] "The unclean spirits," Mark writes, "when they perceived Him, fell at His feet and cried, Thou art the Son of God."[42] Doubtless Mark adds that Jesus commanded them to hold their peace (iii. 12 and v. 7), but it is impossible that these declarations which the evangelist represents as frequently occurring could have passed unperceived by the disciples, and that when hearing them they should not have understood or suspected that Jesus was the Messiah. Thus by the testimony of Mark himself the episode of Cæsarea Philippi had not in reality the importance which the evangelist attributes to it. It is the pivot upon which the narrative is articulated, but not that of the Gospel history itself.

In taking up another point of view, the same conclusion is reached. "Behold, we go up to Jerusalem," said Jesus to His disciples, "and the Son of man shall be delivered unto the chief priests and unto the scribes, and they shall condemn Him to death, and shall deliver Him to the Gentiles" (x. 33). It is in the interest of dogma that Jesus is shown leaving Galilee. "The Son of man must suffer many things, and be rejected of the elders, and of the chief priests and scribes, and be killed, and after three days rise again." The arrival of Jesus at Jerusalem is presented by Mark as a march to execution. It is the Messianic proclamation of Peter which sets in motion the drama. After Jesus has been rejected by the Galilean people, He reveals Himself to His disciples as the Messiah, and goes up to Jerusalem to die there, in accordance with the plan of redemption. Did Jesus really of His own free initiative (as Mark indicates) go up to Jerusalem, and go in order to die there? His departure from Galilee appears to have had other causes than those mentioned by Mark. At the close of the series of conflicts we read: "And the Pharisees went forth, and straightway took counsel with the Herodians against Him, how they might destroy Him" (iii. 6). In Mark this statement is isolated; it could not have been so in the primitive tradition from which he borrowed this fact. No mention could have been made of a plot formed against Jesus without having stated what resulted from it. The primitive tradition has not been preserved in its integrity because a dogmatic construction has been substituted for the account of the real development of the story of Jesus. Of this primitive tradition another fragment is perhaps preserved, in a form, by the way, modified. This is in the episode concerning Herod and his perplexity about Jesus (Mark vi. 14–16). In the way in which we read it, this account is outside the work; it plays no part in the development of facts. It is the débris of a tradition in which Herod had to play an active part in the story of Jesus. Wellhausen has ingeniously conjectured that in the place where we read in Luke ix. 9, "Herod sought to see Him," there was primitively the phrase, "Herod sought to put Him to death." Besides the passage in Mark (iii. 6), the warning given in viii. 15 ("Take heed, beware of the leaven of the Pharisees and of the leaven of Herod") is a trace of this hostility.

There is found in a passage peculiar to the Gospel of Luke an extremely valuable indication with the same significance. At the close of Jesus' stay in Galilee certain Pharisees came and said to Him: "Get Thee out, and depart hence, for Herod will kill Thee" (Luke xiii. 31). This tradition must be historical, for it contradicts the general conception of the evangelists, which always represents the Pharisees as resolutely hostile to Jesus. Otherwise how can it be supposed that a human motive should have been subsequently substituted for a dogmatic motive for the departure of Jesus for Jerusalem?[43]

Jesus did not come to Jerusalem only to die there. His stay appears to have had a longer duration than the Synoptics indicate, otherwise the passage such as that given by Matthew (xxiii. 37) and Luke (xiii. 34), preserved by them from the Logia, would not be comprehensible: "O Jerusalem, Jerusalem, thou that killest the prophets and stonest them which are sent unto thee, how often would I have gathered thy children together, even as a hen gathereth her chickens under her wings, and ye would not."[44]

It is not easy to understand also how within a few days of which the Synoptics speak, the drama of the Passion would have had the time to begin and develop. So far was Jesus from coming to Jerusalem to die there that He carefully organized His entry into the Holy City to impress the spectators, and by His action and His public teaching He did His best to rally the crowd to His cause. Doubtless He must have perceived how dangerous was the part which He played. If He failed, His death was certain, for His enemies would not disarm. He did not retreat while there was yet time, but He accepted in advance the sacrifice which might be demanded from Him.[45]

Nevertheless, so little was His death a dogmatic necessity for Jesus that in the precaution He took of quitting Jerusalem every evening, He attempted to escape from His enemies and perhaps had it not been for the treachery of Judas He would have succeeded. The Gethsemane episode (Mark xiv. 32–42) is in this respect very characteristic. At the last moment, when Jesus sees the circle of His enemies closing in upon Him, He is appalled. The scene in its essential details is certainly historic; it is too much in contradiction with the idea of the Christ accepting with serenity, almost with impassivity, the necessity of His sufferings[46] to warrant the belief that it was created by tradition.

At the time of the composition of the oldest of our Gospels a dogmatic system had already been substituted for the historic treatment of events, and this had happened under conditions such that those who compiled the Gospels found only fragmentary traditions before them. Nevertheless, it is seen that the story of Jesus had a quite different character at its origin. If, as the mythologists say, the Gospel tradition was only the projection upon the plane of history of a myth or of an ideal drama of redemption, the Gospel history would be homogeneous. It would have been instantly manipulated according to dogmatic principles; it would not be possible to find in it, as is the case in our actually existing Gospels, this lack of adaptation which arises from the fact that the tradition was inadequate or difficult to fit into the frame into which it was desired to force it. The character of Mark's narration is only explicable if matter and frame have two different origins. The latter has been elaborated by dogmatic reflection; the elements of the narrative[47] have not been created as a function of this frame, but borrowed from tradition to fill it.

V. CONCERNING CERTAIN FACTORS IN THE DEVELOPMENT OF THE GOSPEL TRADITION

To confirm our conclusions it remains for us to examine various theories by which it has sometimes been desired to explain in whole or in part the origin of the Gospel narratives.[48]

One observation concerning method must be laid down first of all. The Gospel history is not a homogeneous block which suddenly appeared in the form we are familiar with. The observations which authorize us to establish the coexistence of three parallel records prove that the tradition has evolved, and that indeed from the period which preceded the compiling of Mark's Gospel, doubtless since the primitive times of the life of the Church. Concerning this evolution, we can partly recognize and partly conjecture the causes, but it is illegitimate to think that the factors which determined the evolution of the Gospel tradition, its transformations and adaptations, were the same which gave birth to it. Transformation and creation are two very different things, and those factors which explain the first do not suffice to explain the second. This is easily perceived in examining some of the causes which have influenced the evolution of the tradition and by which certain persons have sometimes tried to explain its birth.

1. Folklore

In the Gospels there are elements analogous to certain themes developed in the folklore of different races[49] which must have the same origin, but one can only explain by this fact certain details of secondary importance having no organic relationships with the essentials of the narratives, and which most frequently are only met with in the youngest forms of the tradition. Conclusions which hold good for these details cannot properly be extended to the whole body of Gospel literature. Critics have long since observed that the darkness which covered the whole earth at the moment of the death of Jesus (Mark xv. 33; Luke xxiii. 44; Matt. xxvii. 45), the earthquakes and the resurrections spoken of by Matthew (xxvii. 52, 53), are occurrences which are met with outside the Gospels, in the most widely different circumstances;[50] but it would be no more legitimate to conclude from this fact that the death of Jesus is a myth than it would be to presume that Julius Caesar had never really existed because numerous writers have related that his death was accompanied by signs not less extraordinary.[51] There are among various races legends analogous to the Gospel narratives of the walking upon the waters (Mark vi. 45–52; Matt. xiv. 22–23), or of the multiplication of loaves (Mark vi. 31–43; Matt. xiv. 13–21; Luke ix. 10–17; John vi. 1–13), and the parallels established by M. Saintyves are as interesting as they are instructive. Their relations with the Gospel episode are, however, less direct than those presented by certain Old Testament texts, and, above all, they only bear upon certain subordinate details. In the narratives of the multiplication of loaves the miracle is not the essential thing. The entire interest is concentrated on the meal of Jesus and His disciples, in which the crowd took part. As for the episode of the walking on the waters, nothing proves that it is (at any rate in the form in which we have it) a primary element of the tradition. Doubtless Mark and Matthew in relating it considered they were narrating a miracle. The same may be said of John. But when this last account (especially) is read, there remains an impression (which might at first have seemed to be extraordinary) that Jesus who had made the journey on foot, had reached the Capernaum shore of the lake before the disciples, who had crossed it in the boat. It is possible to conceive a quite natural explanation of this fact. The mythical and supernatural element appears to have intervened, not at the origin of the tradition, but in the course of its literary development.[52] What is there surprising in the fact that the editors of the Gospels, who did not consider Jesus an ordinary man, should have attributed a supernatural power to Him, over the elements?

The presence in the Gospel narratives of certain themes borrowed from myth or folklore is evidence of the already complex degree of evolution shown in the tradition as we have it, but it does not prove that the entire tradition had from its beginnings an exclusively mythical character.

2. Inspiration and Visions

M. Couchoud considers that one of the principal sources of the Gospel history is inspiration, and that in a double sense. In the first place the oracles of inspired persons, considered as direct communications from Christ Himself, have been attributed to Jesus in a so-called historical ministry; then certain acts, particularly certain cures, performed by the Christians and explained by the power of the Christ who guided them, came to be considered as having been accomplished by Jesus Himself. Thus the cures wrought by Peter in the name of Christ, the teaching imparted by Him, the words pronounced in ecstasy by Stephen under the influence of the spiritual Christ, came to be considered as the acts and speeches of a Jesus whose biography was thus constituted by a transference from the history of the early Christians.

The theory is ingenious; it may appear seductive, for many of the teachings of Jesus are portrayed as related, not to His time, but to the situation existing in the early Church when the Gospels were compiled. The fourth Gospel commits an evident anachronism in speaking of exclusion from the synagogue as a penalty with which those who in the lifetime of Jesus recognized His Messiahship were threatened (ix. 22, xii. 42), and the anachronism is none the less evident in the Synoptics, where Jesus is reputed to have spoken of the appearance of His disciples "before governors and kings"[53] (Matt. x. 18; Mark xiii. 9; Luke xxi. 12). There has been no creation here, but merely the adaptation of the tradition to the needs of those for whom the Gospels were written. It is not surprising that the authors of popular books have not carefully distinguished between the teaching of Jesus and its application.

We have shown, in the case of the apostle Paul (Chap. v), that in the primitive Church a very clear distinction was drawn between the word of the Lord and the revelations of inspired persons. In these conditions it is not conceivable that the two things could have been confounded. There is no reason to suppose that the distinction established in the primitive period, which was the greatest flowering time of spiritual gifts, became less clear later on, at a time when the intensity of the spiritual life became less vigorous. It is not possible to explain the origin of the Gospel narratives by visions, as M. Couchoud would like to do. The phrase, "For I have received of the Lord," which Paul uses in 1 Cor. xi. 23, has not the meaning which he attributes to it, as we have seen, but it implies the existence and utilization of an earlier tradition.

It is true at the beginning of the narrative a vision is found—that accompanying the baptism of Jesus—but it is expressly presented by Mark (i. 9–11) as a vision of Jesus; and from the fact that Jesus, like Paul, might have had visions,[54] it by no means follows that He was never an historical personage.

One other vision, the Transfiguration (Mark ix. 2–8), plays a part in the second portion of the evangelist, but this in any case is only a subordinate one, the Transfiguration being only the celestial confirmation of Peter's confession. This it is which is the true pivot of the Gospel history, since it is immediately after Peter has declared to Jesus, "Thou art the Christ," that the story takes a new orientation with the first announcement of the sufferings and death of the Messiah. The Transfiguration, in fact, is ill-placed in the story of Jesus. It must have been originally an account of the apparition of the Risen One, which has not been preserved in its primitive form because it implied a conception of the Messiahship which the faith of the Church had outgrown.[55]

3. The Transference of Material Borrowed from the Apostolic History

It is conceivable that the tradition of the words and sayings of Jesus may have been enriched by aphorisms or declarations which were not originally attributed to Him,[56] but we are unable to discover with certainty any fact of this kind in the Gospel tradition.[57] It would, moreover, only be a question of agglomeration and would presuppose the existence of the Gospel tradition.

It is true that the case of the two sentences spoken by Stephen at the moment of martyrdom has been pointed out: "Lord Jesus, receive my spirit" and "Lord, lay not this sin to their charge" (Acts vii. 60). They have an evident affinity with those which Luke attributes to the dying Jesus: "Father, forgive them, for they know not what they do" (xxiii. 34), and "Father, into Thy hands I commend My spirit" (xxiii. 46). Certain writers have believed it possible to admit that between the two groups of sentences there is a relation of dependence, the book of Acts being the original member. It is true that M. Loisy leans, along with certain other critics, to the idea that this portion of the Acts is prior to the evangelists' account; but even if this were proved beyond all question, it would be inadmissible to draw conclusions of a too sweeping and too rigorous character, since these two sayings of Jesus (the first of which is not to be found in the primitive text of Luke) are in any case subordinate elements foreign to the most ancient tradition of the Passion. The dependence of Luke upon the Acts is, besides, not absolutely certain. The Acts were written after the third Gospel by the same author or the same editor. In telling the story of Stephen's martyrdom he could, even if he knew and used a more ancient tradition, have introduced details which recalled the Passion of Jesus, thus obeying a motive which has inspired the attitude of martyrs and confessors and has had a powerful influence on the whole literature of hagiology.

If from words we pass to narratives, the theory of the transference to the life of Jesus of that which originally belonged to the apostolic history is not more plausible. The fact relied upon here is the analogy (indeed sufficiently striking) which apparently exists between a series of narratives relating to Peter and a series of miracles attributed to Jesus.

There are three passages specially which it is necessary to consider in this connection:

1. That in the Acts (v. 15, 16) referring to the sick brought from all parts to Peter in order that he might cure them by his shadow passing over them. This passage presents certain analogies with Mark vi. 53, 56, in which it is related how, when Jesus returned to Gennesareth after the first multiplication of loaves, they brought to Him from the surrounding country all the sick to the places where He passed, and how those who only succeeded in touching the hem

of His garment were made whole. The analogy between the two accounts should not lead us to ignore and neglect the differences between them. The episode in the story of Jesus possesses an organic importance which it has not in that of Peter. It is found in the Gospel at a time when Jesus was continually on the road. On the contrary, Peter was at Jerusalem at the time referred to in the passage in the Acts. The extraordinary concourse of the sick and their eagerness are not justified as in the case of the Gospel narrative; there is, therefore, a characteristic accentuation of the miraculous element in it. The same conclusion is forced on us if we note that the cures of Jesus took place by actual contact, while those of Peter required only the mere passage of his shadow.

2. At Lydda Peter cured the impotent man, Æneas, who for eight years had lain upon a pallet (Acts ix. 32–35). This has been compared with the healing of the paralytic in Mark ii. 1–12. But two details essential in Mark's narrative are lacking in the Acts. First of all the proof of an extraordinary faith given by the sick man and his bearers, who, in order to get at Jesus, remove a part of the roof of the house. Then follows the discussion upon the forgiveness of sins. The account in Acts is thus a simplification of that in the Gospel; originality cannot be on its side.

3. At Joppa a woman named Tabitha (in Greek, Dorcas, which means Gazelle), who did much good and was extremely charitable, had just died. Her body was laid in an upper room, and messengers were sent to seek Peter at Lydda. The latter having been conducted to the place where the corpse was lying, sent every one out of the room, and after offering a prayer, turned towards the corpse and said: "Tabitha, arise!" The woman then opened her eyes and sat up. Peter took her by the hand and assisted her to rise. Calling the saints and the widows, he presented her to them alive (Acts ix. 36–43). This narration has striking analogies with the account of the raising of the daughter of Jairus in Mark. When Jesus, after His excursion to Gerasa, returned to the western shore of the lake, a ruler of the synagogue named Jairus came to Him, beseeching Him to come

and lay His hands upon His daughter, then at the point of death. While Jesus is on His way, news is brought to Jairus that the child is dead. Jesus replied to Jairus: "Be not afraid, only believe." Arrived at the house, He found a crowd of people weeping and lamenting. He sent them all away, only keeping with Him the father and mother of the child and the three disciples He had brought with Him. He entered into the chamber of the dead, and taking the body by the hand pronounces the words in Aramaic, "Talitha Kumi," which, being interpreted, is: "Damsel, I say unto thee, arise." The child, who was twelve years old, arose. Jesus restores her to her parents, and commanded that something should be given her to eat.

It is improbable that these two narratives—at least in the form in which we are familiar with them—are quite independent of each other. But on which side is the priority? In the Gospel this story is combined very closely with that of the healing of the woman with the issue of blood (Mark v. 25, etc.), while in the Acts it is isolated. This already is favorable to the priority of the Gospel narrative. On the other hand, the story of the resurrection of Tabitha discloses the influence of two Old Testament narratives—that of the resurrection of the Sarepta widow's son by Elijah (1 Kings xvii) and that of the raising of the child of the Shunamite woman by Elisha (2 Kings iv. 33). It is therefore a more developed account than Mark's, where these influences are not revealed. The account in the Acts is also more marvelous, for it is a matter of the resurrection of a person dead already several days, while in the Gospel the child has just died, and certain details lead one to think that originally it was a matter of healing and not of resurrection. The final touch in Mark's account belongs to a very primitive conception representing Jesus as exercising the medical activity of a rabbi. Between the name "Tabitha"[58] and the words "Talitha Kumi" the analogy is quite superficial.[59] If it were a real analogy, taken alone it would not enable us to say which is the original. Here, again, the account in Acts appears subordinate to that of the Gospel, which some have wished to derive from the former.

The two accounts of the cure of the impotent man and the raising of Dorcas are connected in the Acts. Those of the Gospels to which they have been compared belong to two different cycles. And finally, the narratives concerning Peter in the book of Acts are among the least solid and the most recent portions of it. They have, in particular, a very close relationship with the story of Cornelius (Acts x. 1 to xi. 18), designed to attribute to Peter and not to Paul and the Church at Antioch the initiative of the preaching of the Gospel to the pagans—a narrative whose misleading character is obvious, and admitted unanimously as such by the critics.

4. The Liturgy

There remains to examine one last factor through whose action it has been believed the formation of the Gospels could be explained. This is the liturgical factor.

M. Loisy thinks that because of their style a prophetico-liturgical character must be attributed to the Gospels, and he has pointed out that this fact would not be without very serious consequences. Discussions about the historical character of the Gospels would, in his opinion, lose a great part of their import if "these were handbooks relating to the cult of the Lord Christ, if the oracles of the Lord Jesus had been worded by the prophets of the first Christian age, if the account of the Passion was related to the ritual or rituals of the Christian Passover in early times."[60] The idea that the Gospels are only liturgical handbooks cannot in any case be considered as established. In order to justify it, M. Loisy invokes the rhythm, but up to the present, notwithstanding various deliberate attempts (often ingenious), it has been impossible to discover the law of this rhythm. It is hardly to be disputed that there are in the New Testament, in the Epistles of Paul as well as in the Gospel, passages where a certain periodicity is perceptible, and which may be considered as rhythmic. But so long as no one succeeds in defining with precision what constitutes a line and a strophe, it will be impossible to consider the Gospels in their entirety—and with even more reason the whole New Testament—as written in rhythmic form more or less resembling the Sibylline Books. The rhythm discoverable in the Gospels most frequently does not surpass the characteristic forms of Oriental thought, with its predilection for parallelism and antithesis, for opposition, enumeration and gradation, which follow from the dialectical process which it habitually employs. There is nothing which justifies us in calling this a liturgical style properly so called.

There is, besides, a very grave objection to the suggestion that the Gospels were compiled for public worship; it is that there is no trace in first-century Christianity of a liturgical use of the Gospels.[61]

The remark in Mark xiii. 14 and in Matt. xxiv. 15, "Let him that readeth understand," may refer to a public reading,[62] but it is found in the Synoptic Apocalypse, which seems originally to have had an independent existence.[63] The sole texts we possess concerning the Christian cult of the first century, that of Chapters xii and xiv of the first Epistle to the Corinthians and that of the Didachè,[64] contain no allusion to the reading of the Holy Scriptures at public worship, not even the reading of the Old Testament.[65] The first certification of a cultural reading of the Gospels is met with in Justin Martyr (*Apol.,* i. 67). The reading of the Gospels was certainly not in his time a novelty. There is, however, nothing to authorize us to date this custom back to the first century. In the present state of research concerning the formation of the New Testament canon it seems to be established that public reading was one of the causes, not the consequences, of their canonization. That an organic relation exists between the Gospel narratives and the eucharistic ritual is evident, and in particular it is not doubtful that the divergence between the three Synoptic accounts on one side and the Johannine account on the other, respecting the date of the death of Jesus, corresponds to a difference between the rituals of the Roman Church and those of Asia, but this relation is a complex one. If the rites influenced the narratives, these latter, especially at the period of origin, must also have influenced the rites. A perfectly liturgical explanation of the Gospel narratives which is related to the rites would only be possible if the Christian rites could be entirely reduced to those of an earlier age.

Now this is a thesis which cannot be considered as established, especially in the case of the Eucharist. However important the contacts may be, especially in subordinate forms, which it shows with rites foreign to Christianity, there is in it something original which does not owe its existence to borrowing. As confirmation of this statement, the rite of baptism (which in itself seems to be the transformation and adaptation of a Jewish rite) is not connected by Christian tradition with an episode of the life of Jesus. (See *L'Eucharistie des origines à Justin Martyr,* Goguel.)

The interpretation of the Gospel history as a liturgy is not to be set aside only because of its hypothetical character and because it is the explanation of something partly obscure by something totally unknown, but still more because it clashes with this decisive objection, namely that the influence of the cult on the tradition could only be exercised at a time when the tradition was already established—at least in its essential details.[66]

NOTES

1. We may neglect the Apocryphal Gospels, for in what has been preserved to us there is nothing which is not of secondary importance when compared with the Canonical Gospels.

2. For the defense in detail of the theory which we here present in summary we refer readers to our *Introduction to the New Testament,* Parts I and II.

3. Without dwelling on the fact that the attribution of the second Gospel to Mark cannot be regarded as rigorously proved, we shall call its author Mark for the sake of convenience, just as we shall call the authors of the three others respectively Matthew, Luke and John, while the attri-

bution of the third Gospel to Luke is very debatable, and that of the first and fourth to Matthew and John is certainly not established.

4. This is the case, for instance, for a certain number of parables which are only found in Matthew or only in Luke.

5. For instance, the curses only found in Luke (vi. 24–26) and which are in organic relationship with the Beatitudes (vi. 20–23), which later are also found in Matthew (v. 3–10).

6. For example, the Beatitudes in Matthew (v. 3–10) and Luke (vi. 20–23) are in forms too widely different from each other to allow of the differences being explained by editorial work, but which are, however, too similar to permit us to consider them as independent.

7. Jean Reville, *Le quatrième évangile, son origine, sa valeur historique.*

8. Alfred Loisy, *Le quatrième évangile.* In his second edition M. Loisy has modified certain points of the theory defended in the first.

9. Frederic Godet, *Commentaire sur l'Evangile de Saint Jean.*

10. Theodor Zahn, *Das Evangelium des Johannes ausgelegt.*

11. Calmes, *L'Evangile selon Saint Jean.*

12. Only in the feminine and not in the neuter, as in the Christian terminology. The neuter word appears for the first time in Greek. It is found in the plural in an inscription of Priène dating from 9 B.C. (text and translation in J. Rouffiac, *Researches sul le Grèc du N.T. d'après les inscriptions de Priène*). In this inscription concerning the introduction of the Julian calendar into Asia, Augustus is hailed as the "Saviour" of the world, and it is stated that "the day of the birth of the god was for the world the beginning of the good news which he brought." It must be noted that this inscription establishes no relation between the term signifying "good news" and the qualification of Saviour given to Augustus. The use of the plural shows that what is expected from the emperor are material advantages, not spiritual wealth.

13. For instance, 2 Kings xviii. 20, 22, 27; 4 Kings vii. 9.

14. For instance, Psa. xl. 10 and xxvi. 2; Isa. xl. 9, lii. 7, lx. 6 and lxi. 1.

15. Matt. xi. 5; Luke iv. 21, vii. 22.

16. For the justification of this statement see Maurice Goguel, *Introd. au N.T.,* 1. pp. 25–28.

17. It is, of course, necessary to eliminate passages where the word

"gospel" is used by the narrator (Mark i. 1, 14; Matt. iv. 23, ix. 25) and those where it is plainly put into the mouth of Jesus by Mark (i. 15, viii. 35, x. 29), but is not found in the parallel texts of Matthew and Luke.

18. Luke has no parallel to these passages.

19. Maurice Goguel, *L'Evangile de Marc dans ses rapports avec ceux de Matthieu et de Luc,* Paris, 1909; *Introd.,* i. p. 298.

20. We only speak of the first three evangelists, since from what has just been said it follows that it is not admissible to speak of an historical or geographical framework of the fourth evangelist. The appearance of a framework is caused by the evangelist juxtaposing scenes and episodes by making use, as transitions between them, of feasts as reasons for the journeys of Jesus to Jerusalem.

21. The same is the case with the passage in 1 Tim, vi. 13.

22. Their value has recently been defended by Ed. Meyer and by C. Cichorius. The great uncertainty which prevents our dependence on these statements is that we know nothing of their origin. They cannot originate in Christian tradition, which, as we have seen, was not at the beginning interested in these questions. The fact that Jewish tradition, such as we know is through Josephus, has preserved the memory of John the Baptist permits one to suppose, as does Meyer, that it is from a Jewish source that Luke has borrowed them.

23. Papias, bishop of Hierapolis in Phrygia, was born doubtless about A.D. 85. He composed, about A.D. 140, a work in five books entitled *Explanations of the Sayings of the Lord,* of which Eusebius has preserved some fragments, and from which seem to proceed all the information which Irenæaus states he held from the presbyters. Eusebius states that Papias was a man of small mind, and indeed certain stories which he relates show that he must have been a very credulous man (*Ecc. History,* iii).

24. The same idea is found in another treatise of Irenæus, *The Demonstration of the Apostolic Preaching.*

25. Traces of an analogous conception are found in other texts, for example in the letter from Pilate to Claudius which constitutes the most ancient portion of the "Acta Pilati," in the commentary of Hippolytus on Dan. iv. 23, etc. M. S. Reinach also cites the fact that "in a whole collection of Christian works of art, sarcophagi, carvings, mosaics, some of which go back to the fourth century, John baptizing Jesus is presented as

a man of about fifty years old at least, while Jesus is a child of ten to twelve years old. Now, according to Josephus, the Baptist died several years before A.D. 36. If he baptized in the year 30, Jesus would have been born at the earliest in the years 18 or 20, and dying at the age of thirty he would have undergone the Passion towards the year 50 (still under the Emperor Claudius)." This cannot be put in accord with the tradition attested by Irenæus, since the latter states that Jesus died, not at the age of thirty, but at fifty years. At the period from which all these works of art date the authority of the canonical Gospels was uncontested. They should be explained by the liberty which these works of art demanded, which it is not allowable to consider as documents capable of an absolutely rigorous interpretation.

26. Concerning the opinions of Irenæus about the Gospel canon, refer to Zahn, *Geschichte des Neutestamentlichen Kamons*.

27. Hippocrates, according to Philo, *De opificio mundi*, 105.

28. Maurice Goguel, *L'Eucharistie*, p. 51.

29. The few narratives in which other personages intervene have their center of gravity in the special teachings that Jesus attaches to them for His disciples (for example in x. 17–31), or they are inserted in the place in which we read them because tradition located them in Judea (example, x. 46–52).

30. The Gospel of Mark gives no accounts of apparitions of the Resurrected One, its end having disappeared at an early date. Those which are read in the received text have been added afterwards by a man acquainted with the other Gospels. According to a statement made by the Armenian work of Edschmiadzin, this person was the presbyter Aristion.

31. The correspondence is made evident by the fact that the impression produced by the Sermon on the Mount is characterized by Matthew in exactly the same terms that Mark had employed in reference to the teaching in the Capernaum synagogue.

32. The parables given by Mark are completed by others which come from the Logia. The dependence of Matthew upon Mark is evidenced by the fact that the explanation of the parable of the tares, which has no equivalent in Mark, is put after the conclusion of the teaching in parables, and separated in a not very natural way from the parable itself (xiii. 24–30). In essentials it appears to correspond with the parable of the sower in Mark.

33. Exception is made of the addition and suppression of some unimportant details.

34. Some are combined of narratives derived from Mark (xvi.17–19, xvii. 20, xviii. 4), and others are inserted between the narratives borrowed from Mark (xvii. 24–27, viii. 10–35, xx. 1–16).

35. The episode of Beelzebub is found again in a more developed form, and does not seem to be from Mark. It is in a different context (xi. 14). The remark of Jesus about His real parents is given elsewhere (viii. 19–21).

36. One single passage of Mark is not reproduced by Luke. It is the conversation of Jesus with His disciples after descending the Mount of Transfiguration (Mark ix. 9–13). This passage may have been omitted because it discussed a question of Jewish dogma, which had no interest for readers of Luke.

37. See on this point Maurice Goguel, *Introd. au N.T.,* i. pp. 464–81.

38. Omission of Mark (x. 35–45); addition of Luke (xix. 1–27).

39. Luke omits Mark xii. 28–34, of which he gives an equivalent in x. 25–28. He adds xix. 39–44.

40. It may nevertheless be asked if Mark has perfectly preserved the primitive character of the narrative and if he does not represent the people as at least the witnesses of the vision of Jesus.

41. For the evangelist demons are supernatural beings, who see and understand things which escape the knowledge of mankind.

42. Unclean spirits—that is, those possessed.

43. This is so true that in the reply of Jesus Luke has added a phrase (xiii. 32, 33) which explains the departure of Jesus for Jerusalem by the necessity that the Messiah must not die anywhere other than in the Holy City. He has thus in his text a doublet which is not natural. There is, perhaps, also a souvenir of Herod's hostility against Jesus in the nonhistorical account of Luke xxiii. 6–16.

44. John presents Jesus as coming to Jerusalem at the time of the Feast of Tabernacles—that is, the beginning of October. We have attempted to show that the Johannine narrative rests here on a tradition of great value (*Introd. au N.T.,* ii, p. 411).

45. By attaching to it a redeeming value, not in virtue of a dogmatic theory, but in the sentiment that if God allowed Him to perish it could only be because His death was necessary to the accomplishment of His work.

46. Such as is found, for instance, in the triple prophecy of suffering and death.

47. In their totality, of course, and without prejudicing the solution of the critical problem which each one presents.

48. We do not revert here to the function of the prophetic exegesis which was dealt with in the preceding chapter.

49. P. Saintyves, *Essais de folk-lore biblique,* Paris.

50. *Id., ib.*

51. Such as Plutarch (*Cæsar*), Virgil (*Georgics* I), Ovid (*Metamorphoses*).

52. What is here said concerning the walking on the waters may be repeated regarding the account of the stilling of the tempest, which appears to be only a variant of it (see Mark iv. 35–41; Matt. viii. 23–27; Luke viii. 22).

53. The term used by the Gospels may also be translated by "emperors."

54. Visions, however, occupy in the life of Jesus only a very small place. Outside of the account of the Baptism and Transfiguration, where, in so far as one can judge of the first meaning of the narrative, it is a question of a vision of the disciples and not of Jesus, we only note one. It is that referred to in the phrase, "I saw Satan falling from heaven as lightning" (Luke x. 18), and here again it must be asked if this is anything more than a figurative expression.

55. See our study. *Notes d'histoire évangelique,* ii (*Esquisse d'une interpretation du récit de la transfiguration*). *Revue d'hist. des Religions,* lxxxi, 1920, pp. 145 *et seq.*

56. It is thus, for instance, that Acts (i. 15 and xi. 6) put into the lips of Jesus the announcement of the baptism by the Spirit which the Synoptics all give as a sentence of John the Baptist.

57. The Gospels attribute both to John the Baptist and to Jesus the speech about the tree and its fruits, but it is there doubtless an image which must be older than John the Baptist. It is also possible that Jesus had adopted a theme of the teaching of John the Baptist.

58. Which is certified as a woman's name. See Preuschen, *Die Apostelgeschichte,* Tübingen, 1912.

59. It would completely disappear even if, with Wellhausen and Klostermann, the reading "Rabitha Kumi" were admitted on the authority of certain Western witnesses (*Das Evangelium Marci*).

60. Loisy, *Revue critique,* 1923, p. 402.

61. Neither is there any trace of a liturgical reading of the Epistles.

62. It is not certain that this note is primitive. Luke (xxi. 20) has nothing equivalent to it. His text, nevertheless, in spite of the substitution of "Jerusalem besieged" for "abomination of desolation," is closely related to that of Mark and Matthew. The form of the phrase, "and when ye shall see . . . then let them that are in Judea flee to the mountains," is the same. We have tried elsewhere to show that Luke's text is the oldest, and that it has been corrected in Matthew and Mark to dissociate the siege of Jerusalem from the events of the end. If this is so, the note may be considered as a hint to the reader, designed to emphasize the import of the new indication. (See Goguel, *Introd. au N.T.,* i, pp. 301 *et seq.*)

63. The Apocalypses seem to have been, from the beginning, designed for public reading, as is shown by the remark in Apoc. i. 3: "Happy is he who reads and happy are those who harken to the works of prophecy and who keep what is there written."

64. It may even be said that the first portion of the Didachè, which is a summary of the moral teaching of the Gospels for the use of catechumens, would not be comprehensible if the Gospels had been at the time this book was composed the object of a regular reading.

65. There is no allusion made, either, in what Paul says of the Christian cult.

66. With even greater reason may we set aside without detailed discussion the liturgical explanations of certain narratives proposed by M. Saintyves. For example, that of the multiplication of loaves "by a mystery cult analogous to that of Dionysius," which he supposes "existed in Judaism, or at any rate among the Syrians" (*Essais*); or, again, that of the walking on the waters "by a ceremony connected with a seasonal and initiation ritual which was both Jewish and Christian—the ritual of the Passover."

If these are gratuitous hypotheses, what is to be thought of the explanation of the rending of the (Temple) veil by a rite thus described: "When the annual victim which the early Christians sacrificed died, or was on the point of death, in order to show clearly that this victim was fulfilling the part of the Eternal High Priest, perhaps the sanctuary veil was rent in pieces, and the portions were dispersed?" (*Essais,* p. 424). It is unnecessary to add that not one text—and for good reason—is cited to prove the existence of this rite.

CHAPTER XI

THE ORIGIN OF THE FAITH IN THE RESURRECTION AND ITS FUNCTION IN PRIMITIVE CHRISTIANITY

I. THE RESURRECTION PROBLEM

One of the chief objections which M. Couchoud raises against the historical character of Jesus is the difficulty he finds in understanding how, within the space of a single generation, the deification of a man could have taken place, and this upon the territory of Judaism. How did this deification take place, and how did men who had lived close to Jesus come to identify Him with a divine Being, if not (as M. Couchoud says in a phrase which somewhat exceeds the data of the texts) with Jehovah Himself, as least with His Son and Messiah?[1]

Primitive Christianity was not a school of philosophers, but a group of believers practicing a common worship of the Lord Jesus. He did not unite a body of men who admired the teaching of a Master and desired to take Him as a rule for their lives[2]; He brought together worshipers. In the Christian field the word "disciples" possesses a sense quite different from that which it has in the expression "disciples of Plato or Aristotle." It is the equivalent of the word "saints"—that is, of consecrated ones—which is the most usual name for the faithful.

The Christians—and not only thinkers like Paul or the author of the fourth Gospel, but also the humblest and least philosophical among them—only considered the Gospel history as an episode in a cosmic drama of much vaster dimensions. How did they reach this point of view? That which convinced them that Jesus was more than a man was the conviction that He had risen from the dead. Paul expresses the feeling of all believers when he said: "If Christ be not risen from the dead, then is our preaching vain, and your faith is also vain" (1 Cor. xv. 14). The belief in the resurrection is indeed the foundation upon which the whole structure of primitive Christianity is built. The story of its birth is nothing more than the formation of the faith in the resurrection.

In order that we may form an idea of the conditions in which this belief appeared, it is necessary, without neglecting the criticism of the narratives and traditions concerning the apparitions, first of all to examine this problem. In what manner did the early Christians picture to themselves the life of the risen Christ?

The principal problems which are presented by the resurrection narratives may be reduced to three:

1. What is the relation between the discovery of the empty tomb and the apparitions? Upon which of these two facts—or rather upon which of these two beliefs—does the faith in the resurrection rest? Were there really at its origin two facts, real or supposed—the empty tomb and the apparitions—or has one been deduced from the other? And upon this hypothesis, was it believed that Jesus, having shown Himself to His disciples, His tomb must have been found empty? Or, on the contrary, was it the belief in the empty tomb which predisposed men's minds to believe in the resurrection and fulfilled the psychological conditions which prepared and caused the visions?

2. How was the tradition born which fixed the time of the resurrection on the morning of the third day?[3]

3. How can the extreme diversity of the accounts of the apparitions be explained? The anxiety to make them concordant has cost

the harmonizers many efforts, but the results obtained are not proportionate to the wealth of ingenuity expended. This diversity is much greater than is to be observed in any other part of the Gospel history. This fact is all the more striking seeing the very great importance which the resurrection story had for the early Christian faith. The diversity is particularly noticeable on one point: the place of the apparitions. Two forms of the tradition may be distinguished, one which localizes the apparitions in Galilee, the other in Judea.

Criticism has particularly emphasized the considerable influence of apologetic interests on the narratives of the apparitions. The episode of the guard placed over the sepulcher (see Matt. xxvii and xxviii) is a characteristic example of a narrative imagined—in good faith certainly—to reply to a Jewish objection. The Jews explained the discovery of the empty tomb by a nocturnal visit of the disciples, who, according to them, had carried off the body of their Master. The reply was that all necessary measures to prevent such a maneuver had been taken.[4]

But the apologetic factor does not explain the extreme diversity of the apparition narratives. One realizes this in observing the complexity, improbability and arbitrary character of the criticisms by which M. Voelter, of Amsterdam, has attempted to reduce them to one common source, alleged to be a vision of Peter in his home in Galilee, followed by a collective vision of the apostles on the shores of the lake of Galilee. The theories elaborated to explain the empty tomb are scarcely more satisfactory. All of them employ a conjectural factor, apparent death, or abduction of the corpse of Jesus, either by Jews, Romans, or even by disciples. Even if there were not so much of the purely arbitrary in these hypotheses, if all the objections advanced were refuted, if the tomb had, indeed, been found empty, it would still be true that the fact would not have failed to play an important part in the genesis of faith in the resurrection, whereas we are expressly told by Mark that the women kept silence concerning the discovery they had made and the message they had received (Mark xvi. 8). The later accounts have attempted to diminish the strangeness of the simple juxtaposition of the discovery of the empty tomb and the apparitions without establishing organic relationship between them, but they have done so only in a timid and imperfect way which in no degree succeeds in welding the two things together.[5]

Literary criticism alone does not permit us the choice of one out of two hypotheses which are equally possible, and to decide if the accounts of the apparitions have been subsequently introduced to establish the reality of the resurrection and set aside the divergent explanations of the empty tomb, or if the discovery of the empty tomb has been deduced from visions and incorporated into the tradition to establish the reality of the apparitions. Various theories have been proposed to explain the genesis of the formula "the third day." Even if they were less hypothetical than they are, in the conditions of our documentation, they would only have a bearing on a subordinate point, and would leave the true problem existing in its entirety.

II. THE PAULINE CONCEPTION
OF CHRIST'S RESURRECTION

The decisive fact in the genesis of Christianity was neither the discovery of the empty tomb nor the appearances of Jesus to His disciples, but faith in the resurrection. From the religious point of view, it is not facts which have importance, but ideas and sentiments. It is to the study of the conception of the early Christians of the risen Christ that it is necessary to address ourselves. We possess one precise and accurately dated document (it was written about 55 or 56), which shows us how the apostle Paul conceived the person and import of the risen Christ. This is the fifteenth chapter of the first Epistle to the Corinthians. The affirmation of the resurrection (verse 4) is confirmed by an account of the apparitions (verses 5–8). The thought in the text would be exactly rendered by the statement: "Christ is risen; the proof is that He appeared unto Cephas, then unto the Twelve," etc. The discovery of the empty tomb is not mentioned; at the most it might be considered as understood between the interment and the resurrection, each formally attested both as facts and the fulfillment of prophecies. To conclude from the silence of the apostle that he was ignorant of the tradition about the empty tomb would be going too far. It is still none the less true that, for Paul, faith in the resurrection is linked with the apparitions and not with an empty tomb, and this conclusion is not only true as regards Paul, but also for the whole Christian preaching of his time, for all that was transmitted in unanimity and taught equally by Judaic or Gentile Christians.

In the course of the chapter Paul establishes a very close relation, intimate and organic, between the resurrection of Christ and that of believers. He sees in the resurrection of Jesus the guarantee of that of the faithful. Christ inaugurates a series of resurrections; He is the first-born among the dead, the chief of the risen. We are, therefore, able to apply to Christ what is said concerning the resurrection in general. Christ is thus a spiritual being, which does not mean (given the Hebraic anthropology to which Paul remains faithful) that He is "pure spirit," but only that He is endowed with a special organism, whose attributes are different, and in a certain degree opposed to those belonging to terrestrial organisms. Paul characterizes the terrestrial or psychic body of which the earthly man consists by a series of terms such as corruptible, mortal, feeble, dishonor. This being is a living "psyche," constituted by flesh and blood. The body of the heavenly man, on the contrary, possesses immortality; he is the "pneuma zôopoioun," and he is characterized by the terms "incorruptible," "glorious," "powerful." The prototypes of these two species of beings are the first man Adam and the second Adam, who is the Christ.

The risen Christ, therefore, in Paul's view, possesses a body essentially different from that which He possessed during His earthly life. It is formed of a superior substance, the spirit, and is no longer subjected to the contingencies and the necessities which affect humanity; it is no longer subjected (as we should say in modern terminology) to the laws of physics or physiology. This is perhaps confirmed by the fact that when Paul speaks of apparitions he uses the word ὤφθη, with a dative as though he would indicate that in these experiences the initiative belongs to the Christ: He shows Himself *to* the disciples rather than these see Him. However, the expression which Paul uses must not be pushed to the point of reducing the apparitions in his thought to simple visions with no reality outside the consciousness of those who were favored with them.

Thus in Paul's view—and his ideas on this point do not appear to diverge from those of the rest of the Church of his time—the risen Christ lives no longer an earthly life. He is not a human being who, after an interruption comparable to a more or less prolonged slumber, resumes his former life, as might be conceived to be the case for the daughter of Jairus, the young man of Naïn, or Lazarus. The earthly life of Jesus was really ended on Calvary; something new began at the resurrection—a celestial life, but in which Christ has still the power of intervening in the life of those who are His own and of influencing them.

It does not appear that Paul assigns to the period during which the apparitions occurred a definite duration. Those mentioned by him—the last of which is that which he himself experienced upon the Damascus road—cannot in any case be restricted to the short period of forty days spoken of in the Acts (i. 3). Furthermore, although concerning the apparition which he had seen, Paul says, "and last of all, He was seen by me also" (1 Cor. xv. 8), there is no theoretical reason why the series of apparitions should be at an end. The Pauline conception of Christ glorified leaves no place for the Ascension. The vision of Peter or that of Paul on the Damascus road are not differentiated from the visions and revelations of the Lord referred to in 2 Cor. xii, or, rather, since the terms employed by Paul in 1 Cor. xv. 8 imply that the vision upon the road to Damascus closes the series of the first apparitions, the difference between them and those which occurred later can only consist in this, that the later ones are not, like the first, the creative source of belief in the resurrection and of the apostolic vocation.

Thus, in Paul's view, He who showed Himself to the apostles was the Christ glorified, as He existed in heaven. There was a personal identity between this Being and the Jesus whose body was laid in the tomb, but this body had undergone the transformation through which all the bodies of the elect would pass at the second coming of the Lord (1 Cor. xv. 51). In Paul's view the Lord's body did not remain in the tomb, but the fact that he does not consider it necessary to say so expressly is important and significative. An analogous conception, although of a more emphatically spiritualist nature, is met with in certain elements of the Johannine tradition. The activity of the Risen One upon the faithful is therein replaced to a certain extent by that of the Spirit.[6]

The substitution of the Spirit for the Christ is not, however, carried to its extreme consequence—that is, the suppression of apparitions. The influence exerted by the current Gospel tradition was too strong to permit John's full obedience to the inner logic of his thought.[7] Several Gospel narratives contain details which directly recall the Pauline conception of Christ glorified. For example, there is in Matthew the declaration of Jesus: "Lo! I am with you always, even until the end of the world." He who thus speaks is not subject to the ordinary conditions of existence. In the episode of Emmaus (Luke xxiv. 13–32) there are three features, not marked, it is true, with equal distinctness. First of all—and this is only slightly indicated—Jesus seems to appear in a somewhat mysterious way at the side of the two disciples walking along the road. These—and this is the second feature—do not recognize Him at first.[8] The very appearance, therefore, of Jesus had changed. Finally, at the moment when Jesus had just made Himself recognized, He vanishes—literally, He becomes invisible—which seems to imply that the Risen One possessed the faculty of rendering Himself at will either visible or invisible—in any case to appear and to disappear suddenly.

In the account of the apparition at Jerusalem which Luke gives it is expressly stated the disciples thought they beheld a phantom (xxiv. 27). In the Johannine account Jesus said to Mary Magdalene, "Touch Me not" (xx. 17). In the present form of the narrative this seems to suppose that Jesus, having left the tomb, was obliged to undergo in heaven a kind of purification before being able to resume contact with His disciples. But it is possible that this detail signified originally that human hands must not touch the glorified body of the Risen One. In the Johannine account of the first appearance to the apostles, Jesus is found suddenly in the midst of His followers, who had met together, with the doors shut, owing to the fear they had of the Jews (xx. 19).

III. THE CONCEPT OF THE RETURN OF CHRIST TO MATERIAL LIFE

The Gospel narratives also contain an entirely different concept, which may be designated by the term "revivification." The idea seems to be that the life of Jesus is resumed after having been interrupted by the drama on Calvary. Thomas was invited to put his fingers upon the nail marks and his hand into the wound in Jesus' side (John xx. 27). Luke insists that the apostles are dealing, not with a phantom, but with a Being who can be felt and who eats[9] (Luke xxiv. 39–42). In the account of the walk to Emmaus, and less distinctly in John xxi. 13, the disciples recognize their Master when He performs the familiar gesture of the breaking of bread. Finally, in Acts i. 3 it is stated that Jesus, during the forty days which preceded His ascension, gave many proofs to His disciples of His resurrection. These proofs, concerning whose nature the text gives us no information, ought probably to be conceived as confirmations of the reality of the life He had resumed.

That which has been said suffices, without it being necessary to have recourse to more recent and extracanonical narratives, to distinguish in the tradition two concepts of the resurrection. According to one, which is comparable to that of Paul, the Risen One is no longer subject to the ordinary conditions of human existence. He is a celestial being who sometimes shows Himself on earth. According to the other, the risen Christ resumes His terrestrial existence at the very point where death had interrupted it. He possesses a body which may be felt; He eats; He still bears the marks of the nails in His hands and the spear thrust in His side; His wounds are not even cicatrized.

IV. PRIMITIVE FORM OF THE RESURRECTION BELIEF

The Gospel traditions combine these two concepts. The theory of apparitions during forty days is an attempt to harmonize them. They are, however, entirely different, and in reality irreconcilable. They correspond to two different phases of the development of Christian thought. Which is the most primitive? Which had the first Christians in mind when they affirmed "Jesus is risen"? What were the causes which brought about the progress from one concept to the other?

There is already a presumption favorable to the priority of the concept of the resurrection as glorification in the fact that it appears in the first Epistle to the Corinthians, while the other concept of revivification is only found in writings which, in the form known to us, are distinctly younger.

Another consideration has more weight still. The spiritual concept is found in Paul's writings in all its purity, without admixture with any other heterogeneous element. On the other hand, there is no narrative, whether canonical or extracanonical, in which the concept of revivification is not alloyed with some detail borrowed from the idea of glorification. It would, doubtless, be hazardous to affirm that there has never existed a narrative conceived uniquely from the point of view of revivification. The existence of such a record appears, nevertheless, very doubtful. It would have suited later controversies and apologetic needs so admirably that it is not easy to understand how it could have disappeared. The combination of the features which belong respectively to the two different concepts is explicable in two ways. Either the two concepts existed at first as independent and parallel, and it was only afterwards that an attempt was made to combine them; or, on the contrary, primarily there was one simple homogeneous concept to which there were added subsequently certain divergent details which, however, did not possess sufficient plausibility to eliminate others, which logically should not have been capable of association with them. In the case before us the first explanation has little probability. The concept of revivification in itself never appears to have inspired any narrative. The reasons which have caused more and more importance to be attached to the bodily manifestations of the Risen One also enable us to understand the evolution of the resurrection tradition without being obliged to ascribe to it a double point of departure.[10]

Again, it is possible to urge, in support of the priority of the spiritualist conception, the fact that all the features which imply the concept of revivification appear to be inspired by apologetic necessities. They are so many direct replies to objections urged against the belief in the resurrection. It would be, on the contrary, very difficult to suppose, in face of the need to refute the criticisms of opponents, that apologists should have made their task more difficult by sublimating and spiritualizing the belief in the resurrection.

The resurrection was, therefore, first of all conceived as the accession of Christ to a higher life. The concept of the resurrection as a mere suppression of death and a restoration to the former life of Christ is a secondary one, born out of the necessities of apologetics.

This conclusion throws light on the primitive character of the belief in the resurrection. The progress in the history of the tradition has been, if one may so express it, from inside to outside. It has had a tendency, if not to materialize, at least to render faith in the resurrection more concrete. The evolution has been quite spontaneous, without there having existed any plan concerted by any one whatsoever. It is a case in which we may call to mind Pascal's saying: "I only believe the narratives whose witnesses would suffer death."

One is forced to believe at least in the good faith of these witnesses, for a belief founded on dishonest machinations would not have resisted persecution.

In the resurrection faith there are two elements. The first is a conviction of a religious nature: Jesus lives; He cannot be (like other men) vanquished, a prisoner of death. He has escaped the power of death; it is He, in a word, who is the victor. Alongside of this there is a conviction of a material historical fact: Jesus has quitted the tomb; He has been seen by so-and-so. What relation is there between these two convictions? Did the apostles believe that Jesus was living because they found His tomb empty and He appeared to them? Or, on the contrary, did they see Him, and were they persuaded that His tomb must have been found empty because they had the conviction that He was living?

The Gospel narratives, as we read them, express the first of these conceptions. They show us men profoundly discouraged—so little prepared to believe in the resurrection of their Master (which, nevertheless, had been announced to them) that they treated the first news of it brought to them as "idle tales" (Luke xxiv. 11); and when Jesus showed Himself to them they had need to feel Him and to watch Him eat in order to convince themselves they were not in presence of a phantom. In spite of this, Matthew relates that some of them doubted. In the Pauline faith, on the contrary, the fundamental element is the affirmation of the resurrection; no allusion is made to the empty tomb, and the apparitions are only mentioned as confirmatory evidence. If this is not the most ancient concept, the evolution of the resurrection faith must have proceeded in a very strange way. Material at the beginning, in the sense that it was founded upon material facts or on facts held to be such (empty tomb and apparitions), it would have become spiritualized in order later to become material in nature once more. The faith in the resurrection was in its origin an affirmation and a conviction of a religious nature, and it was not an experimental observation. This explains the fertility it has shown in the development of Christianity. The fourth evangelist had an exact appreciation of its true nature when he put into the mouth of Jesus the declaration made to Thomas: "Blessed are they who have not seen and yet have believed."[11]

V. HOW THE BELIEF IN THE RESURRECTION AROSE

M. Couchoud considers that belief in the resurrection arose in a quite spontaneous way, without antecedents directly recognizable, and that the apparitions were only the manifestation of an ideal Messiah whose mythical history included a crucifixion episode. This theory seems to be liable to several decisive objections. The Gospel history is not, as we have seen, the simple transformation of a myth. On the other hand, the belief in the resurrection was in the whole of primitive Christianity intimately associated with the thought of the Lord's death. Under these conditions, how could the resurrection have been for Peter and his first companions, at the primitive period, the object of a direct religious experience, while the belief in the death and sufferings of the Messiah was borrowed from an ancient myth? It is inconceivable that a myth could have included the idea of the sufferings and death of the Messiah without also including the idea of His triumph. The myths of Attis or of Osiris, which the mythologists readily cite as parallels to the history of the Christian Messiah, are on this point characteristic. Death and resurrection of the divine hero in them are on the same plane. Could it be otherwise in Christianity? The belief in the resurrection in the latter stands in organic relationship with an experience of primitive believers, which imposes the following dilemma: either the Gospel drama—that is, the idea of the sufferings and death of the Messiah and that of the resurrection—is only the transformation of an old myth or it was the object of direct knowledge. It is not, however, impossible that a reminiscence of the myth concerning the death and resurrection of the god may have prepared the minds of men to conceive the idea of the resurrection of the Messiah, Jesus, but the affirmation of this resurrection, far from having been deduced from the single fact of the death, represents in relation to it something original and new.

This is confirmed by a study of the conditions in which the belief in the resurrection arose, which did not happen with a group of enthusiastic disciples, but among men profoundly discouraged.

The personality, activity and teaching of Jesus had produced a deep impression on the little circle of disciples formed around Him. Without having translated their sentiments into precise theological propositions, they had closely associated the personality of their Master with the ideal of the Kingdom of God which they had conceived under His influence. Jesus was in their eyes He who was intended to fulfill the divine work, the Son of man destined by God to realize His plan, to destroy the power of the devil and to establish the divine dominion over the world. The Messianic consciousness of Jesus[12] imposed itself on them; if it had been otherwise it would be incomprehensible that belief in Jesus could have survived the drama of the Passion.

Even if it be admitted, as it certainly seems necessary to do, that Jesus had foreseen the eventuality of defeat, and had attempted to prepare His disciples for it, it remains none the less true that the apostles were surprised and disconcerted by the arrest of their Master. Their confusion was complete; they dispersed. This point is beyond doubt; the Gospel tradition which tends, nevertheless, to glorify the apostles, has preserved a very distinct memory of their flight. It makes an attempt, if not to excuse, at least to explain it, by showing in it the realization of a prophecy (see Mark xiv. 27 and Matt. xxvi. 31, quoting Zech. xiii. 7).[13] This attempt at an excuse has the value of a very precise confirmation of the fact.

Even Peter, who seems to have had more assurance and boldness than his companions, and who had protested that, whatever might happen, he would never forsake his Master, according to the fourth Gospel[14] only made the beginning of an act of resistance, and this could not have been very serious, since it did not involve any grave consequences[15] for him. He only accompanied the guard who led away his Master, from a distance (Mark xiv. 54), and he did not even find the courage to admit in the presence of the servants the attachment he had had for Him.

The abandonment of Jesus by His disciples can be interpreted in two ways. The fact of Jesus falling into the hands of the soldiers without any supernatural intervention taking place on His behalf may have killed the disciples' faith and persuaded them that they had deceived themselves in believing they found the Messiah in Him. The disciples of Jesus would thus have been in the same case as the partisans of innumerable Messianic pretenders of the type of Theudas, Judas the Galilean (Acts v. 36, 37), and, later on, Bar-Kochba. Their faith and their attachment to Him would not have resisted the defeat of their hero. Their Messianic faith would have suffered complete collapse, so far at least as this faith was centered in Jesus.

The alternative interpretation is that the crisis was less profound. The disciples' faith did not collapse; it was only shaken. It was primarily the courage to proclaim it which they lacked. There was in them weakness of character, discouragement, eclipse, if you wish, but there was no total bankruptcy of the Messianic faith in Jesus.

It is not easy to decide between these two hypotheses, partly, no doubt, because the memory of the apostles and tradition did not willingly dwell on this troubled and dark period when their faith had at least vacillated. Certain observations impel us, however, to incline toward the second of the two interpretations just mentioned. There is, in the first place, a reason which we shall call one of psychological economy. The later evolution of the apostles is easier to understand under the hypothesis of momentary or temporary weakness than under that of a total collapse of their Messianic faith. If this latter really took place, it would be necessary to admit that the disciples had remained completely impervious to what certainly seems to have been the dominating note in the thought of Jesus in the last days of His ministry, and particularly on the last evening—the thought of His death and return.

Certain significant facts favor the hypothesis of a temporary weakness. It is sufficient to mention them. The first is that Peter, in short, had only denied Jesus because he desired to follow Him—from a distance, it is true. He was not, therefore, completely indifferent to the fate of Jesus.[16] The denial itself is a formal disavowal which still demands consideration to see how far it was sincere and how far it was dictated by fear. But Peter only refused to admit that he knew Jesus; he did not declare He was an impostor. His behavior was not that of a man who had lost all belief in Jesus; it was that of a man who had not the courage to declare his faith. The ancient Church did not consider the behavior of Peter as the equivalent of a renunciation of his apostleship; it has preserved no memory of a new reinstatement which in such a case would have been necessary, and whose record would have been indissolubly linked to that of the forfeiture. The incident in John xxi. 15–19, habitually spoken of as the "rehabilitation of Peter," has a quite different significance. Peter, notwithstanding his denial, plays a part of the first importance in the resurrection narratives, and in the incident which has been taken for his restoration there is found no allusion which implies a denial and its consequent disqualification. (See *Introd. au N.T.*, ii. p. 302, M. Goguel.)

Where did the apostles go in their perplexity? Did they remain in Jerusalem hiding themselves more or less carefully, or did they quit Judea to take refuge in Galilee? The tradition represented by Luke and John (under its first form—that is before the addition of Chap. xxi) supports the first hypothesis. According to the beginning of the book of Acts (i. 4) it was by explicit command of Jesus that His disciples waited at Jerusalem for the inspiration of the Spirit. It was therefore at Jerusalem where the decisive evolution to which the Church owed her existence took place. Events are not presented in the same way in the other accounts. According to Mark (xvi. 17) the disciples were still at Jerusalem, since the women received from the angel the commission to tell them that they had found the tomb empty and that they must repair to Galilee, where they will see Jesus. Owing to fear the women keep silence. The account stops at this point. It must originally have related the apparition of Jesus in Galilee, announced in xvi. 7. But was it in consequence of the women's message or on their own initiative that the disciples quitted Jerusalem? The first hypothesis must be put aside owing to the last phase of the Gospel. If the narrator had intended to relate why, after the event, it came about that the women decided to speak, would he not have linked up this new account by saying, for instance: "At first they said nothing to anyone"? The primitive Gospel of Mark could not have related that the disciples quitted Jerusalem to go to meet their risen Master at the place assigned by the angel. It was not with even a flickering hope in their hearts, it was in despair, that they returned to Galilee. They must have quitted Jerusalem as soon as the tragedy of Calvary had been consummated, leaving only the Sabbath to pass, during which they could not set out on their journey.

It is thus that the Gospel of Peter presents the events:

The women who discovered the empty tomb and received the testimony of the angel fled terrified, and although it is not explicitly stated, they said nothing. It was with tears and distress that on the morning of the third day the disciples set out on the road for Galilee. That which the Gospel of Peter contains more than this—namely the story of the resurrection properly so called—is from another origin, and has not been intercalated in a satisfactory manner in the narrative of the discovery of the empty tomb and the return to Galilee. Neither the women nor the disciples could have ignored such a sensational event as the exit of Jesus from the tomb, as it is related in the Gospel of Peter.

The account of Matthew reproduces that of Mark with some

variations. In the first place Jesus appears to the women (xxviii. 9, 10). These latter deliver the message confided to them (verse 8), and it is after having received it that the disciples go to Galilee, to the mountain which Jesus had given them as the meeting place (xxviii. 16). The return of the disciples to Galilee has, therefore, a character other than in Mark. It was, if not with a sense of certainty, at least in the hope of the resurrection, that they left Jerusalem.

The priority of Mark's narrative compared with that of Matthew is beyond question. The apparition of Jesus to the women is under suspicion; Mark would not have suppressed it if he had found it in the source of his work. It makes a useless repetition of the apparition of the angel. The mission confided by Jesus to the women adds nothing to those they had already received.

Moreover, in stating that the disciples went to Galilee to the meeting place named by the angel, the narrative of Matthew establishes a close relationship between the empty tomb and the apparition; it thus does away with one of the strangest features of Mark's account—the simple juxtaposition of these two facts. It is natural for the tradition to have linked them to each other. It would be more difficult to understand if it had dissociated them.

The tendency to connect organically the account of the discovery of the empty tomb with that of the first apparition is still more distinct in Luke, and particularly in John. In Luke's work the angel's message is so transposed that he no longer speaks of a rendezvous in Galilee, but of a rendezvous that Jesus had given while he was in Galilee (xxiv. 6). The message is delivered to the disciples, but they are not convinced (xxiv. 11). It is not even said that they went to the tomb.[17] In the narrative of the meeting upon the road to Emmaus matters are somewhat more definite. The disciples certainly had been to the sepulcher, but they had seen no angel (xxiv. 22–24). The message of the women had at least disconcerted them. They could not fully believe in what had been told them, but they took the trouble to make some inquiry. When the disciples returned to Jerusalem from Emmaus, they are greeted with the cry,

"The Lord is risen indeed" (xxiv. 34), which implies that the question of the resurrection had been at any rate raised by the discovery of the empty tomb. The reasons why Matthew's version must be considered as of secondary value compared with Mark's maintain all their force for that of Luke. In xxiv. 11: "Their words seemed to them as idle tales, and they believed them not." Here a trace of the primitive conception, which established no relation between the empty tomb and the apparitions, very clearly persists.

In John's narrative (xx. 1–18) the relation between the empty tomb and the apparitions is closer still. Jesus appears to Mary Magdalene, and two disciples come to the tomb to investigate the women's assertion. One of them "sees and believes." The synthesis is thus perfectly realized. It is upon the empty tomb that the belief in the resurrection rests. Such is the case, at least, for the one whom the evangelist presents as a noble soul—as the very ideal of a disciple. Mary Magdalene and Peter are not convinced in the same way; for them apparitions are necessary. They served as confirmation for those who were not directly convinced of the existence of Christ. Their function is thus essential; although subordinate to that of the empty tomb, it is perfectly coördinated with it.

The comparison of the accounts of the resurrection therefore proves that in the most ancient tradition which we can find the empty tomb and the apparitions were merely juxtaposed. This condition of things, to some degree inorganic, could not be long maintained. An obligation was necessarily felt to seek to express in the narratives the relation that could not fail to be perceived between the two facts. Thus two secondary forms of the tradition came to birth. In the older of the two the character of the return of the disciples into Galilee is transformed: it is to go to meet Jesus that they quitted Jerusalem. But, at length, this could not suffice; it was necessary to go farther and associate the empty tomb with the apparitions, not only in the thought of the disciples, but also in time and space. With this object the apparitions were transferred to Jerusalem, where the disciples still remained at the time of the discovery of the empty tomb.[18]

Various objections have been raised to the thesis of the priority of the Galilean tradition. They rest in general upon the a priori dogma—more or less unconscious—that there cannot be any contradiction between the various accounts of the resurrection, and that it is only necessary to find some means to reconcile them. Certain critics have imagined in the environs of Jerusalem, on the Mount of Olives, a place named "Galilee,"[19] but this place obviously has only been imagined for the needs of the case. Others, again, following the example already given by the author of the unauthentic ending of Mark and by the editor who added Chapter xxi to the fourth Gospel, have combined the two traditions by positing a series of Judaic apparitions followed by a series of Galilean apparitions. They misunderstand the fact that in the primitive tradition the Galilean apparition was quite distinctly a first apparition of the risen Jesus.

Johannes Weiss has offered an original theory which seeks to explain the origin of the Galilean tradition through a misunderstanding. It rests entirely on the words of Jesus related in Mark xiv. 28: "After that I am risen, I will go before you into Galilee"—words to which reference was made in the message of the angel (Mark xvi. 7). According to Johannes Weiss, Jesus had announced to His disciples that after His resurrection He would lead them into Galilee, walking at their head. If this theory had any basis, the problem of the resurrection would be much simplified. The Church would be the direct continuation of the communion which during the lifetime of Jesus existed between Him and His disciples. The ingenuity of the system which suppresses rather than solves a whole series of problems demands a very serious examination. The Jerusalemite tradition of Luke arises from downright juggling with the phrase in Mark on which the Galilean tradition rests.[20] In the way it is understood by Johannes Weiss, the phrase concerning the return into Galilee is the sole surviving element of a tradition according to which Jesus had resumed, or considered it necessary to resume, after His resurrection the life which He had formerly led with His disciples. How could Jesus have entertained such a thought when (His declaration before the Sanhedrin proves it) He expected to return upon the clouds of heaven? On the contrary, is it to be supposed (admitting the otherwise weak and improbable hypothesis of an apparent death) that Jesus, after the drama of Calvary, may still have lived for a certain time with His disciples? How is it that this period of His life could pass and leave no other souvenir except one sentence, very soon misunderstood? How is it that tradition had never made use of it as the argument best adapted to refute those who denied the resurrection? And finally, how could a tradition arise which, in opposition to the most obvious interests of apologetics, reduced the manifestations of the risen Christ to a few brief apparitions? It is still possible to suppose that the sentence about Jesus leading His disciples into Galilee originally related to the period which must follow the success He hoped to obtain in Judea and at Jerusalem. It is easy to understand that, the hope of Jesus having been deceived, tradition may not have preserved the memory of it; but how does it happen that a fragment of it has survived, and why should one single phrase, misunderstood by Mark, suffice to give birth to the Galilean tradition and suppress in his version the souvenir of the primitive Judean tradition?

It is objected against the priority of the Galilean tradition that we know nothing about a Christian community in Galilee whose existence was the direct consequence of apparition in that region. Tradition has not preserved the souvenir of the disciples' return to Jerusalem either. The chances as to the preservation of documents may explain the first point. We should know nothing about the existence in the early years following the death of Jesus of a Christian community at Damascus were it not mentioned in the narrative of the conversion of Saul of Tarsus. The same explanation holds for the second point. Moreover, it is comprehensible that the souvenir of the Galilean tradition may have been obliterated when the Judean tradition had become so preponderant that it was possible to speak of an order given by Jesus to His disciples not to leave Jerusalem, but to await there the effusion of the Spirit (Acts i. 4).

VI. THE BELIEF IN THE RESURRECTION AND THE MESSIANIC BELIEF

The religious thought of the early Christians had two foci: the belief in the resurrection and the Messianic belief. Between these two there is an organic relationship. What was precisely the function of each, and what was their relationship? The Messianic belief of the first disciples was earlier than their belief in the resurrection. The first named was born of the impression which Jesus made on them, and was not entirely destroyed by the drama of the Passion. If the failure of Jesus had been also a complete negation of the confidence the disciples had placed in Him, it would not have caused a complete collapse of their abstract faith in *a* Messiah, but it would have radically destroyed the faith they had placed in Him.

Certain passages, however, might at first sight induce one to consider the belief in the resurrection as the origin of belief in the Messiah. Such is particularly the case as regards a passage of Peter's address at the feast of Pentecost (Acts ii. 36), where a conception is found of such an archaic and pre-Pauline character that there can be no hesitation in recognizing in it the echo of a fairly primitive notion. According to this passage, God "has made Lord and Christ" (that is, the Messiah) the selfsame Jesus who had been crucified by the Jews.[21] But it is not asserted that Jesus was not the Messiah before His resurrection; it is, on the contrary, presumed that He was the one whom God destined to fulfill the Messianic mission, but who, during His earthly ministry, was not invested with the attributes of power and glory. The dignity of the Messiah has now been conferred on Him in all its fullness; Jesus is now the Lord—that is, the Messiah transcendent who will return at the end of time to complete the discomfiture of the enemies of God, assuring at the same time the salvation of the faithful and the establishment and triumph of the Kingdom of God. "It is from heaven," writes Paul, "that we await the Saviour, the Lord Jesus Christ" (Phil. iii. 20); and if the continuation of this declaration, with the idea of the similitude of the body of the believer to the glorious body of the Lord, expresses an idea essentially Pauline, the commencing phrase contains the faith common to all Christians. The resurrection was, in the first place, a sentimental satisfaction for the disciples, at once a consolation and a reparation of the indignity offered to Jesus by His ignominious condemnation. By its means Jesus was rehabilitated, and the faith of the disciples, shaken by the drama of the Passion, was restored. But this was not all. The resurrection placed the Messianic faith on a new plane. From the first manifestations of the life of the Church it assumed a character and outlook different from those she had nourished until then. It was no longer an inner conviction, having the character of a secret of which even among the initiated one could only speak with prudence, and which remained surrounded by a certain mystery. It became a certainty openly proclaimed before the world, forming the very essence of Christian preaching. There was in this something more than a change of tactics or the abandonment of precautions henceforward superfluous. The Messianic creed had been exalted; it had passed from the imminent to the transcendental plane. However paradoxical it may appear at first sight, the Christ preached in the primitive Church was not rigorously identical with the Jesus in whom the disciples trusted when He accompanied them on the roads of Galilee or in the streets of Jerusalem. Doubtless He was indeed the same person, but He had now received from God the full Messiahship which formerly had been only promised Him.

The resurrection in itself alone cannot have given this new character to the faith of the disciples. The first Christians believed that Jesus had restored several persons to life, but this did not imply in any way their exaltation. They were considered only as having resumed for a time their preceding life, not as having radically triumphed over death. The resurrection of all these persons has only importance for the evangelists as an activity of Jesus whose power they thus revealed as stronger than death. The belief in the resurrection of Jesus had in primitive Christianity other consequences.

The Risen One, to those who had received the revelation of His return to life, was no ordinary man, but already the Messiah. The resurrection belief was the exaltation of their Messianic conviction; it afforded a striking confirmation.

The Socialist writer, Maurenbrecher, introduces here a racial consideration. He speaks of the faculty acquired by the Jewish race, in the course of the tragic vicissitudes of its history, to surmount all catastrophes and to extract from all disillusions sources of new hopes and new illusions. This interpretation demands reservations of some importance. That which in primitive Christianity survived the drama of Calvary was not alone the Messianic faith in general, but also the personal character which this faith had assumed. It did not attach itself to another Messiah, but continued to see the Messiah and Savior in the crucified of Golgotha. This is not explained by a racial disposition, but presumes a profound attachment to the person of Jesus the Messiah. The first Christians did not make of Jesus the Messiah transcendent because He rose from the dead, but it is because His departure from earth and return to heaven had made of Him the Messiah that they believed in His resurrection and, in a new sense, in His Messiahship. This is the conviction which explains the apparitions. The disciples saw Jesus because for them He was living. This proposition is truer than that suggested by the Gospel narratives—that is, that the disciples believed in Jesus as living because He had appeared to them.

The Messianic faith of the disciples is older than the belief in the resurrection. It is this faith which was the source of the belief. It is because they believed Jesus to be the Messiah and no ordinary man that they believed in His resurrection.[22] As M. Loisy judiciously observes, the disciples of John the Baptist, who never held a similar opinion about their Master, never believed in His resurrection.[23] It would be possible, it is true, to object, as does Maurenbrecher,[24] that this explanation of the origin of the resurrection belief does not hold for the case of those who (like James, possibly, and in any case Peter) did not see in Jesus the Messiah before acquiring the certainty of His resurrection. This is evident, but the causes of the first appearance of the resurrection faith are not necessarily identical with those explaining the conquests it made afterwards. It is very certain that the existence of a group of men who believed in the risen Jesus was, if not the unique factor, at least an essential one in the conversion to the Christian faith of those who, like Paul, had never felt the influence of Jesus during His ministry.

VII. CONCLUSION

We are now able to imagine the conditions in which the apparitions occurred, on which is based the apologetic literature of the first century and by means of which the resurrection faith was vindicated.

They were in the first place independent of the discovery of the empty tomb, since, as we have seen, the most ancient tradition assumes that the disciples had no knowledge of this fact before experience of the apparitions, and because the comparison of narrative proves that in the sequel the narrators must have been forced to subject the tradition to a complete process of retouching in the attempt to coördinate and fuse together the narratives of the empty tomb and the apparitions. Moreover, in this task they never completely succeeded.

It was in Galilee that the disciples had their first visions. They had not returned there expecting them, but they had returned in a period of discouragement.

The time of the first apparition cannot be fixed with precision. The existing accounts, which place the resurrection on the morning of the third day, represent a second phase of the tradition. The primitive formula was not "the third day," but "after three days"; this probably originally meant after a short interval, whose duration was not fixed with precision. It certainly seems from Paul's testimony that it was Peter who had the first vision, which must have been rapidly followed by others, several of which doubtless were collective visions.

It is possible that certain among them had repasts as their occasions, and may have happened at the moment of the breaking of bread. The evocation of the last repast of Jesus and the memory of the words He then spoke, affirming at one and the same time His sacrifice for His friends and the promise of a future reunion, must have played an important part in the genesis of apparitions, the intense feeling of a spiritual presence being easily transformed into the sense of a real presence.

At first there must have been some indifference as regards the details of the apparition narratives, so exclusively were minds dominated by the sentiment of the presence and the life of the Christ. It is this which explains that the narratives, at an early date, took forms of sufficiently varied character, and ended in the extreme diversity which we observe between the accounts known to us, both canonical and extracanonical.

Lastly, it is certain that the resurrection must very soon have become a subject of bitter controversy between Jews and Christians, and the necessity of replying to the varied objections advanced against the Christian faith greatly influenced the narratives and led to the creation of entire groups of traditions such as that of the empty tomb.

The conclusions to which we are thus brought in studying the origins of the resurrection faith have for the problem before us an importance whose meaning it is superfluous to insist upon. The genesis of the resurrection faith not only presumes the historic tradition about the death of Jesus, but it appears to us as the continuation of the activity exercised by Him during His lifetime. The resurrection faith is thus the link which unites the story of Jesus with that of Christianity, making the second the consequence of the first.

We do not, therefore, find at the birth of Christianity this naïve euhemerism which M. Couchoud reproaches historians, from Renan to Loisy, as having so easily accepted, but we find something quite different. The early Christians did not deify a man whose teaching and authority impressed them, and the worship of the Lord Jesus has no resemblance at all to that of the emperors. It is because they had found in Him during His ministry the one destined to accomplish the divine work. It is because, under the influence of the belief in His resurrection (a direct consequence of the impression He had made on them), the disciples of Jesus, in the exaltation of their faith, saw in Him no ordinary man, but directly identified Him with the celestial Messiah. Henceforth the story of the earthly life of Jesus was for them only an episode of a great redemptive drama, and it was in the light of their conception of this drama that they devoted themselves to present and interpret the facts of the life of Jesus and the circumstances of His death.

NOTES

1. The subordination of Christ to God is, in fact, very clearly affirmed by Paul (1 Cor. xv. 27, 28).

2. Even considering this teaching to have been directly revealed to him by God.

3. Behind the present tradition there is perceptible one of older form which attributed to the body of Jesus a period in the tomb lasting three days and three nights (Matt. xii. 40).

4. The accounts of Luke and John have an obviously apologetic character.

5. Matthew (xxviii. 9, 10) mentions an apparition of Jesus to the women, immediately after the discovery of the empty tomb. Jesus renews the message already given by the angel. The disciples go to Galilee to the meeting place Jesus had given them, and there He appears to them (verses 16–20). According to Luke (xxiv. 9–11) the women bring also the message of the angel to the disciples, but these latter do not believe them. However, Luke states that the disciples have been to the tomb and found it empty. This action is directly attributed to Peter (in Luke xxiv. 8), but this verse, which is absent from manuscript D and in several forms of the

old Latin version, is much suspected. It betrays the influence of Luke xxiv. 24, and must originate from John's narrative. In the fourth Gospel (xx. 1–18) Mary Magdalene, on her own initiative, goes to inform the disciples that she has found the tomb empty. Peter and the unnamed disciple run there at once, but it is only of the latter that it is said that he believed. Jesus appears afterwards to Mary Magdalene, who is charged to carry to the disciples the news of His resurrection. She carries out this task, but it is not said how she is received.

6. *La notion Johannique de l'Esprit et ses antecedents historiques,* Goguel.

7. The original Johannine conception was perhaps more distinctly marked in an early form of the Gospel, where the narrative appears to end with the sentence of Jesus to Mary Magdalene: "Go to my brothers and tell them that I ascend to My Father and your Father, to my God and your God" (xx. 27). It is difficult, indeed, to conceive that such a message could have been originally followed by other apparitions of the risen Jesus. The narrative of the apparition to Mary Magdalene might thus be the remains of a tradition in which the Gospel history ended by the return of Christ in celestial glory.

8. The same feature is found in the fourth Gospel, in the account of the apparition to Mary Magdalene (xx. 15) and in the scene on the shore of the lake (xxi. 4).

9. The idea that a phantom cannot eat, and that an apparition which is taken for a spirit offers a decisive proof of his corporeal reality by sitting down to a repast, appears to be widely disseminated in folklore. It serves as the theme of a popular song, composed at the prisoners' camp at Holzminden by a soldier, native of Mayenne (France). It refers to a prisoner whose death certificate had reached his family and who, having returned from captivity in Germany, is taken for a spirit up to the moment he sits down to his meal at table before them. Having announced his continued existence, the refrain runs:

> "In order to reassure you
> I'm going to eat and drink."

Note.—The author states that since his book was published in France it has been proved that the song referred to in the note was composed before the late War.—*Translator.*

10. In the narratives containing details implying the concept of revivification it is easy to convince oneself that these details are not in harmony with other elements in it. Thus in John xx. 26–29 the exhibition of wounds, implying "corporality" of the Risen One, does not harmonize easily with the fact that Jesus passes easily into the room when the doors were shut.

11. Compare with Luke xvi. 31: "Neither will they be persuaded though one rose from the dead."

12. We cannot discuss the problem of the Messianic affirmations of Jesus in the Gospels, nor the various hypotheses proposed to explain them. We think that Jesus really considered Himself as the Son of God, and that if the Messianic conceptions of the primitive Christians may have influenced the manner in which the declarations of Jesus are related in the Gospels, and given them more precision, they do not explain them. In support of our opinion we shall only cite one decisive fact—that is, the reply of Jesus to the high priest. When asked if He was the Christ, the Son of the Blessed, Jesus replies: "I am: and ye shall see the Son of man sitting on the right hand of power and coming on the clouds of heaven" (Mark xiv. 62). If this declaration is a product of Christian faith, the fundamental idea of primitive Christianity is found therein—that of resurrection on the third day. Matthew (xxvi. 64), in introducing the sentence "Henceforward shall ye see. . . ." tends to substitute the idea of glorification for that of return, but he does so only in an imperfect way, since he preserves the idea of return upon the clouds of heaven. Luke goes farther still, and suppresses the idea of return in giving to the declaration of Jesus this form: "Henceforward shall the Son of man be seated at the right hand of the power of God" (Luke xxii. 69).

13. The fourth Gospel (xviii. 8, 9) puts into the mouth of Jesus a sentence which justifies the dispersion of the disciples.

14. The Synoptics also relate the incident, but they do not name Peter.

15. The behavior of Peter was in any case more circumspect than that of the young man who wished to follow Jesus and whom the soldiers tried to arrest (Mark xiv. 51, 52).

16. According to the oldest tradition, it was not before the Sunday morning that the disciples quitted Jerusalem; they desired, therefore, to know the issue of events in the drama.

17. At least, in the version which there is reason to consider the primitive one.

18. Accessorily the evolution of the narratives in this sense has been facilitated, and perhaps partly determined, by the always increasing importance of the Jerusalem Church and also by the need to affirm that the apparitions did not take place in a far-off province, and thus escape more or less the possibility of verification.

19. Rud. Hofmann, *Galilaea auf dem Oelberg;* A. Resch, *Das Galilaea bei Jerusalem; Der auferstandene Galilaea bei Jerusalem.*

20. Matthew (xxviii. 7) slightly transposes the last part of the phrase, which consequently becomes in his version superfluous, and can only be explained as a survival of the version in Mark, whose priority is thus confirmed.

21. This text ought to be compared with that in Rom. i. 4, but in Paul's work it is rather a question of the manifestation of Jesus as Messiah.

22. Meyer, *Ursprung und Anf.,* ii, p. 453, and iii, pp. 216–19.

23. Loisy, *Les Mystères païens et le mystère Chrétien,* p. 215.

24. Maurenbrecher, *Von Nazareth nach Golgotha,* p. 262.

GENERAL CONCLUSIONS

J esus did not create the Church; He did not trouble about establishing institutions or laying down rules to assure, after His death, the continued existence of the group which had formed around Him and to direct its life. His mind was too much dominated by the idea of the immediate end of the existing economy to permit Him to trouble about the future of His friends on earth and to dream of organizing it. Jesus was not, therefore, in the usual meaning of the word, the founder of a religion; He desired only to announce and fulfill by His advent the accomplishing of the promises made by God to Israel. His Gospel implies no rupture with the religious tradition of His people. If He combated the abuses which the Scribes and Pharisees had introduced, He intended to remain faithful to the inspiration of the Law and Prophets.

Christianity, on the contrary, was a new religion, and it was so from the day after the death of Jesus, long before the time when the hostility of the Jews, on one side, and the necessity of freedom to welcome the pagans on the other, had forced believers to organize themselves in a society independent of the synagogue. The Christians did not only preach, as Jesus had done, the nearness of the Kingdom of God, but before all else the doctrine of salvation by the death and resurrection of Jesus—a death and resurrection which have precisely the effect of introducing the Kingdom of God.[1] The Christianity of the primitive Church was neither a form of Judaism[2] nor the transformation of a pagan mystery, and this is true notwithstanding all the elements which it has in common with these two religious species. It was a new religion. If in the course of events Christianity absorbed elements foreign to the thought of Jesus and to Judaism, it was, nevertheless, born out of the preaching of Jesus and the impression He had made upon the few men who had grouped themselves around Him.

Christianity is not the religion of Jesus; it is that of the worshipers of Jesus. It was the personality of the Master which linked together the Gospel preached in Galilee and the religion of the primitive Church, and which explains the organic unity of the entire movement initiated by Jesus.

Not only did the thought of Jesus exercise on the Church (especially in the moral sphere) a decisive influence as the source of her inspiration, but still more was it the impression left by the personality of Jesus which gave the impulse through whose activity the whole system of Christian thought was developed. Between the preaching of the Kingdom of God by Jesus and the doctrine of salvation elaborated and developed in the Church there is more than a simple coincidence in time; there is an organic relationship. It is through the impression produced by Jesus that the Church professed her doctrine of redemption. If this doctrine has some kinship with the Mystery Religions, it is differentiated from them and cannot be reduced to them. While the worshipers of Mithra, Attis and Adonis knew perfectly well that the redemptive story of their heroes plunged into such fabulous antiquity that all reality was lost to it, the Christians were persuaded that it was not at the beginning but at the end of the age that their Christ had lived. His life, for them, could be fitted in a very intimate manner into the reality of history.

If Christianity is a mystery, it is one of a very special type which contrasts with others even more than it resembles them. As M.

Loisy, who has strongly insisted upon the originality of Christianity in comparison with the contemporary religions, has very well observed: "It may be said, if you wish, that Christianity is a mystery, but it must be quite understood that this mystery is unique of its kind, and that it does not enter into the same category and is not of the same type as the pagan mysteries, to which, nevertheless, it is compared and from which it has in some way issued."

If there is in early Christianity any speculation assimilated from preëxisting Jewish and even pagan elements, it is upon the basis of an historical tradition about the life and death of Jesus that this speculation has developed. The historical reality of the personality of Jesus alone enables us to understand the birth and development of Christianity, which otherwise would remain an enigma, and in the proper sense of the word, a miracle.

NOTES

1. Loisy, *Les Mystères païens et le mystère Chrétien,* p. 210.

2. It is true that the rupture between Christianity and Judaism was not brought about at once, but it was nevertheless fatal from the start—that is, from the moment the Christians invoked the name of one who had been disavowed and rejected by the authorized leaders of Judaism.

INDEX